RELIGION AND REBELLION

HISTORICAL STUDIES

The Irish Committee of Historical Sciences inaugurated a series of biennial conferences of historians in July 1953. Since then the 'Irish Conference of Historians' has circulated among the Irish universities and university colleges and the papers read since 1955 have been published as *Historical Studies*. Since 1975 the conferences have been devoted to a single theme, the full list being as follows.

T.D. Williams (ed.) *Historical Studies I* (London: Bowes & Bowes 1958)

M. Roberts (ed.) *Historical Studies II* (London: Bowes & Bowes 1959)

J. Hogan (ed.) *Historical Studies III* (London: Bowes & Bowes 1961)

G.A. Hayes-McCoy (ed.) *Historical Studies IV* (London: Bowes & Bowes 1963)

J.L. McCracken (ed.) *Historical Studies V* (London: Bowes & Bowes 1965)

T.W. Moody (ed.) *Historical Studies VI* (London: Routledge & Kegan Paul 1968)

T.D. Williams (ed.) *Historical Studies VIII* (Dublin: Gill & Macmillan 1971)

J.G. Barry (ed.) *Historical Studies IX* (Belfast: Blackstaff Press 1974)

G.A. Hayes-McCoy (ed.) *Historical Studies XI* (Dublin: ICHS 1976)

T.W. Moody (ed.) *Nationality and the Pursuit of National Independence: Historical Studies XI* (Belfast: Appletree Press 1978)

A.C. Hepburn (ed.) *Minorities in History: Historical Studies XII* (London: Edward Arnold 1978)

D.W. Harkness and M O'Dowd (eds.) *The Town in Ireland: Historical Studies XIII* (Belfast: Appletree Press 1981)

J.I. McGuire and A. Cosgrove (eds.) *Parliament and Community: Historical Studies XIV* (Belfast: Appletree Press 1981)

P.J. Corish (ed.) *Radicals Rebels and Establishments: Historical Studies XV* (Belfast: Appletree Press 1985)

Tom Dunne (ed.) *The Writer as Witness: Literature as Historical Evidence: Historical Studies XVI* (Cork: Cork University Press 1987)

Ciaran Brady (ed.) *Ideology and the Historians: Historical Studies XVII* (Dublin: The Lilliput Press 1991)

T.G. Fraser and Keith Jeffrey (eds.) *Men, Women and War: Historical Studies XVIII* (Dublin: The Lilliput Press 1993)

Mary O'Dowd and Sabine Wichert (eds.) *Chattel, Servant or Citizen. Women's Status in Church, State and Society: Historical Studies XIX* (Belfast: Institute of Irish Studies, 1995)

RELIGION AND REBELLION

edited by JUDITH DEVLIN
and RONAN FANNING

Historical Studies XX

Papers read before the 22nd Irish Conference of Historians,
held at University College Dublin, 18–22 May 1995

University College Dublin Press
Preas Choláiste Ollscoile Bhaile Átha Cliath

First published 1997 by University College Dublin Press,
Newman House, St Stephen's Green, Dublin 2, Ireland

ISBN 1 900621 03 7

Cataloguing in Publication data available from the British Library

Index by Helen Litton
Typeset in Garamond by Seton Music Graphics, Bantry, Co. Cork, Ireland
Printed in Ireland by Betaprint, Dublin

Contents

Preface

The papers in this volume were read to the twenty-second biennial Irish Conference of Historians, held at University College Dublin between 18 and 22 May 1995, under the aegis of the Irish Committee of Historical Sciences (the representative body for professional historians throughout the island of Ireland).

The biennal conference is the principal general meeting of academic historians in Ireland and, from the earliest conferences in the 1950s, the programme has traditionally included a number of distinguished historians from outside Ireland and has been broadly based. 'Religion and Rebellion', the theme of this conference, has likewise been interpreted in the broadest sense.

As conference organizers, we are especially grateful for financial and other assistance to Dr Art Cosgrove, President of University College Dublin, who, by happy coincidence, was one of the joint editors of the corresponding volume when the conference was last held in University College Dublin in 1981. We are also indebted to Dr Fergus D'Arcy, Dean of the Faculty of Arts, and to Professor Seymour Phillips of the Department of Medieval History. We are grateful, too, for financial assistance from the Irish Office of the European Commission; the British Council; the Educational Company of Ireland; and Gill & Macmillan Ltd.

The publication of these proceedings has been made possible through generous grants from the Governing Body and the Faculty of Arts, University College Dublin, and from the Irish Committee of Historical Sciences.

As editors, our greatest debt is to Barbara Mennell, the executive editor of University College Dublin Press, for the unflappable efficiency tempered by unfailing good humour with which she steered us to the point of publication.

Judith Devlin and Ronan Fanning
University College Dublin, January 1997

1 Renegade Religious in Late Medieval England[1]

F. Donald Logan

(Denis Bethell Memorial Lecture)

On the second day of January in 1402 the Cistercian abbot of Baltinglas Abbey sent the following letter to the king of England:

To the most excellent prince in Christ, to the lord, Lord Henry, by the grace of God, illustrious king of England and France and lord of Ireland, your humble and devoted petitioner, Brother Adam, by divine permission, abbot of the monastery of Blessed Mary in Valle Salutis (known as Baltinglas) in the diocese of Leighlin, obedient to its bishop, with all reverence and honour to your royal excellency.

May these presents bring to your royal excellency the knowledge that Brother Richard Hollkey, a monk of this monastery, expressly professed in the regular order of St Benedict, apparently having rejected the world, lived the monastic life among us for some time, wearing the monastic habit, yet, at length, moved by the devil, he left the monastic habit and assumed secular dress. For many circles of years he has not returned. Since he left secretly and without permission, he is apostate. I have learned that he has been wandering about in parts of your kingdom of England, where he continues to live damnably in apostasy in contempt of God as a scandal to our order and as a grave danger to his soul and to the souls of others.

Since, therefore, my powers are unable to restore this long erring sheep to his fold, I am led humbly and devotedly to beg your royal excellency, for the praise and honour of God and for the salvation of the said Richard, graciously to grant your royal writ for his capture according to the rights and usages of your realm, so that he whom neither the fear of God nor the love of virtue can correct may be moved by the force of your sharper discipline.

May the king of kings always protect your royal majesty in the guidance of the people committed to you.

Given in our chapter house on the second day of January in the year of our Lord one thousand, four hundred and one.[2]

Richard Hollkey was but one of the nearly 1100 runaway religious whom I have encountered in studying runaway religious in England from the coming of the friars in the early thirteenth century till the dissolution under Henry VIII. He was the only Irish runaway monk who crossed my screen of vision. Except for a score or so who came from Welsh houses, the rest came from English religious houses.[3] They include men and women from every order. There were Cistercian, Benedictine and Cluniac monks –

only six Carthusians, one of whom, Richard Vyell, later became bishop of Killala, although he got no nearer to Killala than Worcester.[4] There were Augustinian and Premonstratensian and Gilbertine canons. There were members of the four major orders of mendicant friars (the Dominican, Franciscan, Carmelite and Austin friars) as well as some from among the Crutched Friars and Pied Friars. Also, in the number of runaways were members of the Knights Templars and Knights Hospitallers as well as religious from leper and other hospitals. They fled from large, often richly endowed monasteries like Westminster Abbey, Christ Church Priory (Canterbury), Glastonbury Abbey, St Albans, Bury St Edmunds, Ramsey and, in the North, from Rievaulx and Fountains and Furness and Hexham and Whitby and Selby. They fled also from small, often nearly impoverished priories, which are not household names even to medievalists: places such as Chipley Priory in Suffolk, Bushmead Priory in Bedfordshire, Felley Priory in Nottinghamshire, Little Horkesley Cluniac Priory in Essex. So, too, with nuns. Some became fugitive from large, wealthy abbeys such as Shaftesbury in Dorset, Romsey in Hampshire and Godstow in Oxfordshire. Others left from the small nunneries that dotted the English countryside, many of them poor and with fewer than the apostolic twelve in their communities: such places as Pinley Priory in Warwickshire, Kilburn Priory outside London, Sewardsley Priory in Northamptonshire, a nunnery so poor that it closed in 1460 and the nuns were moved to nearby Delapre Abbey. These professed religious who abandoned their vows, their houses and usually their habits can be found in the surviving records in every decade during this three-hundred year period.

I have been speaking of 'runaways' and I have used the word 'flee' and the programme uses the word 'renegade' and, at times, I use the word 'wayward'. None of these words is perfectly appropriate. Not all wayward religious fled their orders. And the word 'fugitive' has a precise meaning in the common law. Even *vagabundi* – wanderers – might bring to mind monks on the move from one monastery to another as, in Hugh Lawrence's phrase, 'professional guests', for by the thirteenth century the wandering religious, scholars or otherwise, had virtually disappeared from the scene. Such terms were not those most commonly used by contemporaries. The term used by popes and bishops in fashioning laws against them, by religious superiors contending with them in practice, by the rules, constitutions and customs of orders is the word 'apostates'. *Apostata* was the word used consistently by contemporaries to describe the religious who climbed over the wall literally or figuratively. The understanding of the word 'apostate' almost exclusively in another sense in modern times makes it hazardous to use the word without explanation. A lecture entitled 'Apostate Religious in Late Medieval England' might have brought you here expecting to hear about grave crises of faith, and you would have been disappointed. In the twelfth century canonists commenting on Gratian's *Decretum* said that the word 'apostasy' had two different meanings. There is, they said, apostasy from the faith (*apostasia a fide*), by which a person who is baptized abandons the Christian faith (like Julian the Apostate). And there is apostasy from religion (*apostasia a religione*), by which a person who made religious profession leaves the religious life and returns to the world.[5] Writing *c.*1160, the canonist Stephen of Tournai said, 'Today when we say "apostate", we mean a person, who, after taking the religious habit, returns to a life in the world.'[6] And so it continued to be used in this sense of abandoning the religious life. Thus, apostates from religion are the subject of this paper.

The definition fashioned by the medieval canonists was quite clear: an apostate from religion was a professed religious who abandoned the religious life. It was not the monk who without permission went into the local village for entertainment and failed to return for a few days, nor the nun who overstayed a visit to her family. Neither had abandoned the religious life: neither left with the intention of not returning. The military distinction between going AWOL and deserting is fairly analogous. The AWOL monk might have been a disobedient monk, even a monk who engaged in unmonklike behaviour, but he was not a deserter, not an apostate.

Apostasy required prior profession. If not professed, then not apostate, not excommunicated, not liable (in England) for arrest by the secular arm. Nothing could be clearer, but life as it is lived and laws as they are applied do not always respect such clarity.

A true profession had to be made freely by an unmarried person who had reached the age of discretion. A boy could enter a monastery at age 14 and a girl could enter a nunnery at age 12, the same age at which they could enter marriage, the age of legal puberty. After a year's probation (*annus probationis*) the candidate would kneel before an abbot or bishop and recite a formula of profession, like Sister Joan of Easebourne Priory, who in 1416 solemnly said

I, Sister Joan, do hereby promise stability, moral conversion and obedience according to the rule of St Augustine before God and his saints in this monastery, which is dedicated to St Mary, in the presence of the lord bishop of Selymbria, suffragan of Chichester, and in the presence of Dame Margery, prioress of Easebourne and her sisters. To Prioress Margery and her successors I promise to live without any goods of my own and in charity until death.[7]

And so she was veiled, and so too young men reciting similar formulas had their habits blessed. In both cases, they made lifelong commitments to the religious life. For the violation of this commitment, they incurred *ipso facto* excommunication (after 1298) and, in England, became subject to arrest and forced return by the king's men acting on the king's writ. Yet, even if

Sister Joan and Brother William and Friar Thomas never recited the formula of profession, even if they never received the veil or had their habits blessed by a bishop or abbot, they were still religious and, indeed, professed religious, for the law explicitly stated that a person who remained in a religious house beyond the year of probation was automatically professed. It was called tacit profession. And leaving after tacit profession was apostasy. The English bishops who met at Lambeth in 1281 said that some nuns think erroneously that, if they have not solemnized their vows and received a bishop's blessing, they are free to leave. They are not free to leave, the bishops reminded them, for they are ipso facto professed and not permitted to leave without incurring apostasy. The bishops at Lambeth continued; this applies also to monks and religious.[8] The bishops were not creating new law but merely repeating the general law of the church, which was in the Decretals of Gregory IX (1234) and which remained the law of the church till the Council of Trent.[9] Problems arose. Take, for example, the nun Clarissa Styl. In 1338 aged eight she entered the preceptory of nuns of the order of the Knights Hospitallers in Somerset. There, after only two months and in patent violation of the canon law, she made solemn profession. Subsequently, at the age of fourteen, Clarissa Styl left, claiming that she was not a nun since she was not of canonical age when she professed and that now as a laywoman she could claim her inheritance. Her relatives, also claiming the inheritance, said that Clarissa was not only a nun and unable to inherit but an apostate nun. And they prevailed not because her profession at the age of eight was ruled valid – it was not – but because Clarissa had remained in the nunnery wearing the habit and veil for a year after reaching the age of puberty: she was tacitly professed.[10]

Clarissa Styl was not the only religious to encounter charges of apostasy by claiming underage profession. There is the touching story of John Hawteyn, who said that at the age of eight he entered the London house of the Carmelites and, when he ran away, his mother brought him back crying.[11] And, in York, in 1358, a prominent merchant and the local Carmelites clashed over his son, whom, he claimed, the Carmelites had ensnared when he was but a boy and had forced him to profess before he was fourteen. His son left before he was fourteen but was called an apostate by the friars, who sought his arrest by the secular arm. The king gave the boy his protection, and the Carmelites backed off.[12]

Not entirely dissimilar was the case of the Franciscan friar John Sillow. Early in the second half of the fifteenth century at the age of seven, while under the care of his stepmother, he entered the friars, as he later said, 'with childish levity'. When aged fourteen, apparently knowing his canon law, he attempted to leave but the friars would not let him and forced him to profess. Sometime later he fled and was considered an apostate by the

Franciscans. Sillow appealed his case to the pope, who, in 1490, declared him not professed and, thus, not apostate. Yet the determining issue was not age but force and fear (*vis et metus*): Sillow, under the pressure from the friars, did not have the necessary freedom to make a valid profession.[13]

Besides the required age of discretion and the necessary freedom, the professed religious had to be single: either unmarried or widowed. (I should add that it was possible, but it rarely happened, for a husband and wife to agree mutually to enter the religious life.) The single state, then, was the rule, but occasionally this rule was violated. For example, in 1268, John de Beverley entered St Mary's Abbey, York, and during his probationary year admitted to the abbot that he had contracted and consummated a prior marriage. He was asked to leave.[14] The friar Robert Trone acted less candidly. He became a Franciscan in 1275, was ordained a priest, and in 1284 announced that he could no longer live a lie, that he must leave because he had previously contracted marriage. And so he left and returned to his wife. But the order doubted his story and had writs issued for his arrest as an apostate.[15] He may indeed have been like the Augustinian canon Thomas de Melton of Hexham Priory in Northumberland, who, in the mid-fourteenth century, wanted to leave his priory without the odour of apostasy, and so he lied to his superiors. He told them that he had been previously married, and his prior asked him to leave, which he did without being pursued by royal writs. Yet he was pursued by a troubled conscience and, in 1350, he appeared at the priory gates, repentant, armed with papal letters and seeking reconciliation. He had, indeed, been apostate.[16]

These cases underline the general principle: if no profession, then no apostasy. Yet in almost every year of this period validly professed religious left the religious life and fled into apostasy. They might never have constituted a very large number, yet they remained a constant feature of the monastic and religious life of these centuries. Many religious houses must have had their own stories, passed from one generation of monks to another. The monks at St Augustine's Abbey, Canterbury, must have told and retold the story of Peter Dene, the canon lawyer and secular priest, who unhappily supported Thomas of Lancaster in 1322 and who rushed south from Boroughbridge, fearing for his life, and made a deal with the monastery to clothe him in the habit to protect him from the royal vengeance. They would recall generations later how Dene, when the heat was off, left by stealth one winter night and how he was brought back under armed guard as an apostate.[17] The apostates of stories told and untold confront their historian with one particularly puzzling question, which, wish as he may, will not go away. It is a question which a lecture in memory of Denis Bethell, who delighted in the hard question, cannot eschew. It is quite simply: Why did they leave? What motivated these hundreds of monks and canons and nuns and friars to renounce their vows and return to the world? Why did the Carmelite friar of Nottingham and the Cistercian monk of Tintern and the nun of Godstow abandon the religious life? We may be dealing here with the final frontier for the historian: the motivation of individual human beings for individual human acts, which is distinct from what motivated institutions (states, political parties, universities, etc.) to establish policies. It is not always easy to know what motivates individuals whom we know and perhaps know well, and, in moments of self examination, we may not be totally certain what motivates us in some of our actions. No student of human nature can be unaware that motives may be mixed. The problem is compounded for us here by the separation of centuries and the presence of scant and always incomplete sources. We can perhaps skate around the edges of this question, and then only on thin ice. And, when on thin ice, one should always speak softly and only in the subjunctive mood.

In the vast majority of cases the sources are totally silent about the reasons for apostasy. Name, order, house and a date are what normally confront us. We are told that John Aconbury fled from the Cistercian abbey at Sawtry in Huntingdonshire in 1422; that William de Dunham fled the Dominican priory at Cambridge in 1302; that Agnes de Landwade, a Cluniac nun of Delapre Abbey at Northampton, left in 1311.[18] Why they left we shall perhaps never know: they are the people who appear but once in history and then are never seen again. In about fifty cases does the veil lift and we get a fuller yet incomplete look and can suggest some possible patterns, albeit subjunctively. We can put heresy and doctrinal dissent to the side for it appears but once in all these cases and it involved four Austin friars suspected of Wyclifite sentiments, two of whom were noticed in 1940 by Aubrey Gwynn.[19]

We should perhaps step back a step or two and see the young person entering the monastic gates for the first time and ask why? Ideally that person entered with a burning desire to lead a fuller spiritual life, to seek perfection without the distraction of property and family and to do so with others sharing the same ideals. That such high idealism existed is beyond question – Bernard, Anselm, Ailred and many others are witnesses to this – but it is equally beyond question that others entered for entirely worldly reasons and others for a mixture of reasons. There were the obvious attractions of food, clothing and housing provided, not always luxuriously, and of course tenure came with profession. To some there may have been the ceremonies, the chants, the flowing habit and the cascading veil – the romance of it all. Just as parents settled their children in marriages, so too they settled children in religious houses, and just as love might follow such a marriage, so too vocation might follow religious profession.[20] Contentment and a defined sense of vocation might have come as the religious matured, but, if not, if vocation did not follow profession, it does not mean that apostasy occurred any more than separation occurred (or, indeed, occurs) in loveless marriages. Yet the discontented religious without a sense of vocation was a ripe candidate for apostasy. But what would impel the unhappy, discontented religious to walk away?

Any one of the three vows – poverty, chastity and obedience – might have made life insupportable. The inability to own personal property no doubt created difficulties for some religious. For example, in 1334, an Augustinian canon of Rocester Abbey in Staffordshire was sent by his abbot to the royal court with a sum of money but, instead of going to court, he went into apostasy and spent the money.[21] Or, again, in the 1380s a canon of Kenilworth Priory in Warwickshire fled with goods from the monastery and he stole £10 from a lay resident.[22] Also, a Cistercian monk left Kirkstall Abbey in Yorkshire in 1304 with chalices and other goods from the abbey. At St Mary's Abbey in York a number of similar incidents are recorded in the chronicle, but let two suffice. In 1310, the *refectorius* of the monastery, Adam de Dalton, was collector of the king's tenth but instead of depositing the money in the king's treasury he fled to Wales.[23] Two years later, another monk there stole the sum of £60, a small fortune, and disappeared into the mist, never to be seen again.[24] One wonders whether in such cases the theft provoked the flight or the flight the theft: an apostate needed some insurance against hard times in the world. And more subtle than crass greed, for example, in taking money from the king's bags, was the sense of loss of self-identity that some might have felt in being unable to possess anything however valueless or otherwise as their own. The difference between having something *ad usum* and owning something *ad proprium* might, for some, have taken on a significance far outweighing the actual value.[25] How many were there like the monk of Rochester Cathedral Priory who demanded a room of his own?[26]

The obligations undertaken by poverty of life went beyond the religious being able to have property and to call something one's own. There was a mutuality of obligation: the superiors were bound to provide adequately for the necessities of life. When William Somerton fled from one of the dependent cells of St Albans, he said that as prior he was unable to provide for the needs of his monks and the demands of the abbot of St Albans, who used the priory's money to support the experiments of a Franciscan friar in alchemy.[27]

The burdens of a celibate life clearly proved more than some religious could bear but probably not as frequently as we might tend to assume. The stereotype of the monk running off with the nun is simply not sustained by the evidence that exists. Only three such cases have surfaced. There was the

Benedictine monk of Eynsham Abbey in Oxfordshire who, escaping from
the monastic prison in 1445, fled into apostasy with a nun of Godstow
Abbey.[28] A Cluniac monk of Pontefract Priory in Yorkshire acknowledged
in 1303 that he had intimate relations before and after his flight with a nun
of Arthington Priory.[29] And, then, there was the nun of St Michael's Priory
outside Stamford, who went off with an Austin friar for a day and a night
and returned, but then ran off with a harp-player to Newcastle-upon-
Tyne.[30] Three cases. Surely not enough to support generalizations. I should
quickly add that there were indeed other violations of chastity, but even
here we are dealing with less than a score. In 1414, for example, the bishop
of Lincoln discovered Joan Horncastle, a nun of Rothwell Priory, living
with a man in the parish of Coningsby and forced her unwilling community to take her back.[31] In another instance, the archbishop of York ordered
Felley Priory to readmit Robert Barry, who had impregnated a concubine
at Nottingham.[32] Then there was the Augustinian canon of Notley Priory
in Buckinghamshire who, in 1447, was serving in a local parish but wore
secular clothes, allegedly refused to leave his lover's bed to administer the
last rites and was labelled an apostate.[33] Even if other examples are added to
these, we are still dealing with a fairly small number of cases of apostasy
where issues of chastity were clearly involved.

An argument could be made that the daily demands of obedience
imposed the greatest burden on the religious. The need to bend one's will
to the will of another and the daily need to follow the prescriptions of rule
and regimen – to rise for matins in the middle of the night, to chant seemingly endless psalms, to take one's same place day after day next to the same
people whose smells and sounds and chatter could be a constant and
swelling source of irritation – these were all requirements of obedience.
Who could be more disobedient to one's superior than the Cistercian
monk of Buildwas Abbey in Shropshire, Thomas de Tonge, who, in 1342,
murdered his abbot?[34] Abbots too had responsibilities to provide a safe,
secure setting for their monks to live the life of the Rule. There was near
rebellion against the abbot at Whitby Abbey in Yorkshire in 1366, when
one of the monks, Thomas de Hauksgard, walked out with more than half
the community. Evidence strongly suggests that the abbot had grossly
misused his authority beyond the limits of human endurance.[35] Likewise,
in 1402, something like a rebellion occurred at Christchurch Priory, an
Augustinian priory in Hampshire, where seven canons swore on the
Blessed Sacrament to overthrow the prior. Their conspiracy discovered,
they fled in apostasy only to be captured and punished.[36]

Not all superiors were arbitrary and tyrannical. When the saintly
Thomas de la Mare became abbot of St Albans after the abbot and prior
and half the community perished in the Black Death, he instituted reforms

that insisted on a strict observance of the Rule. Many of his monks, long used to a more relaxed interpretation of the Rule, simply left. How many left we do not know, but it must have been a considerable number for, as they began to drift back, so large was their number that, in order to avoid public scandal at St Albans, only some were reconciled at the abbey itself, the others in remote cells and priories. At least eight failed to return.[37] I wonder if something similar – a change of prior or cellarer – caused the departure of a monk of Reading in 1286 after more than thirty years as a monk there.[38]

We get tantalizing glimpses, all too brief, of another phenomenon, the bored monk, the monk who, wearied after years and years of seeing the same faces, hearing the same stories, reciting the same formularies perhaps by now denuded of any meaning – how many times a day did he sing 'Domine, ad adiuvandum me festina'? For some, repetition could lead to monotony, monotony could lead to tedium and tedium could lead to boredom and boredom could lead to *acedia*, and at some point there could be apostasy.

Towards the end of the 47-year rule of Abbot de la Mare at St Albans a number of his monks were eager to join Bishop Despenser in his so-called crusade in Flanders. The chronicler candidly states the reason why: 'quibus quies claustri displicuerat'. The quiet of the cloister displeased them: they were bored in the cloister and wanted adventure to give spice to their lives. In the event, seven went and one died.[39]

We get another glimpse of this phenomenon at Malmesbury Abbey, where the abbot asked one of his monks to write a history of the monastery. This anonymous monk wrote in an opening passage of his *Eulogium*:

I often sit bored in the cloister, my senses dull and faculties idle, plagued with wicked thoughts, because of the length of the lessons and the monotony of the prayers, and because of the vain boastings and evil ways of the world (their pleasure and general acceptance and, what is worse, their numerousness). Therefore, I wondered how I could extinguish such burning darts which try to inflict a multitude of wounds on the meditations of a monk. And I decided, at the request of my superiors, to prepare a work from various authors for the information of posterity.[40]

'Bored in the cloister.' How many others were there who were also bored in the cloister but who did not become historians or crusaders and for whom, at some point, boredom led to flight, we shall never know, but one suspects that behind the bare statement of the facts of apostasy, which we encounter so often, there may be hidden a boredom, fertile ground for discontent, violation of vows and, eventually, apostasy.

I am puzzled by the behaviour of a nun of Romsey Abbey, a certain Margery de Rye. In 1369 she began to act in a strange way and, in a sense, became apostate without leaving her abbey. What she did was to leave her community by removing her veil and sitting not with the other nuns in the choir but with laywomen in the nave. Nor did she attend chapter with the other nuns nor eat in the refectory with them nor sleep in the dormitory with them nor go to confession nor receive the Eucharist. Are we seeing here not a bored nun but the sad spectacle of a woman experiencing a mental breakdown?[41]

I have been discussing indiscriminately the motivations of both men and women since they both took the same vows and both lived lives in communities, but there were motives specific to women. The pregnant nun must be one of the sadder figures in medieval history. Her condition convicted her before the world of the most serious violation of her vows. No male religious, no matter how grave his misdeeds, would ever bear such an obvious sign of his unholy behaviour. One can imagine a nun, discovering her situation, spending days, perhaps weeks, in denial, wanting to believe it was just a dream and with awakening the nightmare would end. The awakening never came and the nightmare of reality continued, and her sisters would soon know. It should not surprise us that, faced with scorn and ridicule and recriminations, she might take flight into apostasy in an attempt to preserve her self-dignity. There was, for example, the Cistercian nun of Esholt Priory in Yorkshire, Beatrice de Hawkesworth. In 1303, aware that she was pregnant, she went apostate, fleeing to her family home, there to have her baby. The nuns of Esholt alerted the archbishop of York. He, in turn, gave two orders: one on 17 October 1303, telling the nuns not to let her back, and the other on the following 7 March, telling them to take her back. Presumably between the two orders Beatrice had had her child.[42] I can document only a half-dozen incidents where pregnancy led to apostasy. In addition, there was an apostate nun of Wintney Priory in Hampshire who was reputed to have children, although the records fail to indicate if she left because of pregnancy.[43] Similarly, a nun of the troubled community at Littlemore in Oxfordshire, Juliana Winter, one of three nuns there named Winter, fled in 1508 after being put in stocks by the prioress, whom she had accused of stealing money for her daughter; Juliana had herself had a child two years earlier, but it is not at all clear that her flight in 1508 was related to this.[44]

Another issue specific to women religious can be seen in the events at the great Benedictine abbey of Nunnaminster, founded at Winchester by King Alfred and Queen Eahlswith in the ninth century. In January 1370, the abbess complained to the king that a large number of evil men broke into the abbey and abducted one of the nuns, a certain Isabel Gervays, taking with them not only the nun but also goods to the value of £40. That was in January. Five months later Isabel Gervays begged to be readmitted, but the abbess was puzzled about what she should do, for Isabel Gervays had returned pregnant. The bishop of Winchester, William Wykeham, great man of affairs, then chancellor of the realm, counselled the abbess to receive Isabel with charity and kindness, but she should not allow her to resume her veil. He also warned the abbess to keep a watchful eye on her lest she bolt. Wykeham promised to come after the child was born to sort things out. And there our sources leave us, but they do tell us that Isabel Gervays, who was abducted from Nunnaminster, was called an apostate, i.e., she was a willing accomplice.[45]

The abduction of nuns was not new in 1370. As early as the time of Justinian there were laws against men taking religious women out of their houses.[46] And, in 1285, the great Second Statute of Westminster included the following chapter:

He that carrieth a nun from her house, although she consent, shall be punished by three years' imprisonment and shall make convenient satisfaction to the house from where she was taken, and nevertheless shall make fine at the king's will.[47]

The word 'abduction' in this context needs to be glossed. It meant a taking away and at this time was neutral regarding consent. Writing in 1922, Eileen Power said that, in fact, abducted nuns were 'always willing parties' and that 'all abductions were in reality elopements'.[48] If she was right – and I have found no cases that would contradict her judgement – then an abducted nun, in this sense, was, in fact, an apostate, as Isabel Gervays was so labelled at Nunnaminster.

The inclusion of this chapter in the Second Statute of Westminster in 1285 merits further comment. Why was such a matter included in this great parliamentary statute? I suggest that it might have been included because of a recent notorious case, which involved Sir Osbert Giffard.[49] He came from a substantial West Country family and held lands in nine counties. Two of his cousins were bishops – the late Walter Giffard, archbishop of York, and Godfrey Giffard, bishop of Worcester – and their sister was abbess of Wilton Abbey, the third wealthiest nunnery in England. It was from this nunnery on a dark night in 1284 that Sir Osbert Giffard abducted two nuns: Alice Russell and Anna Giffard. It soon became a *cause célèbre*. Cousin Juliana, the abbess, sought redress from the king, and a royal order seized Sir Osbert of lands in Oxfordshire, Somerset and Wiltshire.[50] Six months later the chapter already recited was entered into Westminster II. A coincidence? Perhaps, but subsequent events make one wonder. Not long after enactment of the statute the bishops held a council at London, attended by Sir Osbert's cousin, Godfrey, bishop of Worcester, and by Sir Osbert himself, now contrite and repentant and seeking absolution for his great crime. The stern Franciscan archbishop of Canterbury, John Pecham, told the repentant knight that he had caused a national scandal and must return the abducted nuns to Wilton Abbey and do public penance.[51] One week later, on Ash Wednesday, 1286, Sir Osbert Giffard appeared at Salisbury Cathedral, barefoot and bareheaded, among the public sinners cast out of the church, not to be readmitted till Holy Thursday. On three holy days during Lent he was flogged around Salisbury Cathedral and on three Tuesdays he was flogged through the marketplace. Also, three times he was flogged at the market at Amesbury and three times at Wilton within sight of the offended nunnery.[52] What lay behind all this cannot be seen at this distance in time, but it has all the appearance of a family feud turned nasty.

If you will indulge me, I should like to conclude with a case which illustrates many of the issues which I have discussed. It involves a Benedictine nun of Yedingham Priory in the East Riding of Yorkshire. Elizabeth Lutton came from a substantial landholding family, the Luttons of Knapton. Her grandfather held the manor of Knapton and West Lutton and held lands and tenements in other parts of the East Riding, including Flamborough. Her father was eldest son and heir apparent to the Lutton holdings. At the age of fourteen, in *c*.1512, Elizabeth entered the nunnery at Yedingham and made her profession in the small chapel, which now serves as the parish church.[53] There were about eight nuns there at the time. In 1530 she was abducted, married one of her abductors, claiming she had been forced to become a nun. The archbishop of York sent his principal ecclesiastical judge, Dr Nicholas Evererd, an experienced canonist, to Yedingham to conduct an inquiry. He interviewed the eight nuns of the priory and the priest who had been their chaplain for over forty years. Were you here when Elizabeth Lutton was professed? Three had been. Why do you remember it? – because the abbot of Rievaulx came with two of his monks, one of whom is now abbot of Rievaulx; also the prioress of Wykeham Priory and a canon of Bridlington Priory and many others. Did Elizabeth Lutton show any hesitation or reluctance in making her profession? No, on the contrary, she appeared to be a very happy girl: 'gerebat uultum hilarem et gesturam'. She wore a happy face and acted cheerfully. Did she then enter into the life of the priory? Yes, she acted as a member of the community.

Dr Evererd discovered that four years before his coming to Yedingham Elizabeth Lutton had been pregnant and had been placed in a house outside the cloister but within the priory precincts. Did she ask to be readmitted? Yes, she came personally before the community and said she was willing to do penance and asked to be readmitted. She even got the priory's confessor, a friar, to intercede for her, and she re-entered the cloister in 1526.

Now, in 1530, she left, allegedly abducted by Thomas Scaseby, whom she then married. We might ask, why did she leave? We could assume that she wanted to be with her lover, father of her child. That indeed may have been the case, although I hasten to add that there is no evidence that Thomas Scaseby was the child's father. A matter of the heart? Perhaps, but other facts intrude.

Coincidental with her leaving was the death in rapid succession of her father and grandfather, which left her uncle, Thomas Lutton, heir to the Lutton lands. She challenged his claims: since she was not a religious and not civilly dead, she could inherit and, as her father's sole surviving child, she claimed the estates. Uncle Thomas was not sympathetic to her claim, and we should perhaps see him behind the visit of Dr Evererd to Yedingham.

Enter at this point Sir Robert Constable, lord of Flamborough, a lordship held by his family since at least the time of King John.[54] Later, in 1536, he was to be one of the leaders of the Pilgrimage of Grace, for which he was to be executed. Now he seized the moment of the uncle-niece dispute to collect rents from the tenants on the Lutton lands at Flamborough. Thomas Lutton acted promptly, taking out a bill of complaint in Star Chamber, charging, among other things, that it was Sir Robert Constable's servants who, with Thomas Scaseby, had abducted his niece from Yedingham.

In Star Chamber Constable responded to these charges somewhat disingenuously by saying that he had only met the woman once. Several years ago, he recounted, he was travelling from Flamborough to Pickering to go hunting with his son-in-law. Passing near Yedingham he decided to call at the priory to have a drink with the prioress. She was not at home, he said, but he was invited in for a cup of ale. When he entered the chapel, he saw a nun, Elizabeth Lutton, looking mournfully out the window. 'Are you pregnant?', he asked her, and she said 'Yea' and that she had been forced to become a nun. And he never saw her again, which was not exactly Thomas Lutton's complaint.

Neither Star Chamber nor the ecclesiastical proceedings have left their results, but, when Thomas Lutton died in 1546, he was in full possession of his lands.[55] What about his niece Elizabeth, nun of Yedingham? In 1539, when the nuns of Yedingham surrendered their priory to the king, listed last among the nuns on the pension list is the name Elizabeth Sutton, age 40.[56] Should we not see here a scribal error of Sutton for Lutton? The age is right and the last place was the place for a returned apostate. Rather than inheriting the Lutton lands, she apparently received the small annual pension of 26s. 8d. Alleged apostasy, disputed profession, pregnancy, abduction, claim of inheritance, marriage and, probably, return – all marked her career, and in the end she left for neither love nor money but to comply with the policies of the king.

The apostates whom we have met, from every order of men and women, acted for reasons that are mostly elusive: glimpses here and there are all we tend to get. Many of the incidents are known to us because contemporaries found them strange or entertaining. Before the ice cracks beneath me, I should add that, if there were fully known to us the thousand and more stories about which we know merely the bare facts, I suspect we would encounter stories of real human tragedies, the knowledge of which the historian might secretly be pleased to be spared.

NOTES

1 The following abbreviations have been used in this paper:
CPL   *Calendar of the Entries in the Papal Registers relating to Great Britain and Ireland: Papal Letters* (London and Dublin, 1894–).
CPR   *Calendar of Patent Rolls* (London, 1901–).
Power, *Nunneries* Eileen Power, *Medieval English Nunneries* (Cambridge, 1922).
VCH   *Victoria History of the Counties of England* (individual counties are referred to by abbreviated county name, eg, Lincs. for Lincolnshire).
All archival references, unless otherwise indicated, are to London, Public Record Office.
2 C81/1788/1 (author's translation of Latin original). A dorsal notation indicates that writs were issued for Hollkey's arrest to the constable of Dover Castle and to the sheriff of Sussex. He was clearly thought to be on the south coast, perhaps on his way to the continent.
3 This paper and my monograph, *Runaway Religious in Medieval England, c.1240–1540*, are going through the press at the same time. The reader is referred, in general, to chapters 1 and 3 of the latter.
4 C81/1787/25; *CPR, 1452–61*, p. 116; *CPL* 12. 92–3, 210–11; E.B. Fryde *et al.* eds, *Handbook of British Chronology* 3rd ed. (London, 1968), p. 360.
5 *Apostasia* is simply a transliteration of ἀποϭταϭία, a late classical form of ἀπόϭταϭιϛ, and has the meaning of standing apart from.
6 'Hodie etiam apostata dicitur qui post suceptum religionis habitum ad secularem conversationem revertitur'. J.F. von Schulte ed., *Die Summa des Stephanus Tornacensis* (Giessen, 1891) p. 76. For the *Decretum* see particularly *D.50, c.69; C.*16, q.1, cc.11, 12, 17; C.20, q.3, cc.1–4; C.27, q.1, cc.1, 18, 19. These texts can be found in E.L. Richter and E. Friedberg eds, *Corpus Iuris Canonici* (Leipzig, 1881), 2 vols, vol. 1.
7 E.F. Jacob ed., *The Register of Henry Chichele, Archbishop of Canterbury, 1414–1443* (Canterbury and York Soc. 42, 45–7, 1943–7), 4 vols, 3, pp. 454–5 (author's translation from the Latin).
8 F.M. Powicke and C.R. Cheney eds, *Councils and Synods II, 1205–1313* (Oxford, 1964) 2 parts, 2, 912.
9 The text is in bk. 3, tit. 31, c. 22 (*Corpus Iuris Canonici*, vol. 2). See Wolfgang N. Frey, *The Act of Religious Profession* (Catholic University of America, Canon Law Studies, 63; Washington, 1931) pp. 23–31.
10 E135/6/173; G.F. Deiser, ed., *Year Book of 12 Richard II* (Ames Foundation, Cambridge, MA, 1914) pp. 71–8, 150–3; See Power, *Nunneries*, pp. 36–8.
11 *VCH, London* 1, 509.
12 *CPR, 1358–61*, p. 19.
13 *CPL* 14. 38–9.
14 H.H.E. Craster and M.E. Thornton eds, *The Chronicle of St Mary's Abbey, York* (Surtees Soc., 148, 1934), p. 12.
15 See H.R. Luard ed., 'Annales prioratus de Dunstaplia', *Annales Monastici* (Rolls Series; London, 1864–69) 5 vols, 3, 314; C81/1792/11, 13.

16 *CPL* 3, 393.
17 The story can be found in Roger Twysden ed., 'Chronica Guillielmi Thorne', *Historiae anglicanae Scriptores Decem* (London, 1652), *passim* cols. 2035–66, and in the more accessible English translation by A.H. Davis, *William Thorne's Chronicle of St Augustine's Abbey, Canterbury* (Oxford, 1934), *passim* pp. 463–81.
18 These examples can be found in C81/1788/46; C81/1792/2; *VCH, Northants.* 2, 114.
19 *English Austin Friars* (Oxford, 1940) pp. 274–6.
20 For individual choice in these matters see the perceptive remarks of Penelope D. Johnson, *Equal in Monastic Profession: Religious Women in Medieval France* (Chicago, 1991) pp. 13–18.
21 H.E. Salter ed., *Chapters of the Augustinian Canons* (Canterbury and York Soc., 29, 1922) pp. 147–51.
22 SC8/251/12547. He was given a royal pardon, 1 May 1389 (*CPR, 1388–92,* p. 34).
23 *Chronicle of St Mary's Abbey, York,* p. 47.
24 *Ibid.,* p. 53.
25 For more on this theme see Jane Sayers, 'Violence in the Monastic Cloister', *Journal of Ecclesiastical History* 41 (1990) 533–42.
26 Christopher Harper-Bill, 'Monastic Apostasy in Late Medieval England', *Journal of Ecclesiastical History.* 32 (1981) 1–18.
27 Thomas Walsingham, *Gesta abbatum,* H.T. Riley ed. (Rolls Series; London, 1867–69) 3 vols., 2, 132–3. Somerton had disputes with the abbots of St Albans, which *inter alia* involved charges of his apostasy in 1319, 1337, 1340 (C81/1786/32, 34, 35; *CPR, 1338–40,* p. 485).
28 A. Hamilton Thompson ed., *Visitations of Religious Houses in the Diocese of Lincoln* (Lincoln Record Soc. 14, 1918) 2, pp. 91, 116.
29 W. Brown ed., *The Register of Thomas of Corbridge, Lord Archbishop of York, 1300–1304* (Surtees Soc. 138, 1925) part 1, nos 255, 259.
30 *Visitations of Religious Houses* 2, 348. See Power, *Nunneries,* p. 449.
31 M. Archer ed., *The Register of Bishop Philip Repingdon, 1405–1419* (Lincoln Record Soc. 57–8, 1963) 2 vols, 3, no. 15.
32 W. Brown ed., *The Register of Walter Giffard, Lord Archbishop of York, 1266–1279* (Surtees Soc. 109, 1904), nos 666, 916.
33 *Visitations of Religious Houses* 2, 257.
34 *CPL* 3. 137; *CPR, 1343–45,* p. 400.
35 W.A. Pantin, ed., *Documents Illustrating the Activities of the General and Provincial Chapters of the English Black Monks, 1215–1540* (Camden Soc., 3rd ser., 45, 47, 54, 1931–37) 3 vols, 3, 277–309.
36 T.F. Kiley ed., *Wykeham's Register* (Hampshire Record Soc., 1896–99) 2 vols, 533–36, 542. For a summary see *VCH, Hants.* 2, 157–8.
37 *Gesta abbatum* 2, 415; *CPR, 1340–43,* p. 444.
38 C.T. Martin ed., *Registrum epistolarum fratris Johannis Peckham archiepiscopi Cantuariensis* (Rolls Series; London, 1882–85) 3 vols., 3, 933–4.
39 *Gesta abbatum* 2, 416.
40 F.S. Haydon ed., *Eulogium (historiarum sive temporis)* (Rolls Series; London, 1858–63) 3 vols, 1, 2. The translation is by Antonia Gransden from her *Historical Writing in England* (London, 1974–82) 2 vols, 2, 103.
41 *Wykeham's Register* 2, 77–9.
42 *Register of Thomas of Corbridge* 1, nos 247, 269.
43 A papal commission was appointed to investigate the matter, 17 Sept. 1405 (*CPL* 6. 55).
44 A.H. Thompson ed., *Visitations in the Diocese of Lincoln, 1517–1532* (Lincoln Record Soc., 33, 35, 37, 1940–47) 3 vols, 3, 11.
45 *CPR, 1367–70,* p. 353; *Wykeham's Register* 2, 100–1, 114–15.

46 Novellae (6th ed.; *Corpus Iuris Civilis*, vol. 3, Berlin, 1954) 123.

47 13 Edward I, c. 34 (A. Luders *et al.* eds, *Statutes of the Realm* (London, 1810–28) 1, 87).

48 *Nunneries*, p. 440.

49 See C. Moor, *Knights of Edward I* (Harl. Soc., Visitations, vols 80–84, 1929–32) 5 vols, 2, 115–16.

50 *Calendar of Fine Rolls* (London, 1911–62) 22 vols, 1, 207.

51 *Registrum . . . Peckham* 3, 916–17.

52 J.W. Willis Bund ed., *Episcopal Registers, Diocese of Worcester, Register of Bishop Godfrey Giffard, September 23rd, 1268, to August 15th, 1301* (Worcestershire Historical Soc., 1902) pp. 278–9.

53 The principal events narrated here are reconstructed from York, Borthwick Institute, CP.G.216, and *Yorkshire Star Chamber Proceedings: Yorks. Archaeol. Soc., Rec. Ser.*, vols. 41 (1909) no. 81; 45 (1911) no. 52; 51 (1914), no. 45. For a summary of this case see G.W.O. Woodward, *The Dissolution of the Monasteries* (London, 1966) pp. 42–5, and Claire Cross, *The End of Medieval Monasticism in the East Riding of Yorkshire* (Beverley, 1993) pp. 15–17.

54 *Dictionary of National Biography* 4, 969–70.

55 York, Borthwick Institute, Wills 13, f. 227.

56 SP5/2/76. J.S. Purvis ed., 'A Selection of Monastic Rentals and Dissolution Papers', *Yorks. Archaeol. Soc., Rec. Ser.*, 80 (1931) 91; J.M.T. Clay ed., *Yorkshire Monasteries: Suppression Papers, Yorks. (Archaeol. Soc., Rec. Ser., 48, 1912) p. 171.*

2   Morebath 1520–1570: A Rural Parish in the Reformation

Eamon Duffy

Morebath, ten miles north of Tiverton, twenty-five miles north of Exeter, is a remote and isolated community on the rain-swept southern edge of Exmoor. The parish forms a compact rectangle, three and a half miles by about two and a half. Flanked to the west by the valley of the river Exe, from which it rises steeply to between two and three hundred metres above sea level, it runs east along the county boundary with Somerset, which forms its northern edge. On its south it stops just short of the market-town of Bampton. Now as in the sixteenth century it is a village without a centre. A handful of farms and cottages, once mostly of cob and thatch, cluster round a small gaunt church, virtually demolished and rebuilt in two drastic Victorian restorations, the last by Butterfield in the 1870s.[1]

Even for this border-country on the fringe of the moor, Morebath was a remote place in the sixteenth century, one of the smallest communities in the Hundred of Bampton and the region generally. A set of regulations for the collection of Peter's Pence dating from 1531 (were they ever used?) reveals that there were just thirty-three households in the parish, five of them cottages, the rest tenant-farmers or 'placeholders'.[2] Most were tenants of the manor of Morebath, held by the local priory of Barlinch, an impoverished and somewhat run-down house of six Augustinian canons and a prior.[3]

Yet, remote as it was, we would be quite mistaken in dismissing Morebath as one of the 'dark corners of the land'. A good road ran from Exeter to Bampton, and Bampton itself was a bustling place, claiming 600 houselling folk in the 1540s, and supporting a community of gentry, merchants, tradesmen, parish and chantry clergy, and lawyers, representatives of all of whom feature in the Morebath accounts.[4] Morebath parishioners and their priest attended ales, employed workmen and transacted business in the surrounding towns and villages like Brushford, Dulverton and Bampton itself, attended the 'sherows towrne' at the court at Bradninch, and regularly travelled on ecclesiastical or civil business to Exeter or, nearer at hand, to Tiverton. At least one parishioner travelled sufficiently regularly to London on business to be given errands to perform for the parish. Books and church-furnishings beyond the resources of Bampton, Tiverton or Exeter thereby found their way to Morebath and, along with them, no doubt, budgets of news of the outside world.[5] A grammmar-school functioned at the priory in the early years of Henry VIII, and there are plenty of signs of literacy in the parish accounts, even among the cottagers and wage-earners.[6]

In economic and social terms, the parish was relatively homogeneous. The lay subsidy for 1524 lists 55 tax-payers, assessed at sums ranging from £1 in wages – the normal valuation for farm labourers – to £14 in goods. Only five parishioners in all – two Normans, two Morsses and a Tymewell – were rated at more than £10. As these modest figures suggest, there were no gentry in the parish, though the nearest gentry household, that of the Sydenhams of Leigh, in the parish of Dulverton, was not far away, just over the parish boundary in Somerset, and members of the Sydenham family were on several occasions called in to help adjudicate parish disputes.[7]

Seventeen parishioners were assessed at £1 in wages or goods, the standard figure for farm labourers or poor cottagers. At Morebath, therefore, they formed a third of the parish, just about the county average. These poor men included Lewis Trychay, the priest's brother. Thirteen parishioners were assessed at £2, while the remaining nineteen were assessed between £3 and £8, the majority in the £3-£4 range.[8]

Sir Christopher Trychay, vicar from 1520 to 1574, arrived in Morebath on 30 August 1520.[9] He was not exactly a local man, having been born twelve miles away at Culmstock, where his father Thomas still lived. There are two Thomas Trychays listed in the 1524 subsidy rolls for Culmstock, assessed at £2 and at £5, and most of the eight Trychays in Culmstock were assessed at £1 in wages, so the vicar's origins were certainly humble. He had been ordained acolyte in September 1514, subdeacon and deacon in March 1514/15, and priest on 2 June 1515, 'ad titulum prioratus de Frithelstock'.[10]

The vicarage of Morebath was recorded in the *Valor* as worth a mere £8, not the poorest living in the region, and certainly enough to live on, but by no means a plum. The living of Bampton was worth £20, and Trychay's own home parish of Culmstock was worth £16.[11] Nevertheless, Trychay's £8 put him at least on a par with most of his parishioners, and by contrast with what may well have been lean years before, he clearly viewed his arrival in Morebath as a homecoming to permanence and security. Twenty years on, recalling his arrival on 30 August 1520, he wrote, jubilantly,

> et in eo anno dextera domini exaltavit me.[12]

For so small and poor a place, the parish had an astonishingly elaborate internal structure, whose practical arrangements were reflected in and were themselves a reflection of the devotional life of the community. The parish church, dedicated to St George, housed a large number of images – of the patron, the Virgin (two images, including one of Our Lady of Pity), St Anthony, St Sunday, St Loy, St Anne, and Jesus, whose figure stood in a tabernacle over the one side altar. In the year of his arrival, Trychay presented the parish with a new carved and gilded image of the Exeter saint, Sidwell, and she too was placed above the side-altar, where, with the Vicar's encouragement, she rapidly became the dominant devotional focus.[13] Most of the images had lights burning before them, and these lights were maintained by a series of 'Stores' or funds, maintained by the return from small flocks of sheep, by ales, by gatherings, and by gifts and bequests. The stores of Morebath were Our Lady's store, St Anthony's store, St Sidwell's store, the store of Jesus, St Sunday's store, the Alms Light store, the Mayden store, and the Young Men's store. They differed widely in character.

The stores of Sidwell, Jesus and the Alms Light were simply lamp funds, whose income was derived from the sale of wool, supplemented by gifts – the Jesus and Sidwell stores had no officers of their own. The Alms Light, a taper burning in a basin before the high cross, had its own warden, elected newly each year: until 1538 most of those who were elected high wardens had already served as Alms Light warden. St Sunday store had its own warden, but unlike the other stores with wardens, this job was done year after year by the same man, John Norman at Courte, described as 'yerly wardyng' of the store: he was the wealthiest man in Morebath, and may have founded the store.[14] St Anthony store had two annually elected wardens, and differed from all the other church stores in having a small number of pigs as well as sheep, presented from time to time by parishioners. St Anthony was normally portrayed accompanied by a 'tantony pig', so these gifts should probably be understood as a distinctive devotional gesture.[15]

None of these stores should be considered as 'gilds': they were purely and simply funds, with the single complication required by the management of livestock. The Mayden store was another matter: the maidens maintained a light before the statue of the Virgin, before the high cross and, once her cult had established itself, before St Sidwell. They had no sheep, the income from the store coming from an annual 'gathering', which steadily grew throughout the 1530s, though the sums involved were never large – 3s.5½d. was gathered in 1529, 7s.4d. in 1538. These gatherings may well have taken place as part of organized ritual games or similar events, like the 'hock-tide' collections common elsewhere. Two wardens were elected each year, almost always young women, though their fathers occasionally seem to have served instead, perhaps because the girls elected were too young to manage the finances.[16]

The Young Men's store played a central role in parish finances and, by implication, its social life. Its main source of income came from an ale, referred to sometimes as the 'grooming ale' and, once at least, held in Lent.[17] The sums raised at these ales varied wildly, but were normally between one and two pounds, and sometimes more, a significant element in parochial finance. The Young Men maintained the taper before the patronal image of St George, and two lights before the 'high cross' or Rood: in the early 1530s they several times accounted to the parish on Holy Rood day. Again, they had two wardens elected afresh each year, and as with the maidens, when boys too young to serve were elected, their fathers were expected to take on the responsibility.[18]

The Store of Our Lady was the most important store in the parish. Like the others, it existed to maintain a light, in this case before the Virgin, but the two wardens of this store derived their income from the church's principal flock of sheep, called 'Our Lady's sheep', normally about two dozen and producing about forty pounds weight of wool each year. Like all the church sheep, this flock was distributed piecemeal to individual parishioners, who were responsible for accounting to the wardens for the sheep in their care at the end of the year, and for handing in the fleeces after shearing. Keeping one or more of the church sheep was a parochial obligation, only occasionally refused.[19] This meant that at any one time very large numbers of parishioners were involved in this aspect of parish fund-raising – in 1529, twenty-one households had church sheep in their keeping, in 1531 twenty-four.[20]

Coordinating all these stores were the two High Wardens of the goods and cattle of the parish, elected afresh each year from among the heads of households. Both wardens served for just one year, and there was no staggering of office, but it is clear that the two wardens did not carry equal authority. Each year the church 'iulis' or plate, the stock, and the contents of the Church house were entrusted to one of the wardens in particular, and that warden was responsible for preparing the account at the end of the year: it is often delivered in the singular – 'I received' or 'he received', and restrospective references to a previous year's accounts were often identified by the name of the senior or accounting warden – 'Harry Hurly's account'. When Robyn Isac, the senior warden, was absent from the parish during the 1562 account, his fellow warden was able to account only for the proceeds of the Church ale: it may be that the ale was the special responsibility of the junior warden. This tendency for one warden to take primary responsibility, evident throughout the accounts, was more marked in Elizabeth's reign than earlier, and reached its logical conclusion in the mid-1580s, when for about ten years the parish elected only one warden each year.[21]

Election seems to have travelled round the parish by farms and small-holdings, and the head of the household was expected to serve when his or her turn came round, even where that head was a widow. There were women high wardens in 1528, 1542, 1543, 1548, 1557, 1561(when both wardens were women), and 1563. With so many offices to fill each year, the refusal of parishioners who 'wolde not doo ther diligens' [22] was a serious matter, and finding substitutes could be difficult. One member of a family might stand in for another,[23] or sometimes the deputy was paid: when William Tayler acted as High Warden 'in vice' George Smyth in 1557, Smyth paid him 3s.10d. 'pro ejus labore'.[24] Sometimes payments were made directly to the parish, in the form of fines. Eylon Norman paid the parish four pounds weight of wax 'for her discharge of the hye Wardynscheppe' in 1546. But allowance was made for circumstances: when the cottager Richard Don was elected High Warden in 1544 he paid only two pounds of wax 'for hys dyscharge', and when the even poorer Exbridge cottager Marke was due to serve 'the parysse forgave hyt hem'.[25]

As that reference suggests, service as High Warden was not restricted to the well-to-do: the essential qualification was headship of a household, and the poor served as well as the prosperous. William Norman of Lawton was assessed at £1 in wages but served as Alms Light Warden in 1529, High Warden in 1533, and Our Lady's Warden in 1537. William Scely, a cottager assessed at £1 in wages, was High Warden in 1536. Richard Robbyns, also assessed at £1 in wages, was Alms Light warden in 1535 and High Warden in 1539. Lewys Trychay, the priest's brother, a cottager assessed at £1 in wages, served as Alms Light Warden in 1537, High Warden in 1541 and 1553, and Sheep Warden (what had been Our Lady's Store) in 1546.[26]

At the other end of the scale, the parish plutocracy also served. William at Morsse, assessed at £14 in goods, was High Warden in 1532, Our Lady Warden 1536, and High Warden again in 1545.[27] John Norman at Court was perpetual warden of the store of St Sunday, High Warden in 1526 and 1539, and Warden of St Anthony Store in 1537.[28] Men of their standing were also likely to be elected to the small group of senior parishioners who comprised the 'Four Men' or 'Five Men' – the number varied – 'that have the churche stock yn governansse'. These men (they were always men) acted as bankers for all the church stores and for the High Wardens. They also appeared at Visitations with the Wardens, met extraordinary demands for money imposed in the manorial or Hundred courts, making 'setts' after-wards to recoup the outlay, and from time to time were called upon to resolve parish disputes, sometimes with the assistance of the Vicar, or under the chairmanship of an outsider, such as the Sydenhams of Leigh, or the Steward or Lord of the Manor. To qualify as one of the 'Five Men' financial security was essential, because from time to time such men were expected to solve cash-flow problems from their own resources.[29] As we shall see, this aspect of their office was to be crucial in Edward's reign.

Throughout the 1520s and 1530s, therefore, in any one year twelve parishioners, eight of them heads of households, held parish office, in addition to the 'Five Men'. The degree of active parochial involvement this demanded from a community as small and poor as Morebath is staggering. It reflects a highly self-conscious community life, of which shared decision-making and accountability were dominant characteristics. This dimension of parish life in Morebath is built into the very nature of our principal source, the remarkable accounts kept by Sir Christopher Trychay.

The first thing to be said about these accounts is that they are only at a second remove Sir Christopher's. Each of the accounting wardens produced their own accounts for their stores or the parish as a whole. These may sometimes have been verbal accounts – the wardens' accounts are often cast in the first person, 'y resseuyd of the pleers at Easter here xijd', where the 'y' is clearly the senior warden,[30] and sometimes in the third person – 'hee made clere of hys ale all costs quytte. . .'.[31] In the latter cases, Sir Christopher may be producing the first written version. But there are a number of references to the retention by the warden of 'the cownter pane of this a cownte' or 'the copy istius competus', which suggests that they were usually in written form when the vicar received them.[32] He then copied them in standard form, for presentation to the parish, a task for which he was paid a token penny. In the process, he frequently corrected the warden's reckoning: in 1565, reporting John Lambert's Young Men's account, he wrote

Sum totalis receptionis ys vere but £4 4s.6d. . . . and y got the wardyn here by my cast xijd in hys ressetis for he cast his ressetis furst £4 5s.6d. where as he resseuyd not so moche by xijd by my cast.[33]

Each account was read aloud to the assembled parish, always on a Sunday: to make this possible, the stores accounted at different times of the year. We can be certain that the accounts were read aloud by the Vicar because of the vocative form into which he constantly breaks as he reports:

Now how many scheppe of our Lady be dede and gon this ere and how many there be as ytt a lyffe and yn hoo ys kepyng they be now schall ye have knolydge of . . .[34]

Sometimes he breaks off the general report to remind parishioners of specific issues, or to address individuals. The High Wardens' accounts for 1538 provide a particularly good sample:

Item of Richarde Webber we resseuyd of the be questh of hys wyfe Jone a gowne and kurtyll: the wyche was sold to John at pole for 13/4 for the wyche mony the iiij men wyll make you a cownt as here after ye schall hyre: and Richard Webber wyll desyre you that ye wyll ley forth this mony a gayn of the churche stoke un remembrans of hys wyfe Jone: when ye bye a new cope to this churche.

Item John Waterus remember yor promysse to the syde auter as ys expressyd the ere be fore a pon Harry Hurlys cownte.

Item Willam at Wode remember your paynter for the hye auter in yor 5s. a cordyng to you promysse of the laste ere a pon Harry Hurly's a cownte.[35]

Accountability before the parish, and consent by the parish to all decision-making, is a striking feature of the accounts. Debts to the church might be settled publicly, 'this day ante parochianos'[36] Similarly, when the Store of Our Lady commissioned 'a nimage of the nativite of our Ladye' from the carver Thomas Glasse, they were careful to make the 'bargyn' at their annual account in 1530, 'ante parochianos'.[37]

For the first twenty years of Trychay's incumbency, this communal sense of Morebath was focussed on the adornment of the parish church itself, and the elaboration of the cult offered within it. The scale of the parish's investment in the fabric and ritual of its church in those years is staggering. Its annual income never exceeded and rarely approached twenty marks, and in the twenties and thirties averaged out somewhere between six and eight pounds a year, yet in that time the parish rebuilt, roofed and reseated the choir, installed new high and side altars, installed a complete set of pews in the nave, commissioned expensive new images of the Virgin, including a tableau of her birth, another set of images of the parish patron St George and his horse and dragon, and had new or regilded tabernacles for the images of Jesus, Sidwell, Loy, Sunday and Saint Anne. New celures or painted ceilings of honour were erected over the side and high altars, and over the new Rood group, commissioned in direct rivalry with the neigh-bouring village of Brushford in 1538. And alongside these parish projects innumerable individual gifts flowed in year by year – vestments, banners, wooden or latten candlesticks, lamps and bowls for lights, rings, girdles, gowns, caps, sets of beads, altarcloths and hangings, pillows, palls, corpo-rasses and kerchiefs.[38] The priest was certainly one driving force behind such gifts. On first arrival in the parish he gave in and had gilded a new image of St Sidwell worth 33s.4d., and subsequently paid for the dressing of her altar, for the new glazing of a window in the choir, and with the aid of a bequest from his father added to a parishioner's gift of a white chasuble the matching dalmatic and tunicle for deacon and subdeacon. When the nave was pewed in 1534 he was the largest single contributor to the project, donating three oak-trees (to the Prior of Barlinch's two). His devotion to St Sidwell triggered a growing tide of gifts by parishioners to her altar, image and cult, and reflected in the fact that at least two Morebath families christened daughters Sidwell.[39]

Such devotional acts, which could be replicated in most parishes in England on the eve of the reformation, were embedded in a sense of com-munal engagement in which sacred and secular are impossible to separate.

In 1531 Joan the daughter of Richard Hucly left her beads to St Sidwell and 6*s*.8*d*. to buy a candlestick of five lights to stand before the new image of Our Lady. The candlestick was duly bought by her father, who was one of the Five Men, but it cost 8*s*.5*d*. Her father donated the 21*d*. difference to the parish, no doubt out of paternal piety towards the daughter's wishes but also, as the vicar reported to the parishioners, 'by cause you schuld se the soner that he mayzth be contendyd for the rayling of Exbryge and thus ys this canstycke y cum fre unto this churche'.[40] This harnessing of a devotional and commemorative gesture to the promotion of goodwill and, in this case, with the express aim of speeding the recovery of a secular debt from the parish, nicely locates for us the piety of Morebath in its proper communal context, the promotion of the social miracle, and the creation of harmony and the balance of justice and charity within the parish community.

The early stages of the Henrician reformation made little impression in Morebath, and there is no evidence of any attempt to implement the provisions of the 1536 Injunctions, such as the purchase of a Latin and English New Testament, until 1538. Barlynch Priory was dissolved in February 1536, a momentous event for the village since most of the inhabitants were tenants of the monastery. The manor itself was acquired by a courtier, Sir John Wallop, and remained in his family's hands until the mid-seventeenth century. But the rectory was acquired by Sir Hugh Paulet, and Paulet probably also became Steward of the manor, for he as well as Wallop held courts in Morebath. This change from ecclesiastical to secular lordship may well have had perceptible economic consequences in Morebath, and certainly 'setts' and gatherings to meet manorial obligations feature more prominently after the 1530s, but the only direct evidence of the change in the accounts is the gift in 1537 of a stained glass window worth £3 from Barlinch, by the Bailiff, John Dysse, 'to pray for hys Master (Hu Powlyth) and him'.[41]

The year 1538 was a watershed. The Second Royal Injunctions marked a decisive turn towards a more radical protestantism, outlawing any overt cultus of the saints, and in particular the maintenance of lights before images. The piety of Morebath had been specially focussed on the provision of images and lights for at least two decades, and as the Injunctions were promulgated the parish was still settling the bills for its latest outlay, the new crucifix with Mary and John. There was far more at stake here than a matter of candles in front of statues. All the stores of Morebath existed primarily to maintain these lights: the whole structure of lay involvement in the parish was tied to the cult which the Injunctions outlawed. As yet the attack was qualified. Lights might still burn before the High Cross, the Easter Sepulchre and the Sacrament, and at Morebath both the Young Men and Maiden stores kept lights before the High Cross: these at least could continue. But the parish was in no doubt about the implications of the

1538 Injunctions for the cult of the saints. At the end of the accounts made in Lent 1539 the vicar added a note signalling the end of all the stores of the saints: 'Lett all the churche scheppe in future be put yn our Lady merke full what store so ever they be of'.[42]

But Trychay knew that even Our Lady's store itself was no longer safe. The new protestant dean of Exeter, Simon Hayes, had greeted the 1538 Injunctions with a holocaust of imagery and funerary inscriptions in the cathedral. His many enemies in a conservative diocese were to see to it that these radical reforming actions later rebounded on his own head, but a clear signal had been sent to the diocese at large, and it was well understood at Morebath.[43] In 1538 'Our Lady's bedis', Katerine Robbyns's gift to adorn the image every high day and principal feast, were sold off: in 1539 the last accounts for the stores of St Anthony and St Sidwell were submitted, the vicar noting that the sheep in St Sidwell's store 'the hye Warden dydd answer for in preteritis but in futuro he schalbe dyschargyd'. The account of the store of Our Lady is now headed the account of the wardens of 'the churche scheppe (quod in preteritis esset de stanzo beatae marie)'. Trychay had been accustomed to introduce the accounts of each store with a pious ejaculation to the patron saint – 'Sancte Antoni ora pro nobis': he did this for the last time for the Lady store in 1539, using his standard formula – 'Auxilium nobis fer pia nunc Sancta Virgo Maria', and then added as an afterthought 'et deinceps sent Iorge', literally 'and next, St George' but in this context implying rather *deinde*, 'from now on', a momentous transfer of patronage from the Virgin to the parish saint, and the symbolic equivalent of the transition from 'Our Lady's sheep' to 'the church sheep'.[44] The Young Men no longer maintain two lights before the Cross and one before St George, but three before the Cross: the Maiden's lights were transferred from Mary and St Sidwell to the Sepulchre.[45] All the other stores, including the Alms Light, disappear permanently from parochial life, together with their opportunities – and obligations – for office-holding and patronage.

In other respects, however, the religious life of Morebath continued as before. Donations to images now being forbidden, their piety was redirected: the routine pious giving of the parish in the early 1540s was directed towards the cult of the dead. As Vicar, Trychay was entitled to the small tithes of the parish. Under his predecessor Sir Richard Bowdyn, these had included the tithing of the wool of the church sheep, but there had been no honey tithe. Trychay, like several other members of his family who display a marked interest in bees and honey, evidently had a sweet tooth. In return for the institution of a honey-tithe in kind in 1528 he agreed to surrender the church wool tithe, the proceeds to go towards the purchase of a set of black vestments for requiems. This black vestment fund had inched up through the 1530s, with the vicar and the custodian, Harry Hurly, as

virtually the sole benefactors. But from 1539 it became the major focus of
parochial pious benefaction, and the vestments were bought, and taken to
Exeter to the bishop to be blessed, in 1547, when Trychay accounted for
the money to the parish:

and now lok ye a pon these vestmentis and the cope and take them at a worthe with
all there fawtis for y have don the best that y can doo yn getheryng of ye small
pensse to gethers y pray God that hyt may be for there sawlis helthe that gave any
gefth un to hyt for thys ys cum with owt any charge of any store by my procure-
ment to the honor of God and this churche and to the worschyppe of all thys hole
parysse as y pray God hyt may soo be. Amen.[46]

This was the last fling of undisturbed pre-reformation piety at Morebath. The
accession of Edward VI brought a series of rapid disasters which dissolved
the internal economy and the social structures of the parish, pushing them
into the maelstrom of disaster surrounding the 1549 Prayer-Book rebellion.
    Parish life had seeemed much as normal till high summer of 1547. The
black vestments were displayed and accounted for to the parish on the
Sunday before St Mary Magdalene's day in late July 1547. On the same day
the wardens of the church sheep accounted, and their successors for the year
1547–8 were elected.[47] Even as the parish voted, however, the Edwardine
visitation of 1547 was getting under way, and the Royal Injunctions on
which the Visitation was based sounded the death-knell for this particular
manifestation of the pieties of Morebath. In particular, Injunction 29,
which required the installation of a poor man's box in every church, also
commanded the diversion of all funds 'which riseth of fraternities, guilds
and other stocks of the church' to the use of the poor man's box.[48] By the
time the High Wardens rendered their account as usual on All Saints' day
1547 the Royal Visitors had reached Exeter and the warden and the
Three Men had been summoned before them to receive the Injunctions.
Accordingly, the new sheep wardens, a year early, made their first and final
account. The entire flock of church sheep (much depleted anyway since the
dissolution of the stores of Anthony, Sidwell and Sunday) was sold off to a
parishioner, the proceeds absorbed into parish funds 'to helppe to make the
cheste with all', the wardens discharged, and no successors appointed. The
hives of bees which had once provided wax to burn before St Sidwell, about
which the accounts had been silent for years, were sold off at the same time.
The vicar, whose relatives had provided most of the swarms, bought them.[49]
    By the time the Chantry Commissioners arrived at Tiverton, therefore,
to implement the dissolution required by the new chantry act passed in
December 1547, Morebath had no stocks set aside for the maintenance of
lights or obits. Its parishioners, however, certainly shared in the general
panic and discontent provoked both by the Royal Visitation and by
the making of the inventories required by the Chantry act. January and

February 1548 brought with it a radicalization of the official reformation, manifested in the attack on and eventual abolition of many traditional cere-monies and sacramentals, such as Candlemas lights, and Holy Bread and holy water, and the outlawing and destruction of all images.[50] West Country discontent with these drastic moves reached a climax at Helston on 5 April, with the lynching of William Body by a traditionalist mob led by an out-of-work chantry priest.[51] Matters were conducted more law-abidingly at Morebath, where William Scely, dying in office as High Warden early in 1548, dutifully left 6*d.* to the new poor man's box, as the Injunctions required him to do. But there was a mounting sense of crisis there all the same. On 18 March 1548/9 the Three Men summoned an extraordinary parish meeting to account for their expenses in connection with the Royal and the Chantry Visitations. Having settled these expenses and paid off some parish building and repair debts, they reported that, apart from a few pence for current expenditure in the hands of the High Warden, Lucy Scely, the parish stocks were now totally exhausted.[52]

The agitation of the parish in all this is revealed in a note added to the end of this March 1548 account by the Vicar. In 1547 the Crown required every parish church to submit an inventory of its valuables, and this measure triggered a wave of pre-emptive concealments and panic sales of church goods all over the country.[53] Morebath was no exception. In place of his usual handsome and neat handwriting, the vicar hastily squeezed a note on to the bottom of a page, with frantic emendations and crossings out, record-ing the parish's attempts to conceal its vestments from Royal depredations. The annotation reveals a chaotic and perhaps panic-stricken sequence of events, as vestments hidden with one household were moved to another. The black vestments, so long awaited, went to John at Courte. John Norman at Pole got the best blue velvet vestments, and the church's banners and streamers, wrapped up to preserve them in a tablecloth. The best cope went at first to Robert at More, who also had the black cope for dirges and requiems, but it was later decided to put the good cope in pledge for 20*s.* with another parishioner, William Hurley. This change of custodian reflects the deepening financial problems of the parish. Hurley had advanced 20*s.* to the parish to meet expenses, including the costs of the appearance before the Commissioners for Church goods at Tiverton, and the cope was lodged with him rather than Robert at More till his 20*s.* was repaid.[54]

In the same year the parish sold off the ritual furniture now under attack by Somerset's government – the candlesticks and light basins, the banner staves, the coverings for the Easter Sepulchre and the furniture of St George and St Sidwell's altars. This may have represented unilateral action by the warden, for Trychay was later to claim that she sold these church goods 'without commission'. By Michaelmas 1548, when William Scely's widow

Lucy accounted on his behalf to the parish, the church had been stripped of much of its ritual furniture, and there was 15*d.* in hand to pass on to her successor: the Young Men had held an ale the previous year, but they then evidently dissolved themselves, for they handed over all their remaining funds to the High Warden, and no new officers were elected. For the first time, there was no parish ale at all. Again for the first time, the parish elected only one warden.[55]

The crisis deepened early in 1549, and the parish celebrated its patronal festival that year by selling off its secular possessions, the furnishings and vessels used for parish commensality at ales and other celebrations, and which were also sometimes loaned out to parishioners for weddings and similar events. By contrast with Lucy Scely's sale of ritual objects the previous year, this sale was 'by the consent of the hole parysse', and the receipts were delivered to the Six Men. Some of the proceeds were absorbed by the expenses of appearing at Tiverton before the Commissioners for Church goods and the provision of Erasmus' *Paraphrases*, and the remaining 20*s.* was lodged with William Tymewyll, at the parish disposal 'at all times'. The table linen from the Church house was given to poor parishioners at the public meeeting. Privately, more odds and ends of linen was divided between the parish clerk and the warden. And to deepen the sense of desolation, the next night, in a sequence of events becoming familiar in parishes all over the country, thieves broke into the church and stole the best surplice and the clerk's rochett.[56]

By the early summer of 1549, therefore, the parish of Morebath had been stripped to the bone. Its images and most of its ritual furnishings were gone, its vestments concealed, its communal social life suspended and the Church house locked and empty, and all its parish organizations dissolved. A decade before there had been a minimum of twelve parish officials active, raising and managing a total annual income of about £10, deployed about a multitude of parish projects. There was now a single warden, operating with a balance in hand of less than two shillings, and, with the disappearance of parish commensality and the church flocks, without a regular source of income to meet the expenses of reformation. At this low ebb, the parish's local problems were swept decisively into greater upheavals.

On Whitsunday 1549 the new Book of Common Prayer came into use all over England. Morebath dutifully acquired a copy, spending 4*s.*4*d.* on it, the price set for one of the best quality bound in calf.[57] But Morebath was not the only community which had been devastated by reform, and smouldering resentment of the religious changes now burst into flame, beginning at Mass at Sampford Courtnay on Whit Monday, 11 June. The West Country erupted into violence, and the rebels laid siege to Exeter at the beginning of July.[58] In faraway London and with a rash of other disturbances on his hands, Protector Somerset was slow to register the seriousness of the Western Rebellion. Lord Russell, the Lord Privy Seal, was despatched to deal with the rebels on 24 June, but found it hard going, since the gentry and commons of the county sullenly refused to put down a rebellion with which most of them were in essential (if ingloriously passive) sympathy. Demands to the Justices of Peace of Devon to 'putt your selfs with such of yor tenants and servants as you best trust, secretely ordered to attend' mostly fell on deaf ears.[59] By 10 July London was aware that even the Devon gentry professing loyalty were not lightly to be trusted, and by the third week of July Russell was at his wits end for lack of adequate numbers of troops.[60] Foreign mercenaries were sent, and the Privy Council ordered Russell to levy footsoldiers from the neighbouring counties of Somerset and Dorset. If they proved reluctant he was to issue proclamations threatening that if they did not show themselves ready 'to fight against the rank rebells and papists of Devon . . . they shalbe both demed and for trators and forfeit theyr landes, Copiholds and goods without redempcion to themselves, wyfes and children, and be without all hope of pardon'. It was thought that this threat about 'the matyr of Copiholds' would infallibly galvanize the reluctant into action, though in fact in Somerset there was little response because of the 'evill inclynation of the people', some of whom 'do not styck openly to speak rash traterous words agaynst the kyng and in favor of the trayterous rebells'. Russell was instructed to hang two or three, *pour encourager les autres*. It was hardly worth doing, for even those who did join up would prove to fight 'most fayntly' against their Devonshire neighbours, and they were disbanded at the earliest opportunity.[61]

Morebath's part in all this is hidden in ambiguity. The Edwardine reform had brought its social and religious structures to the verge of collapse: it can hardly be doubted that the traitorous speeches being voiced just over the county boundary in Somerset would have had a fervent echo among Trychay's parishioners. An enigmatic set of entries in the parish accounts seems to suggest that the village's patience had indeed snapped, and that they sent the young men off to join the rebels. On 18 July Russell complained to Somerset and the Council of the 'dayly encrease of the rebell's numbers'. The Morebath entry gives details of 'another rekenyng' for money laid out 'about sent iamys day', 25 July. This includes a payment of 3s.4d. for the Book of Common Prayer, but also a series of payments to five parishioners – William Hurley 'the yong man', Thomas Borrage 'the yonger', John Tymewyll, Christopher Morsse and Robert Zaer, at their goyng forthe to sent Davys down ys camppe. St David's Down was the main rebel camp outside Exeter. Of these men only Morsse and Tymewyll occur as Morebath tax-payers in the subsidy of 1543, and so far as can be deduced from the accounts, none were householders, suggesting that the group as a whole was made up of 'Young Men'. Whatever their precise identity, they certainly went with the parish blessing and support. William Tymewyll and William Hurley senior had the parish's remaining stock in their keeping. They disposed of it in providing each man with 6s.8d. 'at hys goyng forthe' and in providing them with arms – swords for all but Zaer, who was paid 2s. for his bow. There was a shortfall of 9s.10d., made good by two parishioners, William at Combe and John at Pole, and the tithing man, William Leddon, levied a sett on the parish to recompense them. 2s.6d. for Christopher Morsse's sword was raised by a collection 'at the churche style of viij persons viij groats'.[62]

This is a baffling incident, and its very existence was masked from previous users of the accounts by the editor's mistranscription of St David's Down as 'sent *denys* ys down'. What were the Morebath young men being equipped to do? The 6s.8d. given to each of them seems to have been an officially fixed sum – when the parish stock was exhausted, enabling only 3s.4d. to be given to John Tymwell, Willam at Combe gave him another 3s.4d. 'to make up his nobyll'. So this suggests compliance with some acknowledged procedure, an official routine such as a response to a muster, perhaps. Yet by 25 July there were no royal forces anywhere near St David's Down. If the young men of Morebath marched away to St David's Down in the fourth week of July 1549 they can only have been going to join the rebel forces beseiging Exeter, an act of defiance which Russell's reference to the 'dayly encrease of the rebell's numbers' does indeed suggest was wide-spread. And as we have seen, Morebath had no lack of motivation for such a gesture of desperate defiance.

Yet there are enormous problems in the notion of the parish equipping its sons for rebellion and then solemnly recording the proceedings in the churchwardens' accounts. West country parishes recorded parochial expenses in connection with the 1548 Cornish 'commotions', but those expenses were incurred in support of Royal forces putting down the rebellion, and as part of the secular obligations of the parishes.[63]

The key to unlock this mystery is, I think, a single word in the record of the payment for the prayer-book of 1549 with which the entry begins: the priest writes that William Tymwell paid 3s.4d. for 'the *furst* communion book'. The word 'furst' can only mean that this entry was copied in its present form after the publication of the *second* Edwardine Prayer-Book in 1552 – the keeping of accounts on loose sheets for copying later was com-mon practice in the period and is attested elsewhere in the Morebath accounts. Writing at a distance of three years or more about the events of the summer of 1549, Sir Christopher might well have telescoped the departure of the Young Men as part of a royal muster, culminating several weeks later in the raising of the siege of Exeter, into the phrase about St David's Down.

And in fact we can be fairly sure that such musters were being raised at this precise point. In the midst of general lamentation about the reluctance and failure of the West-Country gentry to mobilize their tenants on behalf of the crown, the Council instructed Russell on 22 July 1549 to convey the King's special thanks to those gentry who had responded to his appeals and done the King 'good, faythfull and paynefull' service. Among these was almost certainly Sir Hugh Paulet, patron of the living of Morebath and Steward of the Manor, at whose Somerset house Russell had based himself on his first arrival in the West Country.[64] After the collapse of the rebellion Paulet would be rewarded for his services to the Crown with the governorship of Jersey.[65] A hawkish professional soldier, he was indeed one of the key figures in the Royalist counter-attack against the rebels, and within weeks of the Morebath meeeting on St James's day would chase the retreating remnants of the rebel forces up the Exe valley, almost to Bampton itself. The young men of Morebath, press-ganged into service by Paulet, may have returned home hard on the heels of an exhausted and hunted group of rebels with whose cause they entirely sympathized.

Morebath's obedient provision of troops to suppress the Western Rebellion highlights the paradoxes of the English Reformation far more vividly than if they had instead taken part in the uprising. As the torrent of destruction swept over their community, annihilating the network of stores and devotions which had helped structure their social and religious life, they did not resist, but doggedly and dumbly bent their heads to the storm. The hostility to reform represented by the attempts at concealment in March of the previous year was not determined enough to force the parish into the gamble of rebellion. Instead deference to authority, the habit of obedience, and maybe fear of the threatened loss of copihold and livelihood, brought them into line.

At any rate, by the time the parish assembled for the High Warden's annual account at All Saints 1549, the Prayer-Book rebellion had been suppressed, and Morebath was obliged to come to terms with that defeat. Certainly their loyalty bought them no favours: the destruction went on. Two sets of vestments and copes were returned to the church, for use in the Prayer-book liturgy, but the missal and breviary were handed over for destruction, the parish salvaging what it could by selling the leather covers. In the following year, the warden sold off the remaining great candlesticks, sixty pounds weight of brass, to an Exeter brazier. From this point onwards, the High Warden's account dwindles in significance, for the parish was now functioning at a massive deficit, and was being kept afloat by loans from the wealthiest parishioners, now augmented for the purpose to 'Six Men': their accounts, now greatly augmented, become the real key to activity in the parish. Some of the expenses they had to meet were directly linked to the process of reform – the removal of the High Cross and the patronal image, the destruction of the altars in 1551. It may be that the parish had destroyed the Book of Common Prayer during the heady days of the rebellion, for sometime before 1551 they had to buy another, together with a psalter. These books were paid for with two collections of groats from parishioners, the first collection not raising enough for the psalter, so that it was bought 'a gode whyle after the boke of communion', the parish having to wait for a further Sunday collection 'to have mony by twyxt masse and matyns for the sawter boke'.[66] The parish also incurred a series of expenses in connection with its 'cooked' inventory of church goods: the Commissioners realized that the parish were concealing items, and the vicar had to go four times to Exeter to answer queries. When the final Edwardine Inventories were ordered prior to total confiscation in 1553, the parish surrendered two copes, two tunaicles, a silver pax and a small paten, which they certified 'was all the churche gooddis that they hadd'. This tallies with the pathetic little list of religious bric-a-brac in the church chest by 1553 – worn out towels and napkins, pieces of ironwork, the foot of the processional cross, a holy-water bucket, the sanctus and lych bells. But it was certainly not the whole truth: it is notable that there were no chasubles among the surrendered items, and no word of the vestments concealed round the parish.[67]

The Rebellion itself hit the parish's tottering finances, for in its wake the Privy Council ordered the removal of all but a single small bell from every church tower in Devon, since it was by the bells the people had been summoned to rebellion. In practice, this meant the removal of the clappers, and the committal of the bells to the notional custody of selected 'honest men' of the parish. In 1550 the Council granted the clappers and bell furniture to Sir Arthur Champernon and John Chichester, a move which proved self-defeating, since they promptly cashed in on this grant by allowing parishes to redeem them, for a price. Morebath bought its clappers back on 27 June 1551, at a cost of 26s.8d., advanced by three parishioners, one of whom was still waiting for his money in 1554.[68] The parish was kept going by borrowing from successive wardens (the obvious explanation for the evident reluctance of parishioners to serve in that capacity between 1548 and 1554), from the more substantial parishioners and from the Vicar, or by attaching fictional future payments to services actually rendered gratis, as in the rebuilding of the Church House in 1542. By the end of Edward's reign the parish had outstanding debts of over £6, and no obvious way of meeting them.[69] The Church House had by now been rented out – to the parish clerk – as a private dwelling house, a symbol of the privatizing of communal resources which the reformation had brought to Morebath. In a well-known passage reviewing the history of the parish in the 1540s and early 1550s, Trychay commented bitterly:

Anno domini 1548 was hye warden of this church Luce Scely and by her tyme the churche gooddis was sold a way with out commission ut patet postea and no gefth gevyn to the church but all fro the churche and this continyd fro Luce ys time un to Richard Cruce and fro Cruce un to Richard Hucly and fro Hucly un to Richard Robyns and fro Robyns un to Robyn at More and by all thes mens tyme the wyche was by tyme of King Edward the vj the church ever dekeyd and then deyd the Kyng and Quyne Majestis grace dyd succed and how the church was restoryd a gayn by her tyme here after this ye schall have knolydge of hyt. . . .[70]

Unsurprisingly, the accession of Mary was greeted unequivocally at Morebath as an opportunity for a return to normality. Henry Wallop held Manorial Court at Morebath at Michaelmas 1553. At that meeting, the assembled parishioners agreed to authorize the Four Men and the Vicar to draw up an account of all the parish debts, and 'to qualyfye all dettis and demandis wt all other contraversy a mong us'. By 27 March 1554 they were ready to report. Every parishioner turned in to the Four Men a detailed account of whatever they had laid out on the parish's behalf, and what they were still owed. To meet these claims there was a collection from every household, which in theory at least was voluntary, the vicar commenting 'how gentylly for the most parte men have payd of there owne devocion with out ony taxyn or ratyng as ye schall hyre'. There was a shortfall of £2 14s., and this was dealt with by securing the agreement of the majority of parishioners to take less than they were owed.[71]

The settlement of debts was not the only step to the restoration of normality. Following the pattern which had emerged in Edward's reign, only one warden, Joan Morsse, had been elected for the year 1553–4. When the time for the High Warden's account at All Saints 1554 came round Mistress Morsse duly made the account, but another warden, Thomas at Tymewyll, had been added, and this return to the Henrician pattern continued thereafter.

Their account shows the beginnings of the restoration of Catholic cultus.[72] The ringing of knells for deceased parishioners, discontinued throughout Edward's reign, commences at once, as do bequests to the church 'to be prayed for'. The high altar was rebuilt, the Easter Sepulchre and its hearse for lights taken out of concealment and repaired. To begin with the parish had no mass-book, and had to hire one from a local priest, but a parishioner, Thomas Borrage, soon presented a missal worth 6s.. Richard Tymewyll gave a tabernacle for the reservation of the sacrament (the Marian church's preferred method, in keeping with Italian precedent: a Marian 'box' of the type used at Morebath survives at Warkleigh[73]). A group of parishioners contributed to the replacement of the paten surrendered to the Commissioners in 1553, and the wives of the parish made a collection of tuppences and pennies to buy a new Manual, the book containing all the occasional services and rites of passage such as christenings, marriage and burial. Once again the vicar meticulously records their gifts individually.[74]

From 1554 onwards the Marian restoration at Morebath gathered momentum. The wardens bought a new pyx for the sacrament, and repaired the lamp to go before it to the sick. A new large-sized breviary in two volumes was bought for the celebration of Matins and Evensong, a new lent cloth was bought and hung, a new crucifix bought on sale and return from a Bampton tradesman pending the commissioning of a complete new Rood group. The Young Men's store was reconstituted, and their first ale for eight years raised 48*s*.5½*d*. The Bible and Erasmus' paraphrases were packed up and sent to Exeter to be surrendered to the Marian authorities. Above all, the vicar and his parishioners began to produce the vestments, hangings, carvings and books which they had rescued or bought from the Edwardine holocaust: unsurprisingly, Trychay had kept a cloth painted with St Sidwell, as well as a more utilitarian fire pick from the Church house, but a host of parishioners had something or other:

Item of John Williams of Bery we received a gain a image of Mary and the kyng and the quyne concernng Sent iorge. And of Willm Morsse at lauton was resseuyd a image of John. And of the wydow iurdyn traylis and knottis. And of diverse wother perssons here was resceuyd pagynttis and bokis and diversse wother thyngis concernyng our rowde lowfth like tru and fayzthefull crystyn pepyll this was restoryd to this churche by the wyche doyngis hyt schowyth that they dyd lyke good catholyke men.[75]

By the end of the year 'all of the churche gooddis was brosth yn a gayn'. It is a sign of growing confidence in the permanence of all this that the Vicar in 1556 once more begins the accounts with 'Sent George ora pro nobis', and that and succeeding years saw all this consolidated, St Sidwell's altar reerected, a new Rood erected, the ceilings of honour over the high and side altar repainted, the Young Men and Maidens paying for the work over the high altar, a new ceiling made and painted over the High Cross. Much of this was supererogatory, but the parish was also straining to meet the requirements of the Marian regime, not easy to do when every parish in the land was about the same task and craftsmen could not keep up with the demand. In 1557 a bequest for painting about the high altar had not been spent, 'but not with stondyng hyt schalbe bestowyd in the churche as sone as we can gette a workman paynter gracia divina': as late as 1558 the parish paid 12*d*. 'at the Visitation' to have a lycense to have a longer day to se suche thyngis redressyd as was in payne in the court'.[76]

By the end of Mary's reign, then, much of the energy and commitment to the adornment of the parish church which had characterized Henrician Morebath was once more in evidence, though as yet only the Young Men's store had been recreated. Older patterns of pious benefaction were nevertheless once more ensconced – women bequeathed gowns and girdles to the church, and the passing of the substantial men of the parish was marked by 'ryngyn for a monyzth every nyzthe the grett bell'. The accession of Elizabeth can have been greeted in Morebath with anything but delight. Once more they conformed: the two altars re-erected in Mary's reign were once more taken down, the Book of Common Prayer bought from Exeter. The Vicar and the Four Men spent 5*s.* before the Queen's Commissioners at the Visitation of 1559, and Leuys Trychay and William at Combe appeared before them again at Exeter with the inventory of Church goods, the names of all the houselling people in the parish and a register of everyone baptized, married and buried in the last twelve months, which Trychay had evidently been neglecting to keep.[77]

We need not imagine that any of this was done with enthusiasm: the whole process was closely scrutinized by the authorities. In 1561, when the process of reformation at Morebath was still in progress, there were no fewer than three visitations at which the Wardens were required to attend – the routine archidiaconal one, Bishop Alley's episcopal visitation, and a metropolitan visitation by Archbishop Parker.[78] As far as the authorities were concerned, this was probably just as well, for the reformation at Morebath was a wheelbarrow, which went only as far as it was pushed. Much had been learned from the events of Edward's reign. In 1549 the parish had dutifully destroyed its missal, but now the missal and the mass vestments were placed in the care of parishioners, ready for the next turn of the wheel.[79] Slowly the demands of the Settlement were met: in 1562 the Paraphrases once more bought, the rood-loft taken down. Yet the language of the accounts is anything but reformed. In 1561 Trychay dates the Young Men's account 'Thomas Beckottis day', and again by 'St Thomas day' in 1562, in 1568 by 'the Visitacion of our Ladye', in 1567 the High wardens' account is dated by St Leonard's day, in 1568 St Clement. The contribution of the Young Men to church expenses each year is referred to into the later 1560s as being 'layd a downe a pon the hye auter'.[80] Perhaps it was actually the high altar: at any rate the parish was in trouble for not having the arrangements around the communion table as they should be at the Visitation of 1570, and only at that stage was the table 'sett.. yn a frame', and properly covered with a silk carpet, made from a tunicle which till then had been in the keeping of Edward Rumbelow, the man to whom the Mass vestments had been given in 1558, and who now surrendered the tunicle in payment for his wife's grave. Rumbelow's surrender of the tunicle was a gesture of accommodation, and acceptance of the inevitable. He was not alone. The Vicar himself accommodated himself to the new regime, and even improved his lot. He was satisfying some at least of the expectations of the reformed hierarchy: in 1561 Bishop Alley reported to Archbishop Parker that though not a graduate Trychay was 'satis doctus', and while not licensed, preached in his own church, a rarity in Devon in 1561, but one which we can well believe in the garrulous Sir Christopher's case. He had also secured for himself the united benefice of Knowstone with Molland, which he must have served with a curate, but which must have more than trebled his income, for Molland was worth £26 10s.8½d. in the King's Book.[81]

One by one the links with the Catholic past were going. In 1571 the parish was forced by the Queen's Commissioners to sell a chalice and to give 20s. of the proceeds to the Crown. In 1572 the parish at last sold off the timber from about the side altar, the old stock coffer of the church, ironwork from the Palm Cross. Ironically, the account was rendered for that year on Palm Sunday, formerly the day of the parish's general dirige, and the vicar described the meeting as taking place 'at the secunde evenyng prayer', a reversion to the language of 'first and second vespers' which had meaning in the Sarum rite, but no relevance at all to the order of the Elizabethan Book of Common Prayer.[82] In 1573, the last year in which he kept acounts, Trychay recorded that William Hurley and his wife Eylon had donated 10s. to the church to buy a new Common Prayer book and psalter from London. The gift marks some sort of watershed, which the old priest's annotation 'deo gracias' confirms. The permanence of the reformation had finally been accepted at Morebath.[83]

What had the reformation meant to Morebath? First and foremost, it meant the drastic and sudden interruption of a lush and busy piety, focussed on the cult of the saints and especially on the images of the saints, and on the commemoration of the dead. This will be no news to anyone who has read the *Stripping of the Altars*, or Chris Haigh's *Tudor Reformations*, or Jack Scarisbrick's *The Reformation and the English People*. But the reformation also meant for Morebath the permanent collapse of a parochial structure which had involved much of the adult population in a continuous round of consultation, decision-making, fund-raising and accounting, a scale of involvement which makes the communal life of this remote moorland village look as participatory and self-conscious as the most sophisticated of European medieval cities. Before the reformation a dozen people each year, men and women, a quarter of the number of households in Morebath, exercised responsibility on behalf of the community, and accounted to it annually, and pairs of young men and young women served an apprenticeship to such responsibility within their own stores. By the mid-1580s only one householder was being elected to office in the parish church, though the Young Men continued to organize ales and contribute to parish funds throughout Elizabeth's reign, and the parish income had stabilized at about £6 per annum, less than the pre-reformation average but adequate for its routine needs. But the nature of parish awareness had certainly shifted. Even before the reformation the parish structures of Morebath had observed no strict division between secular and sacred business: parish meetings and parish officers handled setts and levies to repair bridges, meet feudal obligations, fund crown military demands. All of these activities continued and even grew in Elizabeth's reign: in his last year the Vicar was busy entertaining local government officials such as the mayor of Bradninch in connection with the parish's perennial attempts to evade the 'sherowe towrne', and complaining characteristically that for all his pains 'yet y have no thank nother. God be merciful unto us'.[84] But before the 1540s such secular activities had been more than counterbalanced by the lavish succession of religious projects which the parish set itself, in the provision of new images and altars, new seating, new vestments, new devotional gestures. The secular activities of the parish had themselves often been couched in religious terms, of charity, peace, the language of religious mutuality. It would not be too much to say that before the Edwardine and the Elizabethan reformations, the parish of Morebath was essentially a religious body with some secular functions: from 1558 onwards it was increasingly an organ of secular government with some religious responsibilities. I do not know how one would construct a quantum of profit and loss for these changes, but I have my own opinion.

NOTES

1 I am grateful to the staff of the Devon Record Office at Exeter for much assistance, and to Professor Nicholas Orme for his hospitality and expertise during the research for this paper. E. Hobhouse, ed., *Churchwardens' Accounts*, Somerset Record Society IV, 1890). J. Erskine Binney ed., *The Accounts of the Wardens of the Parish of Morebath, Devon, 1520–1573* (Exeter 1904) (hereafter, Binney, *Accounts*) pp. 34–5. The original is now in the Devon County Record Office in Exeter – DRO Mss 2983A/PW1 (Morebath Accounts): W. G. Hoskins ed. *Devon* (London, 1972) pp. 235–6. D. H. Pill, 'The Diocese of Exeter under Bishop Vesey', unpublished MA thesis, Exeter 1963, *passim*. E. Duffy, *The Stripping of the Altars* (London and New Haven, 1992), pp. 491, 497–503, 550, 570, 587–8, 592; Christopher Haigh, *English Reformations* (Oxford, 1993) pp. 30–2, 34–5, 38–9, 157–9, 177, 180–1, 209–10, 245, 247, 286–8.
2 Binney, *Accounts* pp. 34–5.
3 For Barlinch, F. W. Weaver, 'Barlinch Priory', *Proceedings of the Somersetshire Archaeological and Natural History Society* (1909), LIV, pp. 79–106; *Victoria County History, Somerset*, vol. 2; Nicholas Orme, *Education and Society in Medieval and Renaissance England* (Hambledon Press, 1989), p. 113. For the disposal of the Manor, Joyce Youings ed. *Devon Monastic Lands: Calendars of Particulars for Grants 1536–1558* (Devon and Cornwall Record Society) NS, vol. i, pp. 3, 43–4.
4 Binney, *Accounts*, pp. 4, 26, 41, 42, 65, 82, 90; for the Bampton chantries, Nicholas Orme, 'The Dissolution of the Chantries in Devon, 1546–8', *Reports and Transactions of the Devonshire Association for the Advancement of Science*, vol. 3, p. 93.
5 Binney, *Accounts*, pp. 65, 90, 112, 250. The parishioner was William Hurly.
6 Nicholas Orme, *Education and Society in Medieval and Renaissance England*, Hambledon Press 1989, ch. 7, esp. pp. 113–16. See F. W. Weaver, 'Barlinch Priory', p. 87.
7 Binney, *Accounts*, p. 199: for Edward Sydenham's will (no bequest to Trychay or Morebath) see F. W. Weaver, *Somerset Medieval Wills, 3rd Series, 1531–58* (Somerset Record Society XXI, 1905) pp. 74–5.

8 T. L. Stoate ed., *Devon Lay Subsidy Rolls 1524–7* (Bristol 1979) p. 52.

9 Binney, *Accounts*, p. 20.

10 Ordination lists, DRO. Chanter 13, Register of Bishop Oldham 1504–19.

11 *Valor Ecclesiasticus Temp. Henry VIII* (1814) p. 331.

12 Binney, *Accounts*, p. 20.

13 Binney, *Accounts*, pp. 22–3.

14 Binney, *Accounts*, p. 61, 71, 79: St Sunday is probably the 'Sunday Christ', or a representation of Christ wounded by the implements of the trades pursued on Sundays and hence breaking the law of Sunday observance. In England the cult seems to have originated in the West Country in the fourteenth century: Athene Reiss, 'The Sunday Christ: a church wall painting subject in late medieval England', unpublished Chicago PhD thesis 1995.

15 Binney, *Accounts*, pp. 42, 62, 68.

16 Binney, *Accounts*, pp. 6, 38, and esp. 72.

17 Binney, *Accounts*, p. 103.

18 Binney, *Accounts*, p. 241.

19 Binney, *Accounts*, p. 108 (John Tymewell at Borston).

20 Binney, *Accounts*, pp. 9, 36.

21 Binney, *Accounts*, p. 212: and see pp. 51, 212–13, 223, 229–30, 231: for the late Elizabethan practice, DRO Mss 2983A/PW1 (Morebath Accounts) 303/152 – 304/152 verso, 330/165 verso. The parish reverted to the appointment of two wardens annually in the late 1590s.

22 Binney, *Accounts*, p. 250.

23 Binney, *Accounts*, pp. 202, 250.

24 Binney, *Accounts*, p. 190.

25 Binney, *Accounts*, pp. 146, 141.

26 Binney, *Accounts*, pp. 184, 212, 234, 236, 249.

27 Binney, *Accounts*, pp. 25, 47, 74, 140; T. L. Stoate, ed., *Devon Lay Subsidy Rolls 1524–7*, p. 52.

28 Binney, *Accounts*, pp. 6, 21, 27, 34, 61, 71, 82, 86.

29 Binney, *Accounts*, pp. 6, 12–13, 33–4, 52, 79, 82–6 etc.

30 Binney, *Accounts*, pp. 39, 49.

31 Binney, *Accounts*, p. 223.

32 Binney, *Accounts*, p. 171, 252.

33 Binney, *Accounts*, pp. 98, 223–4.

34 Binney, *Accounts*, p. 66 and *passim*.

35 Binney, *Accounts*, p. 100.

36 Binney, *Accounts*, p. 17.

37 Binney, *Accounts*, p. 16 (Binney has printed this out of place, as if it were part of the account of the Store of St Anthony).

38 A convenient summary of gifts between 1520 and 1540, which does not however reveal all the parish projects undertaken during those years, will be found in Binney, *Accounts*, pp. 20–8.

39 Binney, *Accounts*, pp. 60 and passim.

40 Binney, Accounts, pp. 25, 29, 35.

41 Joyce Youings ed., *Devon Monastic Lands: Calendar of Particulars for Grants 1536–1558* (Devon and Cornwall Record Society) NS vol. 1, pp. 3, 43, 44; Binney, *Accounts*, pp. 91–3.

42 Binney, *Accounts*, p. 102.

43 Pill, 'Vesey', pp. 154–5.

44 Binney, *Accounts*, p. 106.

45 Binney, *Accounts*, pp. 113–14.

46 Binney, *Accounts*, pp. 153–5.

47 Binney, *Accounts*, pp. 151–3.
48 W. H. Frere and W. M. Kennedy, *Visitation Articles and Injunctions of the Period of the Reformation*, (Alcuin Club, London, 1910) vol. 2, pp. 127–8.
49 Binney, *Accounts*, p. 156.
50 For these moves, Duffy, *The Stripping of the Altars*, pp. 448–64: Haigh, *Tudor Reformations*, pp. 168–73.
51 Duffy, *Stripping of the Altars*, pp. 458–9.
52 Binney, *Accounts*, pp. 158–160.
53 Duffy, *Stripping of the Altars* pp. 478–503.
54 Binney, *Accounts*, p. 160: DRO 2983A/ PW1 fol 371/186.
55 Binney, *Accounts*, pp. 160–1.
56 Binney, *Accounts*, p. 162: for church thefts at this time, Duffy, *Stripping of the Altars*, pp. 487–9.
57 Binney, *Accounts*, p. 163: P. L. Hughes and J. F. Larkin eds., *Tudor Royal Proclamations*, (New Haven and London, 1964) vol. 1, p. 464.
58 For the course of the rebellion, F. Rose-Throup, *The Western Rebellion of 1549* (London, 1913). A. Fletcher, *Tudor Rebellions* (London, 1973) ch. 5. J. Cornwall, *Revolt of the Peasantry 1549* (London, 1977). Documents in N. Pocock ed., *Troubles Connected with the Prayer-Book of 1549* (Camden Society, NS vol. xxxvii, 1884). For an account emphasizing the social and economic factors in the rebellion, Joyce Youings, 'The South-Western Rebellion of 1549', *Southern History* no. 1, 1979, pp. 99–122.
59 Pocock, *Troubles*, pp. 12–13.
60 Pocock, *Troubles*, pp. 25–7, 30–3.
61 Pocock, *Troubles*, pp. 30–3, 40, 47.
62 Binney, *Accounts*, pp. 163–4: for the detail about the collection at the church style, *ibid.* p. 169; DRO 2983A/ PW1 fol 375/18.
63 Rose-Throup, *Western Rebellion*, pp. 82–3.
64 Cornwall, *Revolt of the Peasantry*, p. 83.
65 Pocock, *Troubles*, pp. 47, 63–4.
66 Binney, *Accounts*, p. 169.
67 Binney, *Accounts*, p. 172.
68 Binney, *Accounts*, p. 168; 175; Pill, 'Vesey' pp. 313–14: Rose-Throup, *Western Rebellion*, pp. 372–7.
69 Binney, *Accounts*, pp. 166–78 *passim*.
70 Binney, *Accounts*, p. 200.
71 Binney, *Accounts*, pp. 175–81.
72 What follows is based on Binney, *Accounts*, pp. 181–4 and the summary on pp. 200–1.
73 Bridget Cherry and Nikolaus Pevsner, *Devon* (Penguin Books, 1989) p. 888 where it is wrongly and preposterously described as a box to carry the sacrament to the sick in.
74 Binney, *Accounts*, p. 182; DRO 2983A/ PW1 fol 398/199 verso.
75 Binney, *Accounts*, p. 185.
76 Binney, *Accounts*, pp. 187–97, 201–2.
77 Binney, *Accounts*, pp. 202–7.
78 Binney, *Accounts*, p. 247.
79 Binney, *Accounts*, p. 208.
80 Binney, *Accounts*, p. 226.
81 Parker Library, Corpus Christi College Cambridge, Ms 97 fol. 198.
82 Binney, *Accounts*, p. 246.
83 Binney, *Accounts*, p. 250.
84 Binney, *Accounts*, p. 249.

3   Religion, Politics
and the Irish Rising of 1641

Nicholas Canny

The Historiographical Background

The primary concern of the scientists Gerard and Arnold Boate when they set themselves to compiling their volume *Ireland's Natural History*, published in 1652, was to illustrate the potential that existed for the promotion of agricultural and manufacturing employment in Ireland. The opportunity to create such employment would, they contended, be provided by God once the resources of the country had been brought into the possession of zealous and enterprising Protestants, and as proof of this they pointed to the improvements promoted by those Protestants who had settled in Ireland previous to the insurrection of 1641. These, 'the introducers of all good things in Ireland', were credited by the Boates with the pursuit of advanced agriculture, the reclamation of bogs, and the introduction of mining activity in several parts of the country. However, while praising what had been accomplished, the Boates also alluded to the cancellation of all these advances by Irish Catholics who by their display of 'unthankfulness, hatred and envy' when they took up arms in 1641, had proven themselves to be a 'brutish nation'. As they warmed to their theme the Boates made it clear that what happened in 1641 was a total conflict and they reported how:[1]

those barbarians, the natural inhabitants of Ireland, who not content to have murdered or expelled their English neighbours . . . endeavoured quite to extinguish the memory of them, and of all the civility and good things by them introduced amongst that wild nation; and consequently in most places they did not only demolish the houses built by the English, the gardens and enclosures made by them, the orchards and hedges by them planted, and destroyed whole droves and flocks at once of English cows and sheep, so as they were not able with all their unsatiable gluttony to devour the tenth part thereof, but let the rest lie rotting and stinking in the fields.

Other Protestants, commenting on the events of 1641, made reference to the supposed wanton and symbolic destruction of English improvements with such frequency that it became a trope in Protestant writing on 1641 that Catholic detestation of the settlers was such that the outburst had by that point become irrepressible. In the course of advancing these charges the authors could absolve the Protestants from any responsibility for provoking this animosity towards themselves by their further assertion that the uprising had been religiously motivated. They did so by invoking the argument that priests in Ireland were as hostile to the enterprising culture associated with Protestantism as they were to the Protestant religion itself. There was ample support for this opinion to be found in the conservative social comment of several Gaelic poets, for example Piaras Feiritéir, who decried British settlers in Ireland for their material obsessions. Feiritéir did this most effectively in his lament for the death in Flanders of Maurice Fitzgerald, son of the Knight of Kerry. When referring to the keening of the fairies for the deceased captain, Feiritéir explained that the English settlers in Tralee had no reason to fear that the lamentations they heard presaged their own demise since fairies lamented only for noble people and not for mercenaries such as they:[2]

Ní chaoinid mná sídhe an sórt soin.

Protestants needed no such reminders of Catholic social disdain for their way of life because, as Charles Webster has made clear, it was an accepted tenet of English Protestant belief that Providence would reveal the secrets of nature only to the righteous, and it was therefore to be expected that Catholics would have no respect for a culture of enterprise. It is in this light that we must interpret assertions such as that of Sir William Petty that priests in Ireland had 'humble opinions of the English and Protestants and of the mischiefs of setting up manufactures and introducing of trade'.[3]

Because they were thus able to marry cultural with religious polarities, the Protestant authors of the seventeenth century could offer a coherent explanation of the happenings of 1641 which generally proved satisfying for Irish Protestant audiences until the later decades of the nineteenth century. This held that the rising in Ireland had as its purpose, the extirpation of both English civility and the Protestant religion, with a view to replacing the truth of Protestantism with the superstition of Catholicism and a progressive English-style polity with the regressive turbulence associated with Ireland before 1603. Most authors held that the conspiracy had been orchestrated by the papacy in concert with foreign Catholic powers, and all gave a prime role to the Irish Catholic clergy and Old English Catholic landowners in Ireland in leading the assault against their unsuspecting victims.[4]

It goes without saying that Catholics at that time, and subsequently, contradicted this explanation and the evidence on which it was based, but it was not until after the Restoration of 1660 that Catholic writers were publicly able to offer a coherent alternative explanation for the rising. This, when it came, was also couched in religious terms and held that Catholics had been forced to defend themselves in arms because of the intolerance of the Protestant officials in Ireland, and of those Protestants in England and Scotland who were then challenging the authority of King Charles.[5]

The comprehensiveness of these explanations, which was essential to the particular audiences to which they were addressed, is their aspect which has convinced modern historians that they should be rejected. This rejection can be considered representative of a trend because there has been a marked tendency on the part of more secular-minded authors throughout western society of the past century, to discard as simplistic the religious explanations for events that were found acceptable in previous centuries. The most potent of such authors in Ireland have been the ideologues of Nationalism, who have been persistent in their efforts to identify the insurrection of 1641 as a powerful expression of national rather than religious resentment that brought Old English and Gaelic Irish together for the first time in a common political challenge to the authority of crown government in Ireland.[6] This interpretation faithfully reflected the secular preoccupations of European nationalists, but throughout Europe in the years after World War II, it was Marxist rather than Nationalist advocates who were most sceptical of religious explanation for political events. These insisted that the essential divisions in society have always been determined by economic factors, and in their works of reinterpretation they have, among other matters, suggested that the theological differences which were thought to have occasioned the so-called religious wars of the sixteenth and the seventeenth centuries served merely to accentuate divisions that were fundamentally economic in origin. Historians in western society, who were not ideologically committed, confronted such Marxist propositions from the outset, but in doing so they did not attempt to resuscitate, because they did not respect, the religious explanations that had held appeal in past centuries. Instead, they challenged the Marxists on their own ground by questioning their use of quantifiable data, and they substituted novel socio-economic explanations for crude Marxist determinism.[7] Irish academic historians of the middle decades of this century were, both by virtue of their conservatism and their relative isolation from the traumatic events that were disturbing western society, at a distance but not entirely removed from such historiographical interaction, and Irish academic history of the mid-twentieth century remains unique in Europe in that it developed no Marxist dimension. This lacuna must be attributed in part to Robin Dudley Edwards and T. W. Moody, who contributed most to the professionalization of history as an academic discipline in Ireland in the middle of the century. Neither scholar had much interest in or sympathy with Marxism, but neither were they attracted by the opposing socio-political exposition perhaps because of its equally secular aspect, since each, in his own way, remained attached to Christian belief. They were however both appalled at how, previous to their generation, historical explanation in Ireland always seemed to have been related to the religious persuasion of the particular historian, and one purpose of the 'objective and value-free' history that they encouraged, both by teaching and example, was to release their discipline from the vice-like grip of sectarian polemic which, in more recent times, had taken the form of Nationalist-Unionist invective. This release was to be effected not by imitating the historical practice and preoccupation of their contemporaries throughout Europe but by placing renewed emphasis on the role of evidence in historical interpretation and by applying the lessons relating to the appraisal of evidence that they both had imbibed as students in the 1930s at the Institute of Historical Research, London.[8]

We now know that the belated quest of Edwards and Moody for a Hibernian variant of scientific Rankean historiography was illusory, and that even their own writings and choice of subject revealed their personal religious and political leanings. Indeed their philosophical outlook appears to have exerted a more potent influence on the writings of their research students than on themselves, and this influence is nowhere more evident than in the received wisdom on the origins of the Rising of 1641 that has prevailed for the past thirty years. This interpretation was first formulated in the writings of Hugh Kearney and Aidan Clarke, the first a research student of Dudley Edwards and the second of Theo Moody. The work of both scholars complied with the standards of their mentors because they relied ultimately on the authority of documentary sources. They were, however, more attuned than their supervisors to current historiographical trends, and each was able to relate his arguments to what was then being said of the origins of civil conflict in England, and each succeeded in presenting a political explanation for the genesis of conflict in Ireland that dovetailed with the interpretations then being offered on the Causes of the English Civil War and of wider conflict in western society of the seventeenth century. While neither Kearney nor Clarke dismissed religion as a factor that complicated political negotiations, they were both satisfied that, in Ireland as in England, it was considerations of patronage and privilege, and exclusions therefrom, rather than issues of theology, which precipitated the political action that resulted in the rising of 1641.[9] Their publications were favourably received by historians of England to the extent that their findings appeared to corroborate the conclusions of those investigating the origins of the English Civil War. This conflict, although considered of universal importance, was then believed to have been a largely discrete event provoked by divisions within England itself, and the Irish disturbance was thought to have exerted but a momentary influence upon the course of events in England.[10] The immediate influence of the early writings of Kearney and Clarke was therefore upon those working on Irish history, and one of their more enduring influences there was to advance the belief that political events in Ireland of the mid-seventeenth century were largely independent of religious considerations. This assumption was given canonical status in Irish historiography when the findings of Kearney and Clarke were absorbed into the narrative chapters of the third volume of *A New History of Ireland,* and their conclusions have won international endorsement and respect now that historians of England have begun to perceive *their* civil war as but one dimension of a wider conflict within the multiple kingdom of England, Scotland and Ireland.[11]

Since the years of first publication, the subject which Kearney and Clarke developed has attracted the attention of other researchers on Irish history, but while some of these have alluded to socio-economic and religious factors that precipitated the rising of 1641 they have all interpreted that rising as an essentially Ulster phenomenon.[12] To this extent their findings elaborate upon rather than challenge the received wisdom that Ulster holds the key to understanding the genesis of the insurrection of 1641 and that what happened there had little to do with the more prosperous, and Old-English-dominated, eastern part of the country, until the weeks after the defeat of government forces at Julianstown in County Meath, on 29 November 1641. It was only then, it has been repeatedly suggested, that the lords of the Pale, under threat of invasion from Ulster, entered into a compact with the leaders of the northern revolt following negotiations at the hills of Tara and Crofty. Previous to then, according to the accepted version of events, the east of Ireland remained tranquil, and there is a suggestion that the Old English Catholic leaders were embarrassed by the alleged plot of some of the Ulster lords to seize Dublin Castle on 23 October 1641. Allowance is made in the standard account for a disturbance in County Wicklow, led by disgruntled Gaelic landowners who had been deprived of their ancestral lands through recent plantations. Otherwise, it is suggested that the Catholic proprietors and townsmen of the prosperous east remained loyal to the crown and to its government in Dublin until their hands were forced in December 1641 by the threat of invasion from Ulster. Even then, it is implied that the Leinster lords were unenthusiastic rebels and gladly joined with the Catholic bishops in early summer 1642 to check the undisciplined aspects of the uprising, and to establish at Kilkenny a conservative Catholic Confederation, under joint clerical and gentry control. This body was intended to serve as a provisional government to maintain order in that part of the country which remained in Catholic hands and to negotiate terms with the king for greater religious and civil freedom for Catholics once normal conditions were restored to the Three Kingdoms.

I have previously challenged some of the arguments and assumptions of this received version of events and I have made the case that the disturbances of 1641 must be regarded as a popular peasant uprising as well as an attempted coup d'état by a small group of disgruntled Catholic landowners.[13] In doing so I have suggested that the disturbances were used by different social elements among the Catholic population in Ireland to serve different ends and I have drawn particular attention to the role of priests in seeking, from the very outset, to curb the violence of the uprising and to direct it towards godly purposes. What I have to say here will reiterate these points, but it will focus more closely on the religious aspect of the insurrection and it will refer almost entirely to events in the province of Leinster and the city of Waterford, areas that subsequently became the heartland of the Catholic Confederacy. The evidence employed for this analysis is again the testimony provided by the victims who survived the assault – the so-called 1641 depositions – because, as I have argued before, this is the only body of material that makes it possible to piece together the sequence of events in Ireland during the winter and spring of 1641–2, and it is the only place where Protestants detailed the explanations that their Catholic assailants offered them for the attack they were launching upon them.[14]

The Rising in Leinster

The first concern of this paper is therefore to establish that people in Leinster were aware of what was taking place in Ulster almost from the outset, and that many elements of the Catholic population were sympathetic to the Ulster revolt to the point where they imitated what, they believed, was happening there. It will be made clear however that the Leinster revolt while imitative was not a pure replication, and that there was considerable variation in both the actions taken and the legitimization for disturbance offered by the insurgents in the several areas of Leinster. On the other hand, the insurrection in Leinster was not marred, as was the revolt in Ulster, by widespread and wanton slaughter of people, and there is therefore particular merit in analysing the material from Leinster because it is easier to establish what was intended by the leaders of the revolt and to isolate the relative importance of religious motivations and objectives.

A close study of the surviving evidence establishes that people in Leinster were almost immediately aware both of the insurrection that had burst forth in Ulster on 22 October 1641 and of the alleged plot to seize Dublin castle on the following day. Word of the insurrection in Ulster had already reached Dublin city by 23 October (809.127), and we learn from Chidley Coote (814. 204–16) that the 'first intelligence' of what had happened in Ulster had reached Birr in the King's County (now County Offaly) by 24 October and that they learned of the further rising in Wicklow on 9 December 1641. News of the Ulster disturbance had spread southwards to Carlow by 28 October because Thomas Poole of Craniscah (812.6)

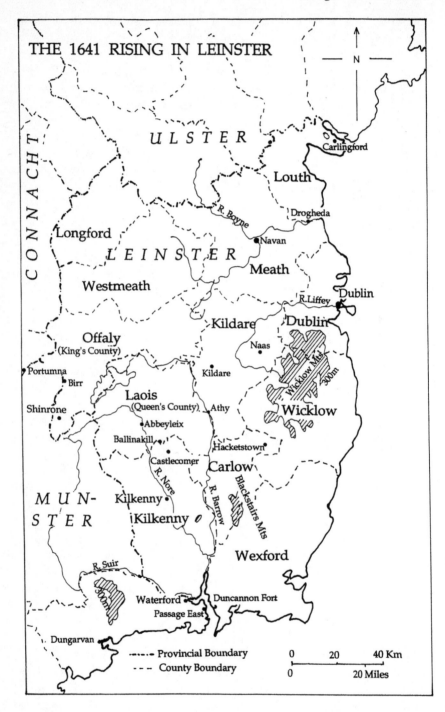

THE 1641 RISING IN LEINSTER

N

ULSTER

CONNACHT

Carlingford

Louth

R. Boyne

Drogheda

Longford

LEINSTER

Navan

Westmeath

Meath

R. Liffey

Dublin

Offaly
(King's County)

Kildare

Dublin

Naas

Portumna

Birr

Kildare

Wicklow Mts

300m

Shinrone

Laois
(Queen's County)

Athy

Wicklow

Abbeyleix

Ballinakill

Hacketstown

Castlecomer

Carlow

M U N-
S T E R

R. Nore

R. Barrow

Blackstairs Mts

Kilkenny

Kilkenny

Wexford

R. Suir

R. Suir

Waterford

Duncannon Fort

Passage East

Dungarvan

- · - · - Provincial Boundary
- - - - County Boundary

0   20   40 Km

0   20 Miles

decided then to abandon his living rather than run the risk of assault. John Bishop, a Protestant settled at Glandomgell, County Kilkenny (812.211), took a similar precaution on 1 November, and William Weldon of New Ross in County Wexford (818.46) was attacked in his place of residence on the following day.

These few references make it clear that word of what had happened in Ulster had reached even the southern extremity of Leinster within a week of the initial outburst, and probably within a matter of a few days. Those counties of Leinster which lay closest to the boundary with Ulster were more immediately aware of what had happened because their communities became involved in the insurrection, either because the military action in Ulster spilled over into their counties or because some Catholic landowners and priests made common cause with the Ulster insurgents. In County Longford, which had experienced a recent plantation, several members of the O'Farrell landowning family resorted to arms as early as 24 October, and the O'Farrells and their associates had within five days taken control of the entire county except for a few fortified positions. Their initial actions were taken on the pretext of defending their region and its residents from attack by rebels who, they alleged, had entered the county from Cavan and Leitrim, and they invited the Protestant settlers in the county to surrender their property and followers to those who could better provide for their protection. This was the experience of Nathaniel Hollington (817.148), the minister of Clogh, who on 27 October surrendered his land, possessions and children to some of the O'Farrells for safe keeping and fled himself to the garrison-town of Athlone. Samuel Price (817.156), a settler at Keenagh in the parish of Killacomoge, was 'standing upon his guard' on 29 October and was not prepared to flee, until he was approached by Irrell Farrell, high-sheriff of the county and other members of the O'Farrell sept. The sheriff then warned him that the county had been invaded from the north, and he offered to take custody of the goods of English men 'that desired to be protected'. Far more ominous for Price was the sheriff's reference to a 'proclamation from his Majesty that all English men's goods should be seized to his Majesty's use, and how that the common people taking knowledge thereof had used cruelty even to barbarism towards the English'. It was fear of such a popular onslaught against him which convinced Price that he should surrender his cattle for protection to the sheriff, but he had no sooner done so than his house was approached by a company of seventy men 'armed with pikes and guns and many others armed with hedgestakes and pitchforks', and his appeal to the sheriff for help then went unanswered.

What happened in County Longford, within days of the insurrection in Ulster, was therefore in direct imitation of what happened in the northern province, with the disgruntled O'Farrells using the disturbances there to recover the status and property they had lost through the process of change promoted by the government during the previous decades. At first, as we saw, the O'Farrells were as concerned as their Ulster counterparts to present their actions within the context of loyalty to the crown, but this veneer was quickly cast aside, or so it appeared to John Edgeworth (817.144) whose goods were seized by the O'Farrells 'upon pretence of distresses for arrears of rent for their land as they say due ever since the plantation of that county'.

Counties Meath and Louth which, like Longford, abutted the province of Ulster were also immediately disturbed by the insurrection but not in the same manner at Longford. Each of these counties had escaped extensive plantation, and most property remained in the possession of Old English landowners who were traditionally loyal to the crown. These proprietors stood to gain little from the rebellion and might have wished to stand aloof but did not have the option to do so because of invasion from Ulster. Already on 26 October 1641 the goods of Amy Briscoe (834.3) of Ardee, County Louth, had been stolen by Collo Mc Bryan McMahon, and those of William Vesey of Dundalk (834.9) were stolen on 31 October by Turlough Oge O'Neill, son to Henry O'Neill of County Monaghan. More general robbery occurred in subsequent days, and some deponents (834.10 and 14) described how their goods had been stolen and 'carried northwards by rebels sent into County Louth by Phelim O'Neill'. Not all thieves in Louth were from Ulster, however, and Thurstan Mawdesley of Carlingford (834.15) complained that he had been robbed and stripped on 26 October 1641 by John White of Margetoges Grange 'an ancient rebel and a notable thief'.

The landowners of County Meath seem to have been in a position to defend their county from raids until mid- or late November, and what attacks on Protestants occurred before that date were perpetrated by residents of the county, several of whom were described as younger sons of land-owners or tenants within the county. Even as late as 24 November those in Meath who had taken to arms could be depicted (816.145) as 'the poorer sort of parish dwellers and others', and insurrection in County Meath up to that point seems to have been a rural phenomenon. However, although limited in scale, disturbances were widespread throughout the county and those who ventured into action at this early stage appear to have enjoyed popular support within the Catholic community. This was certainly the opinion of Roger Puttock, minister at Navan, who reported (816.132) how 'the very first night after this rebellion was known, generally all papists houses near Navan were set upon a merry pin; dancing, singing and drinking as if hell had been broken open among them'. Moreover as riotous behaviour became more frequent, Puttock could not persuade the portrieve and bur-gesses of Navan to keep a watch at the gates 'though the country people were up robbing to the very walls of Navan'. Moreover, as another deponent testified (816.97), the town fathers were kept fully informed of the progress of the rising further afield by John Manning of Navan, 'a common intelligencer betwixt the rebels at Drogheda and the town of Navan'. Finally, when a band of rebels from County Cavan did make their way to the town of Navan on 19 November 1641 they were (816.106) preceded by a priest who so enthused the population of the town, that there was 'great joy and welcoming' for the rebel cause, and (816.97) the portrieve of the town, the baron of Navan and in 'general all the burgesses of Navan in great state and with much joy went out of Navan near half a mile to meet the rebels'.

By this point, rather than at the meeting at Crofty Hill some three weeks later, the loyalty of the Catholic population in County Meath had shifted openly towards the Ulster rebels, and it would seem that the Catholic landowners of the county had little choice in December but to follow the example set by their subordinates. What landowners did to hold the line and to maintain their authority emerges more clearly in the case of County Kildare. There (813.306), on first hearing of the rising in the north, George, earl of Kildare, convened a meeting of the gentry and commons of the county at Naas and they appointed the earl as governor and three gentlemen as captains to provide for the defence of the county. Their efforts were to little avail however and attacks on Protestants became frequent throughout the county from 1 November 1641 onwards. More significantly, Piers Fitzgerald of Ballysonan Esq, one of the captains chosen to maintain order, had become openly involved with the rising by 7 December 1641. In Kildare, as in Meath, the impetus for action came from below and Elizabeth Bradley (813.303) observed 'from the first noise of this insurrection in the north . . . not only their own Irish servants but generally all their Irish begin to insult over them and their Protestant neighbours and to be mightily encouraged and incensed against them insomuch as great threats were made and several forces used by them the Irish'. Once order had broken down, the insurgents formed themselves into armed bands led either by dissident Fitzgeralds or Dempseys, and these, it was alleged, were frequently given moral encouragement by priests to rid that county of Protestants. Disturbances in Kildare, as in Meath, were a rural phenomenon but they soon spread to the towns. Thomasine Martin of Athy (813.380) reported how a fortnight before Christmas she was 'robbed by her neighbours Irish Papists of the said town' who came to her house 'threw her down and trod upon her, and cast clothes over her, that she should not see them'. Despite their efforts, Thomasine was able to identify three of her assailants, two widows and one brogue-maker, 'all of Athy her neighbours'.

The experience of Kildare was therefore that of the inability of the gentry – Catholic and Protestant together – to maintain order and uphold their authority, and this experience was replicated in the more southerly counties

of Carlow, Wexford and Kilkenny. The situation in these counties was complicated by a rising led by some of those landowners in Wicklow who believed
that they had been deprived unjustly of much of their land on several occasions during the previous decades. Some kin of these insurgents – Byrnes,
O'Tooles and Kavanaghs – held property also in the neighbouring counties
of Dublin, Carlow and Wexford, so disturbance in Wicklow triggered an
uprising in parts of these neighbouring counties. Thus George Morres of
Clonemore, County Carlow (812.21) was attacked on 11 November 1641
by one Turlough Byrne of Killalongford, County Carlow, gent, together
with a group of rebels 'his fosterers, accomplices and soldiers'. Similarly in
County Dublin, John Wolverston who was among the first to take up arms
on 1 December 1641 was described (809.299) as a retainer of the 'Grand
Rebel O'Toole near Powerscourt'. Another who resorted to arms early in
County Dublin was William Wolverston of Stillorgan, Esq. who was joined
(809.201) by 'Mary Wolverston alias Cavenagh his daughter-in-law'. There
were some rumblings of discord in County Wexford as early as 2 November
1641 (818.46), but that county was brought into the mainstream of revolt
on 14 November when Luke Byrne of County Wicklow (818.57), 'the first
known and notorious rebel of that county', entered Wexford from the
north with an army of men, estimated as between five and six hundred, and
laid siege to the settlement established by Sir Walsingham Cooke on the
manor of Parsonstown in the parish of Killenoghe.

In all of these instances the first symbol of revolt was the launch of an
attack upon English settlers. The fact that there were few such settlers in
County Kilkenny and that most who were there had been placed on the
property of the marquis of Ormond, would explain why the semblance of
order was upheld for a longer time in that county. When the breakdown in
order did occur, on 26 November 1641, it was in the vicinity of Castlecomer,
where a substantial community of English settlers had been established by
Sir Christopher Wandesford (812.200 and 190). These were attacked by a
large group of insurgents made up of Brennans and Butlers from the
vicinity of Castlecomer and some of the septs of Byrnes and Kavanaghs
from counties Carlow and Wicklow. The insurgents, supposedly to the
number of five hundred men, were armed with guns, pikes, pitchforks,
swords, darts and skeans (*scian* is the Irish word for knife or dagger) and the
English settlers had no choice but to take flight for the town of Kilkenny.
The same group of insurgents also turned its attention to those settlers
associated with the ironworks close at hand at Ballinakill in Queen's County
(now County Laois) (815.358) and they then marched to Abbeyleix
(815.210) where they robbed and spoiled the English tenants who would
have held property from Sir Charles Coote in that vicinity. These incursions
into Queen's County merely exacerbated disturbances which had been

evident in that county since early to mid-November (815.142,159), and similar disturbances made headway in the neighbouring King's County from that time forward despite the best efforts of the Protestant landowners of that county to maintain order.

When all this evidence is pieced together it becomes clear that public order had broken down in most areas of Leinster by the middle of November 1641. The leaders were in most instances those who had cause to be dissatisfied with the existing social order, or who had little to lose, but it is clear that their show of force enjoyed initial popular support in the countryside but that rejection of existing authority soon manifested itself also in the towns. We have already noted this in the disturbance at Navan in County Meath, and what occurred there was replicated in the other counties of the province, as can be illustrated in the instance of County Kilkenny.

One settler in Kilkenny, John Jessop of Cloynmoore (812.188), had taken flight to Dublin as early as 5 November because of his conviction that all papists in that county and in neighbouring County Wexford were 'actors, abettors or at least secret well wishers unto this rebellion'. His suspicion was borne out by the onslaught on Castlecomer and the flight of the settlers there towards the town of Kilkenny. Their movement provoked a popular assault against Protestant settlers everywhere in the county. John Moore, a prebend of St Canice's Cathedral (812.197–9), described how settlers in the county were robbed and stripped of their clothes over a process of ten days, and he bewailed how the rebels had 'not so much respects unto their promises as Othnicks [Ethnics] or Turcks would'. Then he described how on 17 and 18 December the insurgents turned their attention to the town of Kilkenny, which now included Protestant refugees from as far afield as Castlecomer as well as those Protestants previously resident in the town, and how the rural insurgents were 'welcomed by the citizens being for the most part all papists' who both opened the gates to them and joined them in robbing all Protestants within the town. Moore was able to name some of the more prominent citizens who joined the 'discontented gentlemen as they termed the rebels' but he asserted that the 'implacable fury' which these displayed against the Protestants was shared by the urban population at large. More immediately, one William Lucas (812.220), a Protestant tailor in the town, complained how one Peirce McPatrick a Catholic merchant 'brought a lantern in the night and an axe and guided the other rebels to the house of this deponent and to other houses and assisted them in the robberies'. Moreover, Lucas was able to identify Patrick O'Fillon broguemaker, Richard Laughlin, butcher, William McShane, butcher, Patrick Roe, greymerchant, and Perse White, broguemaker, among his assailants.

Such a popular onslaught would have been in defiance of the wishes of the marquis of Ormond, himself a Protestant and resident of the town.

He could do no more than negotiate with his grand-uncle, Lord Mountgarrett (812.1979), to escort the Protestants in the town to Waterford and even then they were not permitted to enter the confines of that city until they had paid further protection money to William Butler, Toby Butler and Mr Sweetman. The departure of Protestants from the town did not bring an end to their humiliation because a small number decided to remain there. James Benn, a resident of Kilkenny (812.213), then witnessed the stripping of Mr Smith, a Protestant minister of Ballinakill, and Mr Lemon, a Scottish schoolmaster, in St Canice's cathedral, and he saw in the houses and shops of Andrew Murphy, James Archdeacon, Piers Archer and other merchants of the town 'the Protestant bibles and prayer books and other good English and Protestant books . . . torn in pieces and employed as waste paper to wrap in soap, starch, candles and wares that they sold'.

Even more traumatic for the Protestant settlers in both Kilkenny and Queen's County, if we are to judge from the frequency of its telling, was the treatment accorded the heads severed from the corpses of those killed at the siege of Ballinakill. That town was the location of an iron-smelting operation established by the earl of Londonderry, and the band of marauders who went to disturb it were resisted by Lieutenant Gilbert and Captain Richard Steele (815.358). After a prolonged siege, Ballinakill was taken and the settlement dispersed, and the assailants then beheaded the minister Thomas Bingham and six other Protestants of the town (815.305, 361). Then, these heads were carried by the insurgents in triumph from Ballinakill to the town of Kilkenny with their 'pipes for joy playing before them on horseback on a market day' (812.202). The populace of the town then became so aroused that 'the rebels but especially the women there' commenced to mock and ritually humiliate the heads, and prominent among 'those lewd viragoes' was 'Alice Butler a reputed mother of bastards yet the daughter of the said Lord Mountgarret' who 'stabbed, cut and slashed those heads' and 'drawing her skeine slashed at the face' of William Ahfrey, one of the victims, 'and hit him on the nose'. The example of Alice Butler apparently provided a lead to the other women of the town to the point where 'those that could but get a blow or stab at those heads seemed to account themselves happy'. Humiliation became desecration in the treatment accorded the head of the Reverend Bingham because the insurgents put a gag in his mouth 'and laying the leaf of a bible before him bade him preach, saying his mouth was open wide enough'. The verdict of the rebels was that the heads were 'the heads of heritics' and having denied them Christian burial they interred them in a hole at a cross roads which gave rise to an oath 'frequently used' by the 'roguish boys' of the town 'by the cross of the seven devils' heads buried on St James's Green'.

What occurred in the town of Kilkenny was similar to, and connected with, what happened in Waterford. That town, like Kilkenny, had remained under the control of Old English merchants, and those Protestants who lived in the town, either as artisans, clergymen or merchants had to accept that their position was altogether more precarious than that of their co-religionists in the planted parts of Ireland. Unlike Kilkenny, they lacked a local protector of the stature of the marquis of Ormond, but they did enjoy the local presence of crown officials associated with the collection of customs, and their ultimate security was the crown garrison at Duncannon fort, under the command of Lord Esmond. Another factor that Waterford had in common with Kilkenny was that most land in its immediate vicinity remained in Catholic possession, and Waterford was also closely connected both by water and land with Kilkenny for which it served as an outport. In this sense, it had more in common with the rich heartlands of Leinster than with the western parts of County Waterford which had been included within the Munster plantation and had been densely settled with Protestants by the earl of Cork and his associates. It was logical therefore that the Protestant refugees from Kilkenny should have headed for Waterford because it seemed they would be safe once they got within the walls of the city, since the mayor, Mr Francis Briver, as well as the aldermen and 'the best of the city' (820.15) were determined to provide for their protection until they could gain passage for England. The arrival in December 1641, of further refugees from Tipperary and the planted lands in west Waterford must have placed a strain on the resources of the city, but we learn from several deponents that the presence of Protestants, whether local or refugees, had become an issue of controversy before then. Thomasine Osbolderston testified (820.8), that when the 'Lady Marquis of Ormond' and her entourage were passing through Waterford on their way to the security of England, 'she heard some of the town and other rebels in Waterford say and wish in Irish that they had the stripping of all that brave company'. Such mutterings persisted but the corporation continued for three months to protect the Protestants (820.15) 'not only from the common people of the city from being spoiled but from others'. Several deponents testified that these 'others' included one Francis Wise gent., of Newtown in Waterford, apparently a member of the corporation, and we learn that the mayor 'was not only threatened but several times in danger to be killed for taking of the Protestants' part both by the inhabitants and some others of the country'. The task of the corporation became both more difficult and hazardous after 1 December when (820.1, 820.3), Dermot Mac Dowlin and others of the Kavanaghs, already in arms in Wexford, 'with boats came over into those parts'. The countryside around the city of Waterford was immediately brought under the control of the insurgents, and land outside the walls belonging to Waterford Protestants was seized. Within the walls, Francis Wise (820.5) 'was a chief instrument in stirring up the city', and he 'with

one John Ilaed of Waterford set open the city gates to the rebels'. These
came from County Tipperary as well as Counties Waterford and Wexford,
and it was (820.15) Sir Nicholas Walshe who insisted that all Protestants
be imprisoned for their security and that their property be placed in a common store house. There are several depositions from Protestants detailing
the privations they then suffered, but there is only one report (820.46) of a
Protestant being killed within the city. In the meantime the incarceration of
the Protestants was taken by some Catholics to mean that their property
within the city might be seized with impunity, and Thomasin Osbalderston
(820.8) was, like Thomasin Martin of Athy and William Lucas of Kilkenny,
able to identify some of her former neighbours who joined with the outsiders
in pilfering the goods of Protestants. The three she recognized, Thomas
White, Henry Poore and James Barnard, 'were disguised with strange caps
that they might not be seen' but she 'at length discerned who they were'. It
was also alleged (820.29–31) that, after Candlemas 1642, such acts of
pillage came to enjoy some official sanction, and that the 'merchants' and
William Woodlocke, sheriff, began 'to strip and rob all the Protestants there
under colour of searching for arms and ammunition'. Then, as we learn
from the testimony of Judith Phillips, at Shrovetide 1642 the 'citizens of
Waterford did appoint constables in every parish in the said city to fetch
and bring with them out of their houses all the English Protestants (men
women and children in the said city)'. Then, it is suggested that 350, or even
as many as 500 (820.15), of these unfortunates were conveyed to Passage
where they endured further privations, injuries, and even death at the hands
of one Captain Strong (820.219) until survivors were evacuated to safety in
a ship provided by the earl of Cork.

A Religious Revolt

It seems appropriate at this juncture to ask what was specifically religious
about these disturbances of 1641 in the heartland of the Old English areas.
The leaders of the insurrection, whether landowners or townsmen, did not
have the compelling reasons of their rural counterparts in the intensively
planted areas of Ireland to attack those English who had settled in their
midst. When they articulated the justification for their action, as they did to
the Irish Protestant clergyman John Kearny (812.237), they were able to
cite no more than general politico-religious justifications for having had to
resort to force. They had, Kearny's assailant told him, 'good reasons' to take
up arms 'in so much as the Catholiques (as he termed themselves) never
attained to any height of dignity or office worth speaking of in this kingdom
when as every pedlar or other (as he termed them) that came out of England'
were 'masters' and were entrusted 'to bear a great sway in this kingdom and

curbed the natives'. Such a sense of exclusion on religious grounds was undoubtedly a prime motivation for action, once the authority of the government could be seen to have been weakened. Others who joined in the onslaught against the Protestants might be considered to have been merely taking advantage of the developing breakdown in public order to rob, humiliate, and even murder those who were but recently settled in their community, and whose customary props had collapsed. There certainly was an opportunistic aspect to the disturbances we have just considered, but social collapse in the Old English areas was not complete and the disturbances in the towns were clearly sectarian in that only Protestants were attacked. This denominational selectivity was mentioned specifically by John Jessop of Cloyamoore, County Kilkenny (812.188), who noted that while his tenants and followers had been robbed and stripped by the rebels they had 'used one John Manselle, gent, with all favour and courtesy for that he was a papist although he came but lately out of England and no acquaintance were between them'. Many English besides Jessop recognized that it was their religion rather than their national origin that made them most vulnerable, and some tried to avoid their fate by going to Mass or even taking part with the insurgents against their own countrymen. The Protestant deponents who ruefully noted these defections admitted no sincerity in such conversions and the attitude of John Lowther, a shoemaker of Waterford, as it was reported by Judith Phillips (820.219), might be considered typical. When he was challenged about what his fate would be when the expected military aid came from England he 'answered and said (with a great oath) do you expect (quoth he) aid out of England and they being up there one against another, the king having lost his crown . . . by losing Ireland? For if you live saieth he . . . a hundred years you shall see Ireland never recovered again by the English'. The deponents took some consolation from the fact that defectors like Lowther, a shoemaker, or (820.246) 'old Nicholas the miller without St Patrick's gate in Waterford and his wife' were base mechanics. A far more serious blow to their morale would have been the loss to the other side of 'Mr Williams of the Cathedral church of Waterford, organist', and the Protestants of Waterford must have been truly perplexed when they were stopped and interrogated at St John's gate as they left the city for Passage, by a man bearing a halberd whom they recognized as one Cary 'formerly a Protestant and free schoolmaster of the diocese of Waterford but then turned Papist'.

While such changes of side make it clear that the defectors believed that the lines of division were strictly sectarian, the fact that a public change of religious allegiance was sufficient to guarantee security of life and property suggests that a higher moral authority still held sway in these Old English areas than had been the case in Ulster. Those who wielded this moral force

were the Catholic clergy who attempted everywhere to stem the violence of
the revolt and to direct its energies towards religious purposes. Their efforts
to do so in Ulster clearly failed but, as I have indicated elsewhere, they
nonetheless strove to prevent Protestants there being murdered and to have
the settlers, when they became the objects of attack, given the choice of
'turning to Mass' or leaving the community.[15] Their efforts in the Old
English areas appear to have been more successful than in Ulster, and we
get a particularly good insight, in the deposition of Robert Wadding
(812.27), into the efforts of one priest in County Carlow to take control of
the situation. This priest insisted that Protestants be given the opportunity
to convert to Catholicism but before being given the protection of the church
they had to have their spiritual condition investigated by himself. Wadding
found the priest 'so busied in giving absolutions' to those Protestants who had
been brought to him 'by some rebel captains' that it took some time to gain
admission to his presence. When Wadding was eventually brought before the
priest, he told him that his 'only course was to go to Mass and to hold with
them', and that if he did so he would be restored immediately to his property.
Before being 'reconciled (as they termed it)' that particular priest tendered an
oath to the Protestants 'that they should continue true and faithful subjects to
the king of England and should honour and obey him in all matters temporal;
that they should acknowledge the Holy Church of Rome to be the true church
and the Pope of Rome to be supreme head over the church of Ireland and
should honour and obey him in all causes spiritual whatsoever'.

Besides their efforts to promote what are recognizable Old English
politico-religious ambitions through the tendering of oaths, the Catholic
clergy also sought to direct the leaders of the insurgency to employ their
energies to achieve the restoration of the Catholic church to its previous
glory. The clergy of Kildare led the way in reclaiming the traditional
revenues of the church from Protestant control. One deponent (813.385)
mentioned that Ross McGeoghegan, 'titulary bishop of Kildare', took away
the 'chapter chest' of the diocese, and that the Catholic clergy began immediately to claim the tithe that had previously been paid to the Protestant
clergy. John Huetson (813.261) reported that he had heard Dominic
Dempsey, guardian of the Franciscan friars in Kildare, remark 'that the king
had long usurped the tithes and rights belonging to the Catholic church
but now God was pleased to bring it to them to whom it did belong, and
that the world was now towards the end, and it was God's will that true
religion should be established and therefore we must all go to Mass which
was the true religion'. The clergy of the Old English towns were especially
active in recovering their traditional places of worship and their traditional
burial places from Protestant control. Lay participants in the insurrection
were certainly impressed by the effort of the Catholic clergy to lay claim to

tithes because this would have relieved them of the obligation to pay voluntary subscriptions to their own clergy as well as official payments to the
Protestant ministry. In Longford, John Stubbs reported (817.203) how the
rebel leaders had exulted that they would never 'be more troubled with the
bishops' courts and paying of tithes' while John Stirling, a minister in County
Meath, complained (816.139) how his proctor, who had demanded duties
and fees at a funeral service, had been taken by the beard and thrown into
the grave by one James Cusack with the expressed hope 'that Mr John
Sterling should never be minister there any more but that the priests and
friars should be in his stead'. The seizure and desecration of Protestant
Bibles and Prayer Books seems also to have been encouraged by the clergy,
and this was frequently conducted by rebel captains or lay participants in
the revolt without a clerical presence. We have already witnessed the
initiative taken by the merchants of Kilkenny in this matter. Similarly in
Waterford, when Elizabeth Hoop (820.50) 'reproached' one Mr Baker for
'tearing the singing psalms out of [her] Bible and Testament', it was he,
rather than any priest, who responded in paternalistic fashion: 'I am sorry
honest woman that you are so deluded for ther's nothing in that book but
Devil's inventions'.

While Baker acted independently of the clergy his behaviour would
have enjoyed clerical approval. There were, however, several instances where
the leads given by the clergy were carried to extremes that, we can assume,
would not have been endorsed by the priests who had identified the religious objectives they believed the insurrection should serve. For example,
there appears to have been a general clerical ambition to rid the churches
and churchyards that were recovered into Catholic hands of the corpses of
Protestants buried there. This appears to have been pursued systematically
in County Kildare and under the direction (813.260) of Bishop Ross
McGeoghegan and James Dempsey 'the popish vicar-general there', saying
that they could not sanctify ground which included 'heretics bones'. The
removal of such bodies, under clerical supervision, always caused grave
offence to Protestant witnesses, and even more so the undignified dumping
in ditches of the remains of their relatives. However we can take it that the
more extreme humiliations accorded to such corpses were manifestations of
a cultural detestation of an English presence in the community that did not
enjoy the approval of the Catholic clergy even when these cultural expressions
were given a religious overtone. For example, the practical bent of the
sectarianism of the Kilkenny merchant community, which we have already
noted in the use to which they put the torn pages of Bibles and Prayer
Books, almost certainly did not have clerical endorsement when it extended
to the exhumation of Protestant corpses (812.202) from 'the tombs and
graves in the churches in Kilkenny under colour of getting up moulds

whereof to make gunpowder'. Indeed, the suggestion that Protestant corpses were so degraded would be unbelievable were it not that a detailed description from Waterford (820.29–31) of two people engaged in the manufacture of saltpetre from the rotting remains of Protestants, conforms so closely to what was then best scientific practice as to render it entirely plausible.[16] The trouble there began when a Protestant clergyman, Thomas Haylin, and his wife were buried in the grounds of the cathedral against the wishes of 'a Mass priest'. Then, after Whit 1642, when the city had been cleared of living Protestants, the insurgents 'caused to be digged to make gunpowder' the grave of Haylin and his wife and four other Protestants. The 'corpses [which] had some bones and flesh on them' were then taken over by Richard Neyler of the city, apothecary, and one Wars 'formerly a Protestant but now turned Papist, an Engineer and Master of their Ordnance' and 'these they boiled in a great furnace till they came to salt petre and made them gunpowder'. Such improvisation, our narrator tells us, was persisted with until gunpowder for the Confederate army was imported from the continent through the port of Dungarvan. There is no evidence of any Catholic clerical presence at, or approval of, these gruesome obscenities, and while the Confederates were certainly desperately short of gunpowder it could only have been an intense animosity towards all English and Protestant presence in their midst that drove them to so degrade the memory and remains of former residents within their community. In this sense, the use made of Protestant corpses as a source of saltpetre can be likened to the practice of ritualised cannibalism which social anthropologists have interpreted as an expression by groups of extreme emotion towards other people rather than the use of human flesh as a source of protein.[17]

Even if we can only assume that Catholic priests would have wished to restrain their followers from such excesses there are a great many instances in the depositions where Protestants acknowledged the intervention of priests as responsible for their escape from humiliation or even death. William Pillsworth, a Protestant clergyman in County Kildare (813.1), believed he owed his life to God's deliverance, but he then acknowledged that this deliverance had been greatly assisted by a Catholic priest who had procured his release from the hands of the rebels even when they had placed him on the gallows and had mockingly commanded him to preach from there. This priest, whom Pillsworth had never before seen, 'made a long speech' on his behalf, saying that Pillsworth's father, who had 'lived for long amongst them, did not deserve his child should be so miserably used', and the priest warned that the 'bloody inhuman act' that they then contemplated would bring God's vengeance upon them.

While the uprising was religious in the sense that it was designed to remedy particular religious grievances identified by the Catholic clergy, it was also religious in that it was intended as a pre-emptive strike against a further erosion of the already precarious position of Catholicism in Ireland. The belief that such an erosion was in prospect derived partly from the reports that Irish Catholic parliamentarians and their associates brought back with them from England, and partly from the stories of what was happening in England, Scotland and Continental Europe that were circulated throughout Ireland by Catholic priests. It is likely that each area of Leinster had its own source of information and this would explain why the rumours circulating in the different counties were not precisely the same. That clear lines of communication with Britain existed is evident from the rumours themselves as also from the testimony of deponents such as that of Job Ward (810.98) that 'one Nicholas Barnwell who married the Countess of Tirconnell gives the best and truest intelligence out of England and is very intimately acquainted with some that are near the queen'. Such connections with those who were closely associated with the court of Queen Henrietta Maria would explain why so many of the stories in circulation related to the sufferings endured by the queen at the hands of English Protestants. Stories concerning priests in the queen's household won favour in most counties. In County Longford it was alleged (817.154) that 'the parliament of England had ajudged Father Philip her higness' confessor to be executed and quartered in the queen's presence'. This same allegation was narrated in more elaborate form in Queen's County (815.295) where it was stated 'that some about London had most cruelly put to death two or three of the queen's religion men; broiled the heart of one of them on the coals and so presented it to the queen on a platter'. Even more gruesome was the version spread in Longford by Cormack Farrell and one O'Meehan 'a popish priest' (817.140), 'that the English had cut off the head of the queen's priest, and cut off his privy members and threw them in his face, and had quartered him before the queen'.

To these gross exaggerations of the indignities that the queen actually did suffer were added stories of hardships imposed on Catholics in England which presaged what would happen to Catholics in Ireland. Donatius or Donogh Connor, a Protestant clergyman in Wexford (818.110), who had once been a Catholic priest but who had 'by the light of God's truth' become a Protestant, explained that the 'rebels from time to time divulged that the cause of their insurrection was for that ten thousand at least of Protestants in England and Ireland had put their hands to a note to hang all the papists at their own doors unless they came to their church with them'. Connor also had knowledge of Catholic fears that this intended assault was but part of a universal Protestant offensive because priests had spread rumours of atrocities committed by Protestants in France against the Catholic population there.

Religion was not a discrete matter however and allegations relating to the humiliation of the queen and the proposed assault upon Catholicism quickly gave way to stories about challenges to the royal prerogative by the English parliament. Some Catholics (813.236) reported that the parliament had used the king so 'harshly' that he had 'departed into Scotland'. It was only a short step from there to suggest that the king had been dethroned by the parliament (817.140) 'and would not return into England for the English had a king, the Palsgrave, and had banished the queen to France'. Then, it was suggested (812.27), that the queen had found refuge in Ireland and 'that this kingdom of Ireland was the queen's jointure', and that she would take up residence there 'and clear this kingdom of all Protestants even as the parliament goeth about to clear England of all Papists'. Some went further to claim that the king also was on their side and (817.161) 'that the English were proclaimed traitors, and that the king was in Scotland and would be in Ireland within nine days and would banish all the English'. Finally it was reported (818.88), that one Welsh, an innkeeper, of Kilcullen, County Kildare had asserted:

that the king was in the north of Ireland and ridd disguised and had glassen eyes because he would not be known and that the king was as much against the Protestants as he himself and the rebels were, for that the Puritans in the parliament of England threw libels in disparagement of the king's majesty making a question whether a king or no king: and this, said the said Welsh, is your religion speaking to this deponent and other Protestants in his company and meaning them and all other Protestants against whom he spoke very disgracefully.

Conclusion

When pieced together, all these reports, allegations and suggestions show how those who became involved in an insurrection designed to frustrate an anticipated blow against Catholicism in Ireland could convince themselves that their actions were also intended to support the king and queen. This lent credibility to the frequently-made claim that the insurrection had been previously approved by the king, and all these rumours and claims were widely believed by Catholics because they contained sufficient elements of truth to make them plausible. What the relative roles of priests and laity were in devising these justifications for revolt is unclear, but several contemporaries gave prime credit to the clergy. Indeed some went so far as to pronounce the priests responsible for the insurrection, and those who did so suggested that they had undermined the authority of the Catholic landowners by stirring up the populace over religious issues. Those Protestant deponents who were convinced of this alluded to meetings convened by the Catholic clergy previous to the insurrection, and special mention was made of a meeting (817.144) held at Multyfarnham, County Westmeath, on 3 and 4

October 1641. The clear implication was that plans were there laid for the revolt without any reference to the Catholic laity, and Randall Adams, a minister at Rathcouragh in the same county, reported (817.42) on a conversation he had overheard on 1 November 1641 between some of the 'chief gentlemen' of the county and a group of friars. The gentlemen, mostly members of the Tuite family, laid a charge against the friars 'that they and their fellows were the cause of this great and mischevious rebellion'. The gentlemen then asserted that the friars had had no cause of grievance that would justify such extreme measures because of:

the great freedom they had in religion without control, and that they generally had the best horses, clothes, meats, drinks and all other sort of provision delightful or useful . . . and they had these and many other privileges beyond any of their own function either regular or secular through the Christian world, and therefore most bitterly them to their teeth said that they hoped God would bring that vengeance home to them that they by their cursed plots laboured so wickedly to bring upon others.

This discourse, if we are to take it at its face value, alludes to a tension that had been developing between the Catholic gentry and continentally trained priests in Ireland ever since the 1620s, and that was to become even more acute after 1642 when the clergy began to play an active role in Irish politics. Previous to then, as far as the Catholic landed interest was concerned it was they, through their parliamentary representatives and delegations to court, who had negotiated toleration for Catholicism, and they obviously wanted toleration to be on the terms they sought after. This involved Catholicism and the Catholic clergy functioning under the protection of their patrons but within a state system that was officially Protestant. The Catholic clergy for their part were becoming impatient with this arrangement, first because it made them reliant upon the support of Catholic lay patrons, and second because it denied them the right, or indeed the opportunity, to practise Catholicism openly with the panoply of power associated with the Counter-Reformation church. It would seem therefore that the clergy, led by some of their seminary-trained bishops, looked for and welcomed the opportunity to make a bid for the full public recognition of Catholicism which would have involved a recovery of cathedrals and churches that had been lost to the state religion, as well as the lands, tithes and other duties that had traditionally belonged to the Catholic church. It has long been accepted, and has recently been detailed by Tadhg Ó hAnnracháin who has worked from Catholic ecclesiastical sources, that these ambitions were in the minds of some senior Catholic clergy before 1641 and were expressed openly by them from the moment the Confederacy was established, and most especially from the time that it received official recognition from the Papacy.[18] One of the arguments of this paper is that such ambitions had been fostered by the Catholic clergy in Ireland long before the onset of disturbances and were articulated by them from the moment the authority of the government was challenged. Thus what Donatus Connor had to report from County Wexford seems entirely credible. He had, he said:

frequently heard the rebels say they would never give up (even if pardoned) unless that all the church land of Ireland were restored to the churchmen of the Romish religion and that they might enjoy that religion freely and the Protestant religion might be quite rooted out of this kingdom and that the church of Rome might be restored to its ancient jurisdiction, power and privilege within the said kingdom of Ireland.

Those landowners, like the Tuites of County Westmeath, who were secure in their property would have had no time for such an agenda, first because they were themselves likely to have been owners of former church lands, but also because they would have recognized that the agenda could only have been achieved through revolutionary action which would have placed their lands and positions in jeopardy. This explains why the Catholic clergy had to speak over the heads of such conservative landowners, and in so doing unleashed a peasant fury which they were only partially able to control.

The inability of the clergy to keep the uprising on a strictly religious course even in the areas dominated by the Old English is explained by a variety of factors. First, as we saw in the case of County Wicklow, not all landowners in Leinster were content with their lot, and those who fostered a sense of grievance over what they had lost in the various plantations believed they had an opportunity to recover their losses at one fell swoop. Besides the Byrnes, O'Tooles and Kavanaghs of Wicklow, there were some landowners in counties Wexford and Longford as well as King's and Queen's counties who were ready to take advantage of the breakdown in authority to meet these purely material ends. These were willing to echo the religious message of the clergy or to express concern over the plight of the queen and the royal prerogative but their ultimate concern (871.183) was that their lands had been assigned to English and Scots who now 'liveth bravely and richly' while 'they and the rest of the Irish were poor gents'. Their objective therefore was to cancel all the plantations that had been established in Ireland after the principle that as 'the English held their own lands in England, and so did the Scots in Scotland and so should the Irish in Ireland'. The fulfilment of this principle required that since 'both the English and Scottish which were in Ireland were all beggars when they came into Ireland so should they be turned thence'. But besides clearing the settlers from their former possessions these landowners were, as we saw, interested also in spreading the insurrection outwards from their own counties. They were concerned to do so because they recognized that their gamble could succeed only if they could gain political control everywhere in Ireland, and create a situation whereby 'they would never have any more chief governors, judges, justices or officers of the English or Scots but would name and appoint such themselves'.

While the effort of the higher Catholic clergy to dictate the course of events was thus complicated by the articulation of a parallel set of objectives by discontented Catholic gentlemen, it was also made difficult because their subordinates among the ranks of the clergy frequently derived their own crude interpretations from the justifications for action being outlined by the continentally-trained priests. Thus, for example, Thomas Fleetwood a minister in the parish of Kilbeggan in County Westmeath (817.37) learned from one Brian O'Grieve, a local farmer, that a friar had exhorted them, 'to fall to this course of rebellion or commotion' and swore them to take action 'assuring them that though the English did discharge muskets and that some of them should be killed yet they should not fear for such as so died should be saints. And they should rush on with a multitude and kill all the Protestants and so receive arms from them'.

While priests might direct the Catholic Irish towards courses of action that were not contemplated by senior ecclesiastics, it is altogether more difficult to establish what motivated the poorer element of the Irish population. Tenant farmers, merchants, artisans and even servants who had a reasonably fixed position in a hierarchical order might be expected to have followed the guidance of their spiritual or social betters, but every locality in Ireland also contained a sizeable number of masterless men and women whose actions could not be predicted once a challenge to the authority of the government was launched. Prominent among these would have been soldiers recently discharged from the army that had been organized in Ireland by Thomas Wentworth, earl of Strafford, and we encounter frequent references to the early involvement of individuals such as (817.32) 'John Hussey who had recently fled from Lord Dillon's troop in Dublin'. The insurrection also attracted the early involvement of people such as Lawrence McArt in County Wexford described (818.97) as 'an ancient rebel', by which was meant somebody associated with Tyrone's rebellion half a century earlier. Regular reference was also made by deponents to the presence of women and even children among their assailants and it was sometimes implied that they had been driven to their actions by economic need as when Ralph Turner in County Westmeath mentioned (817.27) that 'the women rebels' who 'were very forward actors in the rebellion' took it upon themselves to 'take, sell or otherwise dispose of all the robbed, stolen goods that came to their hands'. And to these who might have been expected to take early advantage of the breakdown of order were those who cynically took possession of the goods of Protestants who, from being the most

secure, had dramatically become the most vulnerable people in the community. Among these was Henry Fitzgerald who (813.360) 'took up all that he
could get of the English Protestants for the earl of Kildare's rents' alleging
that he had been appointed by the earl to this task. Such fraud led to the
dramatic economic improvement of some who previously lived on the
margins of society. These included Morris Bawne (812.45) 'who lived about
Bourghall Moore near Hacketstown' who was 'formerly a cowherd but then
turned by his robbery and pillaging to be a famous and rich rebel and a
commander of rebels'.

Social upheavals of this kind were hardly unexpected in the circumstances, and Protestant victims were most distressed by the cancellation of
social and commercial bonds that they had taken to be permanent. William
Bailie, a merchant of Hacketstown in County Carlow (812.45), was
particularly perturbed when he was robbed and mocked by Mr Samuel
East, a Justice of the Peace for Wicklow and formerly a Protestant, and 'one
that owed him some money and was (as he remembered) his special friend'.
Deponents were also bewildered when they witnessed their former tenants
and servants among their assailants, and those Protestants who had been
tenants to Catholic landowners also expressed horror at the cancellation of
agreements they had previously assumed to be sacrosanct. When rebellion
broke out in County Meath, George Boothe (816.108) fled for safety leaving
behind his cattle 'thinking Thomas Geoghegan (who is this deponent's
landlord) to be a loyal subject and upon his the said Thomas his faithful
promise to be true and just to this deponent'. Some, when challenged,
could justify even such unscrupulous behaviour on religious grounds as for
example one Long in County Kildare (813.287) who, when accused of
having broken the commandment against taking his neighbour's goods,
'said that the Protestants were not neighbours of theirs but they were heretics
and therefore no breach of conscience to take away their goods'.

Not all on the Catholic side were as unscrupulous as this, and deponents
noted how some of their former friends among the Irish had remained
steadfast even in the face of adversity. Thus Robert Wadding of Kelltown in
County Carlow (812.27) acknowledged his rescue effected by Owen Byrne
at the point when the rebels had taken 'his coat and hat and were unbut-
toning his doublet', presumably to strip him naked. The rebels, he said,
'were aggrieved' at this interruption of their work 'but durst not oppose him
being powerful amongst them yet swore they would inform against him
that he was a protector of Protestants'. This particular episode implies that
the expulsions were justified on grounds of religion but the assault, when it
gained force, was more sweeping than that. William Collis of Kildare town
(813.285) reported how one Lawrence White remarked that he thought
'the worse of himself the day he saw any of the seed of the English walk

along the streets'. The experience of Ralph Walmsly, (814.264) an English
Catholic who had settled near Birr, was similar. When the uprising began,
several of his former acquaintances among the Irish helped and assisted him
in getting to the house of the Catholic, earl of Clanricard, in Portumna.
However he found that others of the rebels refused to be guided by the
principles that were laid down by priests and proved themselves so antagonistic towards the English that they would spare none 'not so much as any
of the old Roman Catholics if they were of the English kind or race'.
Moreover, as the Boate brothers were to report, the antagonism was not
confined to people, and the symbolism of revolt extended from the destruction of all things Protestant to all things reminiscent of the English presence.
This was put most graphically by Marmaduke Clapham of Shinrone, also
in King's County(814.162), in words that may well have proved inspirational
for the passage we recited from *Ireland's Natural History*. He complained
how the Irish:

made such havoc of our cattle and sheep, killing the lean and young breed . . . in
such multitudes that for want of salt much were corrupted and stank, and the very
dogs that were English breed they killed so transported they were . . . with an invet-
erate malice to extirpate the very memory of our nation.

Moreover, claimed Clapham, (in a statement reminiscent of the symbolism
of Irish revolt in the sixteenth century),[19] the Irish women who 'formerly
used the English habit as bands, ruffs, hats, cloaks, gowns . . . now wear
kerchefs, mantles, trousses and all Irish habit', and he bewailed how 'forty
years improvement of peace' was destroyed 'by these miscreants in one year'.

   Descriptions such as this would suggest that the struggle that happened
in Ireland was essentially a struggle between cultures, and that the ambition
of those who led the revolt was to return to the Gaelic order that had been
forcefully brought to an end a half-century before. On closer inspection, it
seems that the rebels, or those of them who articulated their objectives, had
no such vision. Some, as we saw, could think of change only in terms of
Catholicism taking the place of Protestantism as the official religion of the
country, others looked forward to Irish Catholics resuming their rightful
positions in government, and yet others believed that the queen and king
were on their side and were even present in Ireland to supervise such a
change. However still others, and possibly a majority, could think no further
than the immediate future and (815.313) publicly said that 'now the day
was their own, and that they had been slaves to the English a long time but
now they would be revenged to the full and would not leave (before
Christmas day) an English Protestant rogue living'.

   Such expressions cannot be taken as statements of policy because they
would have never been stated openly if government authority had held
firm. Furthermore what would happen after Christmas day was no more a

concern of these individuals than it was of the common participants in any European peasant revolt during the seventeenth century. Nonetheless, it does seem that the prime factor that drove the peasants to take up arms was a sense of grievance over the loss of property and status. To this, must be added related annoyance over questions of religion. This was possibly felt deeply by lay people, and particularly by those who had been exposed to the doctrines of the Counter Reformation, but it was best articulated by a clergy who had a keener sense of outrage over this matter than their lay patrons. Priests were, after all, the principal losers because of the clandestine status of Catholicism, but they would also have felt aggrieved because they appreciated, from their continental experience, just how scandalously shabby was the profession of their faith in Ireland as compared with the public manifestations of religious fervour where Catholicism enjoyed the fulsome support of the state. Priests, therefore, had every reason to be advocates of change, and their sense of grievance must have contributed to the general sense of dissatisfaction that made it so easy for the different elements of Irish Catholic society to cast aside their political allegiance once the authority of the state had been challenged. It appears, from the evidence cited, that resentments associated with religion were, in many instances, engulfed in an outpouring of hatred against all things English. This was to be shortlived, however, because the more politically astute recognized from the outset, that this course would only lead to anarchy and would prove disastrous for everybody who enjoyed property and status. Faced with this prospect, these Catholic leaders had no choice but to look to the clergy to save them from impending disaster. By doing so they effectively became prisoners of their priests and were brought to endorse politico-religious principles they would never previously have countenanced. Gaelic poets also quickly identified the struggle as a religious one and it became a stock motif in Gaelic verse composed after the Cromwellian defeat that the fate of the Irish was the mark of God's vengeance for their failure to back the Papal nuncio, Rinuccini, against those of the Confederates he had been obliged to excommunicate. This was put most graphically by the anonymous author of *Aiste Dháibhí Cundún* who in chronicling the woes that had befallen Ireland attributed all to the curse of the pope:[20]

Sé is cúis bhunaig, mar thuigim, don méid sin:
Mallacht an Phápa gach lá dá léirsgrois.

The long sad story of the Confederate War, recently analysed in its different aspects by Tadhg Ó hAnnracháin and Pádraig Lenihan,[21] shows that the Catholic lay leaders failed to resolve this tension, and thus found themselves engaged, against their better judgement, in what, by any standards, was a war of religion.

To describe the conflict, and the uprising that gave rise to it, as religious, may appear provocative or even atavistic when considered within the Irish historiographical tradition discussed at the outset of this paper. It proves a less shocking description when the conflict is situated in a broader setting, and the true nature of the conflagration was first, and uncontroversially, recognized by Dr John Morrill some years ago.[22] That author was more immediately concerned to rescue the civil conflict in England from the socio-political interpretations that had been imposed upon it by the plethora of authors who had viewed this, as but one dimension of a General European Crisis of the mid-seventeenth century. By placing an emphasis on the religious nature of the English civil wars and of the wars that the English parliamentary armies subsequently launched against Ireland and Scotland, Morrill was seeking to situate these events in an early-modern context and to counter the anachronistic arguments of those who were determined to show that events in England (whatever about Scotland and Ireland) exemplified the first experience of a Modern Revolution. In the course of his re-contextualization Morrill alluded to the violence of words used by some English people against their government which, they believed, was betraying the fruits of the Protestant Reformation, and he also referred to the violence of action subsequently employed by some Englishmen against those Irish and Scots who they considered to be proven enemies of all true religion. Dr Morrill referred also to the misgivings of some Scottish people that the government of King Charles I was undermining the victory of their Reformation, but the violence he identified within Scotland was again verbal rather than physical, and he portrayed the Scots as having taken up arms against the forces of the crown only after all diplomatic channels had failed them. When it came to Ireland, Morrill recognized that the conflict there was more extreme and more sectarian, and he spoke of that country in the 1640s having become 'a seventeenth-century Lebanon, but with a fundamentally Protestant/Catholic alignment which most *sixteenth-century* Europeans would have had no difficulty in recognizing'.[23]

The comparison with contemporary Lebanon was unfortunate because it dated this particular piece of writing and hindered rather than helped Morrill's effort at re-contextualization. Nevertheless Morrill's endeavour has proved fruitful in that it has pointed to real differences between the role of religion in the conflicts in each of the three kingdoms. My own investigation into what happened in Scotland suggests that more than persuasion was employed by the Covenanters to establish a common politico/religious front,[24] but Morrill has been completely correct in alluding to the relative economy of physical violence employed by those in England who sought to promote agreement on a form of Protestant worship. Moreover the riotous behaviour and religious symbolism that was used in England to complement the violence of words,[25] pales to insignificance when placed beside the blood-curdling episodes in Ireland that have been considered in this paper. However if we are to accept as valid Dr Morrill's proposition that every early-modern revolt in Europe was, to some extent, religious in character, and if we further follow his advice that we should consider events in the three kingdoms of England, Scotland and Ireland as part of a single process then we must declare the events in Ireland to have been characteristically European and those in England only marginally so, with those in Scotland lying somewhere between those two extremes.[26] The validity of this proposition becomes apparent when we acknowledge that the essential conflict dividing Europe at this time was the collision between militant Protestantism and resurgent Catholicism of the Counter-Reformation. Within the Stuart dominions, it was only in Ireland that these forces engaged in a head-on collision and it was this fact, added to the sense of deprivation deriving from the loss of land and office, that explains the particular intensity of the conflict there. Acknowledgement of the religious character to the disturbances in Ireland should therefore not occasion embarrassment (as it did for an earlier generation of Irish historians) or involve us in portraying these events as some throwback to the sixteenth century (as John Morrill has done). The truth is that while the conflict in Ireland did have much in common with the communal discord associated with the religious tumults in France and the Netherlands of the sixteenth century, these animosities, and the horrors associated with them, were still alive in Continental Europe and were to occur many times over, not only during the course of the Thirty Years War, but in France and the Austrian dominions to the end of the seventeenth century. To describe the Irish rising of 1641 as a religious disturbance is therefore to portray it as both an essentially European and an essentially seventeenth-century event, and to invite comparisons with contemporaneous tumults on the continent of Europe as well as within the other dominions of the British monarch.

NOTES

1   Gerard and Arnold Boate, *Ireland's Natural History* (1652), in *A Collection of Tracts and Treatises . . . in Two Volumes* (Dublin, 1860), I, pp. 1–148, esp. p. 77. This paper has benefited greatly from the comments offered by those who engaged in the discussion following its delivery at the Irish Conference of Historians at University College, Dublin, and I am especially grateful for the remarks of Aidan Clarke who chaired that session.
2   'Mo Thraochadh is Mo Shaoth Rem Ló Thú', in Padraig Ua Duinnín ed. *Dánta Phiarais Feiritéir* (Dublin, 1903), p. 74.
3   Charles Webster, *The Great Instauration: Science, Medicine, and Reform, 1626–60* (London, 1975). William Petty, *The Political Anatomy of Ireland* (London, 1691), pp. 94–5.

4   This interpretation was initiated in Sir John Temple, *The Irish Rebellion* (London, 1646); see also Toby Barnard, '1641: a Bibliographical Essay', in Brian Mac Cuarta ed. *Ulster 1641: Aspects of the Rising* (Belfast, 1993), pp. 173–86.

5   For the private explanations for their actions offered by Catholics to the Papacy, almost from the ontset of the revolt see Tadhg Ó hAnnracháin, ' "Far from *Terra Firma*": The Mission of GianBattista Rinuccini to Ireland, 1645–9' (Doctoral Thesis, European University Institute, Florence, 1995), pp. 136–75, esp. 144; for the first printed Catholic explanations see Barnard, '1641: a Bibliographical Essay', p. 177.

6   This interpretation was given a public endorsement in the 1916 Proclamation of the Irish Republic, but is considered too crude an explanation by most academic historians of today. Exceptionally however this teleological quest for the roots of Irish nationalism still preoccupies Brendan Bradshaw, for whose pronouncement on the present subject see 'The Invention of the Irish: Was the Ulster Rising Really a Bolt from the Blue?', in *Times Literary Supplement*, no. 4776, 14 Oct. 1994, pp. 8–10.

7   The first such debate to make an impression on historians of early modern Ireland was that relating to the origins of the English Civil War or Puritan Revolution of the mid-seventeenth century, but see also Roland Mousnier, *Fureurs Paysannes. Les Paysans dans les Révoltes du XVII siècle* (France, Russie, Chine) (Paris, 1967) which was extensively discussed in Irish universities.

8   The term 'value free' has been coined by Brendan Bradshaw, to describe the history favoured by Edwards and Moody, in a series of onslaughts that display no sympathy for the efforts of either author; see Brendan Bradshaw, 'Nationalism and Historical Scholarship in Modern Ireland', in Ciaran Brady ed., *Interpreting Irish History; the Debate of Historical Revisionism, 1938–94* (Dublin, 1994), pp. 191–216; the positions of Edwards and Moody are conveniently set out in this same volume. The only Marxist writing, besides that of James Connolly, with which a historian of early modern Ireland would have been necessarily familiar was Erich Strauss, *Irish Nationalism and British Democracy* (London, 1951).

9   Hugh Kearney, *Strafford in Ireland 1633–41: a Study in Absolutism* (Manchester, 1959); Aidan Clarke, *The Old English in Ireland, 1625–42* (London, 1966). For a more recent statement of Kearney's views see the introduction of the 1989 re-issue of his Strafford book (Cambridge, 1989), and for a modern restatement of the Clarke position see Aidan Clarke, 'The Genesis of the Ulster Rising of 1641', in Peter Roebuck ed. *Plantation to Partition* (Belfast, 1981) pp. 29–45.

10 In this context it is relevant to note that the *Past and Present* debate anthologized in *Crisis in Europe 1560–1660,* ed. Trevor Aston (London, 1965) was later supplemented by Aidan Clarke, 'Ireland and the General Crisis', *Past and Present,* 48 (1970) 79–99.

11 T. W. Moody, F. X. Martin, F. J. Byrne eds., *A New History of Ireland* III, *Early Modern Ireland, 1534–1691* (Oxford, 1976); Conrad Russell, *The Fall of the British Monarchies, 1637–42* (Oxford, 1991), esp. pp. 373–99.

12 Raymond Gillespie, 'The End of an Era: Ulster and the Outbreak of the 1641 Rising' in Ciaran Brady and Raymond Gillespie eds. *Natives and Newcomers: The Making of Irish Colonial Society, 1534–1641* (Dublin, 1986) pp. 191–213; Brian Mac Cuarta ed. *Ulster 1641: Aspects of the Rising;* M. Perceval-Maxwell, *The Outbreak of the Irish Rebellion of 1641* (Dublin, 1994); Jane Ohlmeyer ed., *Ireland: From Independence to Occupation, 1641–1660* (Cambridge, 1995).

13 Nicholas Canny, 'What Really Happened in Ireland in 1641', in Jane Ohlmeyer ed., *From Independence to Occupation,* pp. 24–42.

14 This material is housed in the library of Trinity College, Dublin, and I refer to the individual depositions here in brackets within the body of the text citing the TCD manuscript and folio number. Thus the first citation (809.127) is to TCD Ms. 809 f. 127. See Nicholas Canny, 'The 1641 Depositions as a Source for the Writing of Social

History: County Cork as a Case Study', in Patrick O'Flanagan and Cornelius Buttimer eds., *Cork: History and Society* (Dublin, 1993) pp. 249–308.

15 Canny, 'What Really Happened?'.

16 I am grateful to Dr Joan Thirsk for guiding me to Drs Glenys and Alan Crocker who are the leading authorities on the manufacture of gunpowder in earlier times. I am especially grateful to Glenys Crocker for having assured me that the boiling of rotting remains in a sophisticated cauldron was an essential element in the process of making saltpetre, and for informing me that the Swedish army made use of clay in cemeteries for this purpose. Dr Crocker also guided me to the following pertinent literature: A.R. Williams, 'The Production of Saltpetre in the Middle Ages', *Ambix*, XX (1975) 125–33; O. Guttman, *The Manufacture of Explosives* (London, 1895), 2 vols.

17 Anthony Pagden, 'Cannibalismo e contagio' in *Quaderni storici*, L (1982), pp. 147–64.

18 Ó hAnnracháin, '"Far from *Terra Firma*"', especially pp. 106–33.

19 See Nicholas Canny, *The Elizabethan Conquest of Ireland: a Pattern Established, 1565–76* (Brighton, 1976) pp. 136–53, esp. 142–3; some details of this interpretation of revolt in Elizabethan Ireland but not the symbolism associated with rebellious action, have been questioned in David Edwards, 'The Butler Revolt', *Irish Historical Studies*, XXXVIII (1993) 228–55.

20 'Aiste Dháibhí Cundún' in Cecile O'Rahilly ed., *Five Seventeenth Century Political Poems* (Dublin, 1977) pp. 31–49; see especially p. 48.

21 Tadhg Ó hAnnracháin, '"Far from *Terra Firma*"'; Pádraig D. Lenihan, 'The Catholic Confederacy, 1642–9: an Irish State at War' (PhD thesis, National University of Ireland, University College, Galway, 1995).

22 John Morrill, *The Nature of the English Revolution* (London, 1993) esp. pp. 1–117.

23 Morrill, *Nature,* p. 36; italics mine.

24 In the Maxwell of Orchardton papers, for example, we find the wife of the absent, royalist and Catholic Robert Maxwell complaining that their property would be confiscated by the Covenanters if he did not immediately return to support their cause; on this see Marion Mc Clellan to John Maxwell of Miltown, 29 Oct. 1640 (Edinburgh, S.R.O. RH 15/91/20/5).

25 David Underdown, *Revel, Riot and Rebellion: Popular Politics and Culture in England, 1603–60* (Oxford, 1985); David Cressy, *Bonfires and Bells: National Memory and the Protestant Calendar in Elizabethan and Stuart England* (London, 1989).

26 I made this same point in my concluding sentence to *The Upstart Earl: a Study of the Social and Mental World of Richard Boyle, first earl of Cork, 1566–1643* (Cambridge, 1982) p. 150. The point was then lost to Anglo-centric historians, but scholars are now beginning to accept that people in seventeenth-century Ireland and Scotland were much more directly connected than English people with movements on the European continent.

4   Biblical Language and Providential Destiny in Mid-Eighteenth Century Irish Protestant Patriotism

Jacqueline Hill

Ye are the light of the world. A city that is set on an hill cannot be hid. Neither do men light a candle, and put it under a bushel, but on a candlestick; and it giveth light unto all that are in the house. Let your light so shine before men, that they may see your good works, and glorify your Father which is in heaven. (Matthew, v, 14–16).

Matthew's familiar text, which immediately follows the Sermon on the Mount, has provided inspiration for numberless sermons and exhortations. The following is particularly well known:

Wee shall be as a Citty upon a Hill, the eies of all people are uppon us; so that if wee shall deale falsely with our god in this worke wee have undertaken and soe cause him to withdrawe his present help from us, wee shall be made a story and a by-word through the world.[1]

Thus John Winthrop addressed his fellow Puritans on board the *Arbella* sailing for New England in 1630, in words that have been taken to sound the keynote for American history, 'providential destiny'. In similar vein over a century later, the electors of Dublin were urged to set their sights high:

Consider, my dear Friends, that you are not a *hidden People,* you are neither placed in a *dark Lanthorn,* nor *put under a Bushel.* You are the *Metropolis* of a great Nation, a Light set upon our highest Hill, to illustrate your whole Country by the bright Shining of your Example.[2]

Here the writer and politician Henry Brooke, under the pen name 'The Farmer', addressed the electors during the Dublin city parliamentary by-election of 1749. Although this election has been subjected to detailed scrutiny,[3] the theme of 'providential destiny' has not been highlighted; and it is the intention of this paper to consider the origins, nature and wider significance of this dimension in Irish Protestant Patriotism in the mid-eighteenth century.

Brooke did not content himself with sounding this portentous note. He had already ascribed to one of the candidates, the Dublin apothecary Charles Lucas, prophetic powers:

Prophecy and Patriotism are Endowments of a Peculiar Nature. . . . they are Sparks, which Heaven alone can kindle. . . . To what, if not to such a Spirit as this, can we ascribe the *Powers* of your Fellow Citizen? a Man despised for his Trade, his Poverty, his Pretensions! a Fool (we have said), a Madman! . . . can he Dream that . . . his *Chymistry* can *sublime* a whole People to his Notions of LIBERTY and VIRTUE?[4]

Visionary as a mere tradesman's ambitions to win a parliamentary seat might seem to be, Brooke was anxious to impress on the voters the great importance of the contest, and to highlight the voters' own potential role in the regeneration of freedom throughout the world:

. . . while the *American, African* and *Asian* Worlds groan under universal bondage; while most of Europe hath bowed to the *Yoke* . . . while even in *Britain* the terms Liberty and Patriotism are secretly ridiculed as *chimerical* – it is to Ireland alone, as to the *Heart,* where the *Animal Spirits,* the *Vital Heat* of *Political Nature* appear to make their Retreat; from hence I trust to re-expand, to . . . carry Life and Health anew throughout the whole System.[5]

It is apparent that besides its debt to the New Testament, and to metaphors based on the circulation of the blood, Brooke's appeal had also been influenced by civic republicanism, which drew on classical and Renaissance thinking and stressed the need for citizens to be vigilant in defence of liberty and public virtue.[6] In holding out such an exalted role for the Dublin electors in the regeneration of liberty at home and abroad, it is tempting to suspect Brooke of indulging in histrionics: he was, after all, well known as a playwright. However, his appeal is worth looking at seriously. For it is difficult to think of a parliamentary election of greater significance in eighteenth-century Ireland, and if Brooke's language sometimes seemed inflated, this was no more than the issues demanded.

This Dublin election marked the first major defiance of oligarchy in Irish politics.[7] Lucas's running mate James Digges La Touche[8] was a wealthy merchant, but Lucas himself lacked wealth, position, and highly placed friends. The two stood on a platform dedicated to civic reform, loosening the aldermanic grip on the city's government, and a more 'Patriot' role for the Irish parliament. And although Lucas was forced to flee on the eve of the poll, when his fiery electioneering style incurred the condemnation of the Irish house of commons, La Touche did win sufficient votes to be elected (his election was later overturned by the house of commons). By endorsing reform in the teeth of official disapproval, the voters were defying virtually the entire political establishment in Ireland, and heralding the rise of 'independent' politics in the 1750s and 1760s.

It is worth noting that although it has been generally acknowledged that Patriotism in mid-eighteenth century Ireland was an essentially Protestant phenomenon, relatively little attention has been paid to purely religious aspects. One reason for this is to be found in the conceptual framework that has hitherto prevailed among scholars: that Patriotism is best regarded as a form of nationalism, with the implication that it was an essentially secularizing force, influenced by the Enlightenment, and increasingly tolerant in its attitudes to Catholics.[9] Recent scholarship has begun to reassess these verdicts, and this is something that will be discussed further below. But first, it is necessary to return to Henry Brooke and the invocation of 'providential destiny' in his appeal to the Dublin voters. How common was the use of biblical language and concepts in political discourse at this period?

In the case of England, it has been generally accepted that the heyday of Scripture as a public idiom was the seventeenth century. Steven Zwicker has made the point:

in 1650 the central book of English culture was Scripture; by 1700 the texts men chose to talk about themselves were those of Roman history and Roman politics. By 1700 . . . the Roman senator, not the Mosaic lawgiver, [was] embraced as the paramilitary ideal . . . Roman virtue, not Hebraic righteousness . . . defined civic morality.[10]

This judgement is endorsed by the author of the principal work on the political and cultural role of the bible in England: in the public sphere by the eighteenth century the bible had become marginal.[11] So much for England; though even there it would be wrong to suppose that Scripture as a public idiom vanished overnight. For the American colonies, the work of scholars such as Ernest Tuveson and Ruth Bloch provides plenty of evidence for the continuing vitality of Scripture in the public sphere down to the age of the American revolution and even beyond.[12]

What about Ireland? Some attention has been paid to the role to religion in the politics of Protestant dissent. But outside Ulster (and certainly in Dublin) the bulk of Irish Protestants were members of the Church of Ireland, and the political thought of members of the established church has been comparatively neglected. A recent probing essay by Robert Eccleshall, 'Anglican political thought in the century after the revolution of 1688'[13] is concerned almost exclusively with the clergy; the views of the laity remain to be investigated. Consequently, it is not easy to answer the question, were the voters of Dublin, over eighty per cent of whom were members of the Church of Ireland, likely to be stirred by scriptural appeals and the offer of a providential role?

There are, however, a number of pointers. The fact that Henry Brooke addressed the voters in this way was significant. Although he has been curiously neglected by historians, Brooke was a well-known figure, who had been active in both English and Irish politics. Son of a Church of Ireland clergyman and educated at Trinity College, Dublin, he had gone to London in the late 1730s where he formed part of the opposition circle that grew up around the Prince of Wales. He knew Pope, Swift, probably Sir Richard

Steele, and Bolingbroke. His talents as a writer meant that he was in demand as a publicist for many causes: at different times he was asked to write on behalf of such diverse bodies as the Irish government and the Irish Catholics. However, he was not a mere hack. His political writings and satires have a strong moral and spiritual dimension, and his novel, *The Fool of Quality* (1766), was hailed by John Wesley as the most excellent work of its kind he had seen.[14] Moreover, he knew Dublin well, and following Lucas's flight in October 1749 he was requested to stand as a candidate in the election himself.[15] It seems unlikely, therefore, that he would strike an entirely false note with the electors.

If we turn from Brooke to Charles Lucas himself, the most important Irish Patriot politician of his generation, then a cursory examination of his voluminous writings shows that he too was apt to put a religious gloss on his political activities and exhortations. Like Brooke, he was a member of the Church of Ireland, although he recorded his sympathies with Presbyterian tenets: for him, the only important issue between Presbyterianism and the established church was the question of church government, which he did not consider to be worth quarrelling over.[16] His political ideas, though not particularly original, were drawn from several different sources, including civic republicanism, common law, and corporate rights. But what is important to emphasize is that his thought was not simply secular.

Lucas was above all a conviction politician. As Sean Murphy has shown, from the outset of his career on Dublin corporation in the 1740s Lucas became a thorn in the side of the aldermen (a self-selecting group of twenty-five of the city's most wealthy Protestant merchants), who presided over a city of more than 120,000 people, the 'second city of the empire', and among the ten largest cities in Europe.[17] One particular discovery appears to have set him on the course that resulted in his campaign for civic reform, and (on returning from exile) his subsequent political career in the 1760s. Arising from his challenge to the aldermanic powers in local government, Lucas found himself consulting Dublin's medieval charters, and thanks to his apothecary's training, he had enough Latin to ascertain that they did not appear to sanction the existing oligarchical arrangement. The 'commons' (lower house of the corporation, selected from the guilds) and citizens also had rights, which it became Lucas's mission to reassert. Only by limiting the powers of the nonrepresentative aldermanic board and by strengthening the representative commons (in approved civic republican fashion) could public virtue in Dublin be revitalized. In 1744, long before the question of standing for parliament had arisen, Lucas described his reaction to these ancient charters in a tract addressed to the 'free citizens' of Dublin (the exclusively Protestant freemen, members of the guilds), some three to four thousand in all, who represented the body politic of the city:

I must lay before you . . . some Account of the *Constitution* of this CITY. This I should not have judged necessary, were it not for the great Difficulty I myself found in acquiring any Knowledge of these Matters, which is owing to our *Charters* being, till lately, like the *Sacred Scriptures,* in these Nations, before the Reformation, in an unknown Tongue, and in the Custody of a Few, who, as they grew more corrupt, fell into Ignorance . . .

He also informed the free citizens of their rights:

LIBERTY, my brethren, the best Gift of Heaven, is your Inheritance; granted, indeed, to all the Sons of *ADAM* in common, by the first Law implanted in Man's Bosom, and established and confirmed to Mankind, by the Great CHARTER of civil and religious *Liberty,* the *Christian Dispensation;* . . . This is that *happy Estate,* in which alone, *sacred Property* is secure, and *true* Religion can flourish. This is the Stock on which alone, Arts, Sciences and Trade can be ingrafted, grow, and bring forth all *delicious,* all *desirable* Fruits . . .[18]

Thus, while there were echoes of Locke here (besides references elsewhere to Roman virtue), in this passage Lucas relayed the basic millennial promise of future happiness on earth. The religious element is clear: and repeated references to the Reformation and to the vernacular bible indicate that Lucas's Christianity had a strongly Protestant flavour. The positive side of this Protestantism has been somewhat obscured by an excessive concentration on the question of Lucas's anti-Catholicism. That anti-Catholicism was present in Lucas's thought is difficult to deny, but efforts to rescue him from the charge of 'bigotry' by attempting to trace a softening of his attitudes towards Catholics seem misguided.[19] Lucas's anti-Catholicism is best interpreted not as blind prejudice, but as the obverse to what he judged to be beneficial in Protestantism; namely, that it freed the laity from a priesthood claiming intermediary powers with God, and was most compatible with 'mixed' or limited monarchy.[20] Hence he wrote that Catholic peoples such as the Spanish and French, though they still retained 'the Titule of *Christians,* are, notwithstanding, obprobrious to that divine Appellation, nay even to human Nature; having all the most horrible Characteristics and Badges of *Slavery;* their *Lives* and *Properties* dependent on the . . . *absolute Will* of the reigning *Tyrant,* and their *Souls* at the disposal of mercenary *Monks* and *Priests'.*[21] Lucas was ill informed about the nature of Catholicism and the government of Catholic countries; but his real targets were Catholic kings and priests, and his views about them were at least consistent with his belief in the virtues of Protestantism.

The same blurring of religion and politics was apparent in Lucas's newspaper the *Censor* (1749–50), founded to promote his campaign to win a parliamentary seat in Dublin. In November 1749 the paper carried a eulogy on the liberty of the press:

To the Freedom of the Press, We are indebted for all the Blessings of the *Reformation,* for loosing the dark Fetters of Superstition, in which our Consciences were bound, and letting in upon our Souls the clear and glorious Lights of the Gospel. . . . [To it we owe] the Restoration of *Liberty* and our *Constitution,* in Church and State, under which we enjoy all the blessings of the present happy Establishment.[22]

Was there anything novel in such blurring of religion and politics, and the use of biblical language in political appeals? In the Dublin context, the most obvious precedent, in the 1720s, was Jonathan Swift's *Drapier's Letters.* Drapier, attacking the scheme for William Wood of Wolverhampton to obtain a patent for coining Irish halfpence, used biblical quotations and allusions to reinforce his case. The first letter, inscribed to shopkeepers, tradesmen, farmers and common people of Ireland, addressed the readers as men, as Christians, as parents and as lovers of their country. Swift compared the halfpence 'to the accursed Thing, which as the Scripture tells us, the Children of Israel were forbidden to touch. They will run about like the Plague and destroy everyone who lays his Hands upon them.'[23] In the second letter, readers were informed, 'You have all the laws of God and man on your side.'[24] In the third letter, Drapier compared himself to David, and Wood to Goliath, 'who defied the Armies of the living God'.[25] As a result of his campaign, Swift became a popular hero in Dublin. When in 1724 the authorities offered rewards for the discovery of the author of the letters, the reaction in his favour was expressed, appropriately enough, in a verse from 1 Samuel, xiv, 45, which was 'got by rote, by men, women, and children, and takes . . . wonderfully':[26]

And the people said unto Saul, Shall Jonathan die, who hath wrought this great salvation in Israel? God forbid: as the Lord liveth, there shall not one hair of his head fall to the ground, for he hath wrought with God this day. So the people rescued Jonathan, that he died not.

Swift, of course, was not known simply for his opposition to the single issue of Wood's halfpence. The cheap edition of his *Works* published in Dublin by George Faulkner in 1735 contained this plea (first printed in 1709) for the moral and spiritual regeneration of society by reserving public office only for those of known piety and virtue (the plea was echoed by Lucas in 1748).[27] For Swift, such a policy would produce almost millennial results:

If virtue and religion were established as the necessary titles to reputation and preferment . . . our Duty, by becoming our interest, would take Root in our Natures, and mix with the very Genius of our People; so that it would not be easy for the Example of one wicked Prince to bring us back to our former corruptions.[28]

At this point it is appropriate to inquire into the ethos of the Church of Ireland, the church of Swift, of Brooke, and of Lucas. Was there anything in its outlook to foster the idea of 'providential destiny' in the Irish context?

The most obvious indication is to be found in the commemorative tradition of the 1641 rising, which, thanks to Toby Barnard, we know still retained much vitality at mid-century.[29] The annual commemoration, laid down by act of the Irish parliament in 1662, stipulated that each 23 October in every parish church throughout the land, the minister must read the preamble to the act. This affirmed that although many Protestants had been massacred in 1641, yet God 'hath in all ages shewn his power and mercy in the miraculous and gracious deliverance of his church, and in the protection of religious Kings and States, so even in the midst of his justice he was graciously pleased to extend mercy to this his kingdom and good subjects therein'.[30] A religious service would then take place, with prayers and thanksgiving appropriate to the occasion. In this way the idea of the Irish Protestants as an 'elect nation' continued to be cherished.

In the 1740s this anniversary tradition was still being observed by the political elite, and anniversary sermons were still being published. But we know very little about how these services were received by the faithful. Did they attend, as they were enjoined by the act to do? Did they take the services seriously, or did familiarity breed contempt? Did they snigger at possibly outdated sentiments? These questions are impossible to answer. However, it is possible to point to the great interest in Dublin in religious matters, as measured by the response to the visits, among others, of the evangelical preacher George Whitefield in 1738,[31] the Moravian John Cennick in 1746,[32] and the Methodists (though they had yet to break with the Anglican church) John and Charles Wesley in 1747.[33] Thousands flocked to hear them preach, and interest came from all denominations, including the Church of Ireland. It might be thought that the episcopal authorities would respond with hostility to such incursions, but it appears that these preachers received a generally positive response from the Church of Ireland clergy;[34] there was, after all, a reforming tradition in the established church, much of it directed not at the conversion of Catholics but at the rehabilitation of lapsed Protestants.[35]

It appears, therefore, that in offering the Dublin voters the chance to cooperate with and promote 'providential destiny', Lucas and Brooke were tapping into a still lively religious tradition, and directing it into political channels. But – to return to a question raised earlier – did the prevalence of biblical language and religious allusions mean that the Enlightenment had had little impact in Dublin? By no means. Although the Enlightenment has usually been seen in terms of a straightforward tension between reason and revelation, that perception has recently come in for review. Freethinkers, deists, and others who rejected traditional Trinitarian forms of Christian belief were not so much opposed to religion as to 'corrupt Christianity', and in particular, the authority of the priest and the clergyman, commonly denigrated as 'priestcraft'.[36] Frequently, it has been argued, this concern crystallized over the issue of the role of the church in politics.[37]

For a case in point, the example of Henry St John, Viscount Bolingbroke, is worth considering.[38] Bolingbroke was the foremost English opposition politician of his age (the 1720s and 1730s); he was posthumously revealed to have been a deist. His newspaper the *Craftsman* was in certain respects a forerunner of the *Censor*. Like many of his contemporaries, he drew much of his inspiration from classical history, and in that sense conforms to the general pattern outlined by Zwicker. But his targets included the voters in those constituencies that were relatively 'open', and when addressing such voters – some of them tradesmen and shopkeepers more likely to be familiar with the bible than with the *Aeneid* – he drew heavily on biblical language, and even produced millennial allusions ('*Liberty,* like the Dew from Heaven, fructifieth the barren Mountains').[39] He also denigrated the clergy. Thus his *Freeholder's Political Catechism* (1733) involved transposing the familiar catechetical model from the religious to the political sphere, and elevating the role of elected representatives. One way in which this effect was achieved was by juxtaposing the (arbitrary) mode of selecting bishops ('a Conge d'Elire . . . *where the King nominates*') with the '*Freedom of voting*' that Bolingbroke contended was essential to guarantee 'a *House of Commons genuine and independent*', able to secure 'the *Liberties of the People*'.[40] The king, no matter how dedicated to Justice, was after all only 'a *mortal and fallible Man*'.[41] His power to create peers and nominate bishops to fill the house of lords must therefore be balanced by an independent house of commons, and voters must scrupulously resist all attempts to influence their choice:

Q. *How is [taking a bribe] contrary to the Law of God?*

A. The Law of God saith expressly, *Thou shalt not wrest Judgement: Thou shalt not take a Gift.* If it is a sin in a *Judge,* it is much more in a *Lawgiver,* or an *Elector,* because the Mischiefs occasion'd by the *first* reach only to Individuals; that of the last may effect whole Nations, and even the Generations to come. The *Psalmist,* describing the Wicked, saith, *his Right hand is full of Bribes. . . .*

Q. *What thinkest thou, of those, who are bribed by Gluttony and Drunkenness?*

A. That they are viler than *Esau,* who sold his Birthright for a *Mess of Porridge* [sic].[42]

It is significant that during the Dublin election campaign, Lucas brought out an edition of this catechism, changing only the title (to *The British Free-Holder's Political Catechism*), and addressing it 'to the Free Citizens and Free-Holders of the City of Dublin' (Dublin, 1748). Because of the size of the Dublin electorate, and because most voters enjoyed some degree of economic independence and could contemplate defying their employers or customers, they were a particularly apt target for such appeals. Henry Brooke, too, was eloquent in conjuring up a glorious role for voters who voted on principle, rather than observing the demands of deference:

[When you] demonstrate to the World [that] . . . you tread superior to private Influence . . . you will give a singular Example of living Illumination, to all other Counties and Corporations in the Kingdom. You will give a public Testimony and Sanction to Virtue. You will render it fashionable, approved, and applauded . . . You will deliver down the signal Precedent to many Generations; and when you shall have passed away, future Centuries who shall reap the Harvest of your Truth, in all the blessed Enjoyments of Liberty and Prosperity, will recognize the glorious Ancestors by whom the Seed was sown.[43]

In the Dublin context, the issue of the church in politics was present in Lucas's campaign even before any question of a parliamentary contest arose. In *The Complaints of Dublin: Humbly offered to His Excellency William Earl of Harrington, Lord Lieutenant General of Ireland* (Dublin, 1747), Lucas turned the tables on those who had accused him and his supporters of being 'Tories and Jacobites'. What was the point, he asked, rhetorically, in passing laws against the further growth of popery if at the same time clergymen were being recruited and brought to Ireland 'from a turbid or polluted spring' (Oxford)?[44] This was apparently an attack on George Stone,[45] who had recently been appointed archbishop of Armagh and primate of all Ireland, and whose brother Andrew (also Oxford-educated) had risen from being private secretary to the duke of Newcastle to holding public office and acquiring great influence with the ministries that followed on the fall of Walpole. Lucas conceded that Christianity was once again becoming '*fashionable* in *England*', but this was thanks to 'the Labors of some eminent Lay-men'; meanwhile 'Liberty' remained far from fashionable, and for this Lucas blamed the clergy, although he accepted that '*some* clergy have disclaimed the bad principles'.[46] A year later, having embarked on his by-election campaign, Lucas hit out at an anonymous clergyman whom he suspected of having been hired to attack him in print. Condemning the '*antichristian Religion,* or *Priest Craft*' displayed by the writer, Lucas gave thanks that 'We own no Laws Ecclesiastical, or Civil, here, but what derive their being and Force from the *Municipal* or Common Law'.[47]

Lucas was not the first to sound an anti-clerical note in Dublin. During the 1720s a 'moderate anti-clericalism' had been one of the hallmarks of the Molesworth circle[48] of freethinkers and others whose leader was Robert Molesworth, author of *An Account of Denmark* (1694), which broke new ground by raising the spectre of constitutional liberty being undermined by the actions of Protestant clergy. The circle also included Francis Hutcheson,[49] then managing a dissenting academy in Dublin. But there can be no doubt that through the *Censor* Lucas helped to bring anti-clericalism to a wider and more popular audience. 'Your Constitution', readers were informed, 'is the noblest Improvement of human Reason.' But the constitution was not being supported in its full purity. Just as in the case of the Athenian and Roman commonwealths, luxury and avarice, detrimental to the virtue of the citizens, had made their appearance, brought in by judges, kings, and bishops: 'the Infection came down industriously wrapped in Ermine, Purple, and Lawn.'[50]

Down to the time of Lucas's flight, such veiled attacks on the clergy appear to have caused no very great reaction among those fearful for the reputation and interests of the church. After all, Lucas was a member of the established church himself, and he retained (as did many others at this time) a good deal of what may be called 'institutional loyalty' to the church. And the *Censor's* references to the clergy were by no means all critical. The late Archbishop King, author of the great defence of Irish Protestants during the Jacobite period, was held up to public approval; so was Swift, and so were contemporary clergymen who for one reason or another had ingratiated themselves with the reformers.[51] But following Lucas's condemnation and flight, a 'new light' Presbyterian merchant, Thomas Read, was fielded as a candidate in the approaching by-election.[52] At this point there appeared in Dublin a new publication, *The Church Monitor* (October-November 1749), which accused the reformers of talking of liberty while really paving the way for 'Independents' (freethinkers) to take over the management of the city: kindred spirits with those who had been responsible for the overturning of church and state in the 1640s. Accordingly, those who wished to uphold the established church should vote for the aldermen, whose worth could be judged by the fact that they had the backing of the most eminent men in the kingdom.[53] Not surprisingly, at the poll, the bulk of the Church of Ireland clergy voted for the aldermen.[54]

In conclusion, and to return to the theme of the conference, is it possible to describe this Dublin phase of Patriotism, with its biblical and millennial overtones, as revolutionary? Scarcely in the conventional sense of that term. It was not particularly anti-British. It did not stand for any radical recasting of society or overturning of monarchy. Nor, perhaps surprisingly, was it concerned in any very urgent or practical way with the conversion of Catholics. Even its anti-clericalism, which was typical of the Enlightenment, was of a moderate kind. Its chief targets were the Irish Protestants themselves (particularly the voters), urging them to a change of heart.

Nevertheless, it was of great significance in the history of Patriotism in Ireland. The immediate issue in 1749 was whether the electorate could be induced to defy oligarchy. Given Lucas's failure to win over the aldermen or the civil authorities to endorse his programme, by the time of the poll the reformers were faced with voting against virtually the entire political and clerical establishment. It is hard at this distance to imagine how difficult it must have been, in the absence of the secret ballot, political parties, or more traditional inducements, to persuade the voters to act in this way. Yet enough of them did so to elect La Touche; and within little more than a decade Lucas had been rehabilitated, had won a Dublin seat in parliament, and a measure of corporation reform was on the statute books.[55] For these changes to come about, a more than ordinary commitment on the part of the 'free citizens' was necessary. Could they have been mobilized on the strength of civic republican ideas alone? There is no doubt that those ideas were compelling, particularly in the Dublin context, where the history of corporate life appeared to provide a classic example of the loss of liberty. But Ruth Bloch has stressed how conservative, how pessimistic, even, civic republican ideas were, with their emphasis on the fragility of liberty and insistence on the cyclical patterns of liberty and slavery.[56] Millennial visions, on the other hand, were fundamentally more positive and optimistic. Without the element of 'providential destiny', it is doubtful whether the Dublin voters could have been brought to the point of defying oligarchy; and without their example, it is difficult to conceive of the subsequent rise of 'independent' clubs in the 1750s and 1760s, or the Volunteers of the 1770s.

By then, the visionary element in Patriotism was becoming more secular. However, as we have recently been reminded, there was a millennial element in the ideas of the United Irishmen;[57] and the anti-clerical strain, too, persisted, as exemplified by Henry Grattan's labours in the 1780s to reform the tithe system.[58] Millennialism may even have been strengthened by the accession of Ulster Protestants, many of them dissenters, from the 1770s onwards.[59]

Finally, a parallel development with the American colonies may be noted. Across the Atlantic, in the middle decades of the century the idea that America had a providential destiny was being propagated more and more vigorously as a result of the great awakening:[60] though there too at that period there was little that was revolutionary or anti-British about it.[61] In Ireland, while earlier Patriots such as Molyneux and Swift had contended that English liberties ought to be upheld across the Irish sea, it was these mid-century developments that fostered the view that *Ireland* (and especially Dublin) had a special role to play in apocalyptic history by reviving public liberty and 'true religion'. Such ideas, though in more revolutionary and sometimes more secular forms, were to continue to be influential for later generations of Patriots and nationalists.

NOTES

1 Quoted in Daniel J. Boorstin, *The Americans 1: The Colonial Experience* (Harmondsworth, 1985 edn), p. 15.
2 [Henry Brooke], *A Tenth and Last Letter from the Farmer, to the Free and Independent citizens of Dublin* (Dublin, 1749), p. 6. Matthew's gospel (Authorised Version) is the main source, but there is also an echo of Luke's wording (xi, 36).
3 See Sean Murphy, 'Charles Lucas and the Dublin Election of 1748–1749', *Parliamentary History*, vol. 2 (1983), 93–111.

4 [Henry Brooke], *An Occasional Letter from the Farmer, to the Free-men of Dublin* (Dublin, 1749) pp. 3–4.

5 *Ibid.*, pp. 4–5.

6 See J. G. A. Pocock, *The Machiavellian Moment: Florentine Political Thought and the Atlantic Republican Tradition* (Princeton and London, 1975).

7 Murphy, 'Charles Lucas and the Dublin election'; Jacqueline Hill, *From Patriots to Unionists: Dublin Civic Politics and Irish Protestant Patriotism, 1660–1840* (forthcoming).

8 See David Dickson and Richard English, 'The La Touche Dynasty', in David Dickson ed., *The Gorgeous Mask: Dublin 1700–1850* (Dublin, 1987), pp.17–29.

9 See e.g., T. W. Moody and W.E. Vaughan eds., *A New History of Ireland, IV: Eighteenth Century Ireland, 1691–1800* (Oxford, 1986), liv, p. 233.

10 Steven N. Zwicker, 'England, Israel, and the Triumph of Roman Virtue', in Richard H. Popkin ed. *Millenarianism and Messianism in English Literature and Thought 1650–1800* (Leiden and New York, 1988) pp. 37–64.

11 Christopher Hill, *The English Bible and the Seventeenth Century Revolution* (Harmondsworth, 1994) pp. 6–7.

12 Ernest Lee Tuveson, *Redeemer Nation: the Idea of America's Millennial Role* (Chicago and London, 1968); Ruth Bloch, *Visionary Republic: Millennial Themes in American Thought, 1756–1800* (Cambridge, 1985).

13 In D. George Boyce, Robert Eccleshall and Vincent Geoghegan eds., *Political Thought in Ireland since the Seventeenth Century* (London and New York, 1993) pp. 36–72.

14 See *D.N.B.*

15 [Henry Brooke], *A Ninth Letter from the Farmer to the Free and Independent Electors of the City of Dublin* (Dublin, 1749) p. 14.

16 Charles Lucas, 'A letter, etc.', in id., *The Political Constitutions of Great Britain and Ireland, Asserted and Vindicated* (London, 1751) 2 vols., vol. 2, p. 442.

17 Sean Murphy 'The Lucas Affair: a Study of Municipal and Electoral Politics in Dublin, 1742–9', MA Thesis (NUI [UCD], 1981).

18 Charles Lucas, *Divelina Libera: an Apology for the Civil Rights and Liberties of the Common and Citizens of Dublin* (Dublin, 1744), pp. 5, 9.

19 Sean Murphy, 'Charles Lucas. Catholicism and Nationalism', in *Eighteenth Century Ireland*, (1993), vol. 8, pp. 83–102.

20 See Lucas, *Divelina Libera*, pp. 5, 7, 21; A. F. Barber and Citizen [Charles Lucas], *A Third Letter to the Free-Citizens of Dublin* (Dublin, 1747), p. 14.

21 Lucas, *Divelina Libera*, pp. 7–8.

22 *Censor*, i, no. 25, 11 Nov. 1749–21 Apr. 1750.

23 *The Works of Jonathan Swift, D. D.* (Dublin, 1735), 4 vols, vol. 4, 51–62, at pp. 51, 61.

24 *Ibid.*, vol. 4, 63–74, at p. 72.

25 *Ibid.*, vol. 4, 75–101, at p. 100.

26 Quoted in J. A. Downie, *Jonathan Swift, Political Writer* (London, 1985 edn.), p. 243.

27 [Lucas] *A Tenth Address to the Free-Citizens, and Free-Holders, of the City of Dublin* (Dublin, 1748) p. 5

28 'A Project for the Advancement of Religion, and the Reformation of Manners', in *Works*, vol. 1, 130–54, at pp. 149–50.

29 T. C. Barnard, 'The Uses of 23 October 1641 and Irish Protestant Celebrations', *English Historical Review*, cvi (1991), 889–920.

30 *An Act for Keeping and Celebrating the Twenty-Third of October, as an Anniversary Thanksgiving in this Kingdom* 14 & 15 Chas. II, c. 23.

31 R. Lee Cole, *A History of Methodism in Dublin* (Dublin, 1932) p. 16; John Pollock, *George Whitefield and the Great Awakening* (Tring, 1932 edn) p. 67. See also David Hempton and Myrtle Hill, *Evangelical Protestantism in Ulster Society 1740–1890* (London and New York, 1992) ch. 1.

32 F. M. Harris, 'John Cennick in Ireland 1746–1755', *Irish Baptist Historical Journal*, vol. 15 (1982–3), 21–9.

33 Cole, *History of Methodism in Dublin*, pp. 16–26.

34 Pollock, *George Whitefield*, p. 67; Harris, 'John Cennick in Ireland', p. 22.

35 See David Hayton, 'Did Protestantism Fail in Early Eighteenth-Century Ireland?', in Alan Ford, James McGuire and Kenneth Milne eds., *As by Law Establishment: the Church of Ireland since the Reformation* (Dublin, 1995) pp. 166–86.

36 Mark Goldie, 'The civil religion of James Harrington', in Anthony Pagden ed., *The Languages of Political Theory in Early-Modern Europe* (Cambridge, 1987), pp. 197–222.

37 Justin Champion, *The Pillars of Priestcraft Shaken. The Church of England and its Enemies, 1660–1730* (Cambridge, 1992), pp. 9–10.

38 A selection of Bolingbroke's writings were brought out in a Dublin edition: see [Henry St John, Viscount Bolingbroke], *A Collection of Political Tracts* (Dublin, 1748).

39 *The Freeholder's Political Catechism* (1733), *ibid.*, pp. 199–213, at p. 206.

40 *Ibid.*, pp. 209, 212.

41 *Ibid.*, p. 209.

42 *Ibid.*, pp. 207–8.

43 *A Ninth Letter from the Farmer*, p. 15.

44 Charles Lucas, *The Complaints of Dublin: Humbly Offered to his Excellency William, Earl of Harrington, Lord Lieutenant of Ireland* (Dublin, 1747). Lucas was expressing the popular notion that Oxford was synonymous with Toryism and Jacobitism.

45 See *D.N.B.* Stone's career in Ireland is discussed in Robert E. Burns, *Irish Parliamentary Politics in the Eighteenth Century* (Washington, 1990) 2 vols, vol. 2, chs. 3–6, 8.

46 Lucas, *The Complaints of Dublin*, pp. 35–6.

47 [Charles Lucas], *A Sixteenth Address to the Free Citizens and Free-Holders of the City of Dublin* (Dublin, 1748), pp. 21–2.

48 David Berman, 'The Irish Counter-Enlightenment' in Richard Kearney ed., *The Irish Mind* (Dublin, 1985), 119–40, at pp. 129–30; Ian McBride, 'The School of Virtue: Francis Hutcheson, Irish Presbyterians and the Scottish Enlightenment', in Boyce, Eccleshall and Geoghegan eds, *Political Thought in Ireland*, pp. 73–99, at pp. 82–5.

49 For Hutcheson, see McBride, 'The School of Virtue'.

50 'To the people of Ireland', *Censor*, i, no. 5, 24 June–1 July 1749.

51 *Ibid.*, i. nos. 7, 9 and 23 (8–15 July, 22–9 July, 28 October–4 November 1749).

52 Murphy, 'Charles Lucas and the Dublin election', p. 105.

53 *The Church Monitor*, no. 1, 27 Oct. 1749.

54 Murphy, 'Charles Lucas and the Dublin election', p. 106.

55 Dublin City Corporation Act, 1760 (33 Geo. III, c. 16). This act removed from the aldermen and vested in the guilds the right to choose their representatives for the city 'commons'; it also gave the commons rights in respect of the election of the lord mayor and aldermen.

56 Bloch, *Visionary Republic*, p. 5.

57 Nancy Curtin, *The United Irishmen: Popular Politics in Ulster and Dublin, 1791–1798* (Oxford, 1994) pp. 189–91.

58 W. E. H. Lecky, *A History of Ireland in the Eighteenth Century*, abridged edn., with introduction by L. P. Curtis, Jr. (Chicago and London, 1972), pp. 214–16.

59 Although Ulster did not experience the revivalism that affected the west of Scotland and the middle colonies in North America in the second half of the eighteenth century, it was not untouched by evangelical religion: see Hempton and Hill, *Evangelical Protestantism in Ulster Society*, pp. 18–19.

60 Bloch, *Visionary republic*, ch. 1.

61 *Ibid.*, pp. 42–50.

5   The Sovereign as God? Theophilanthropy and the Politics of the Directory 1795–99

James Livesey

The French Revolution produced an intense compression of experience for those who lived through it. So many assumptions were undermined, expectations confounded and hopes dashed that by the Year V the Minister of the Interior, writing to the Commissaires in the departments, could speak of 'the centuries that have passed from 1788 to 1797'.[1] In the recent turn to the study of the political culture of the revolution historians have been very sensitive to the great pace of events and the effect it had of revealing tensions and inconsistencies in the attitudes and assumptions of the revolutionaries. Furet used the term *dérapage* precisely to capture the sense in which the logic of the revolution escaped the grasp of those who had made it. We have not been attentive, however, to what the revolutionaries themselves learned from this *dérapage*, how they reviewed, revised and restructured their ideas about politics as a consequence of it. The methodological postulate of a *discours révolutionnaire*, a relatively coherent world-view that underpinned and conditioned the nature of politics in the revolution, has turned our attention away from the efforts of the revolutionaries to respond to the disintegration of their assumptions, particularly, but not only, in the face of the Terror.[2] We have operated under the rather incredible assumption that the ideas of 1789, as compromised as they were, remained unrevised in 1796, 1797 or 1798.[3]

Since we have not seen revolutionary political culture as developing, or even degenerating, we have a distorted and overly-rigid view. Thus, despite the often brilliant work done in the past few years on that culture, we do not understand its dynamics and so our view of the meaning of many of the central core concepts that were used in political life is distorted. When we turn our attention to the latter half of the Revolution, Thermidor and the Directory, we discover a much richer and more varied political lexicon than that of 1789–94. More importantly, we can see in the political culture of the Directory the openness of revolutionary political culture to creative interpretation. This holds true even when we turn attention to core elements of revolutionary political culture, such as the concept and practice of sovereignty.

The most powerful and compelling account of national sovereignty was that presented by Sieyès in his *Qu'est-ce que le Tiers Etat?* of 1788. Sieyès's innovation was to take the debate on the relationship of sovereign to society of 1788 and turn it on its head. Constitutionalist parlementarians, neo-republicans like Brissot or social theorists like Condorcet had configured the debate as an account of how society, or the nation, could represent itself and so limit the sovereign power of the monarch.[4] Sieyès ignored this debate about limits to assert that the nation should exercise sovereignty; in a dazzling metaphorical leap he transferred the powers of the crown to the nation.[5] Of course in doing so he made use of Rousseau's notion of the sovereign General Will, developed in the Social Contract. But it would be a disservice to Sieyès to argue that he simply followed through the implications of a theory already immanent in Rousseau. For one thing Rousseau's was not at all a theory of national sovereignty but one of popular sovereignty. Moreover the conditions for a possibly legitimate sovereign people laid down by Rousseau were so strict as to be unfulfillable. Rousseau's argument in many cases ran directly contrary to Sieyès's. Where Rousseau argued that the society of the General Will only came into being at the moment of the creation of the explicit political contract, Sieyès asserted the pre-existence of the nation in the community of productive members of the society, which only needed to be represented.[6] Moreover, Rousseau had expressly denied the possibility of representing the sovereign and the thrust of Sieyès's theory was to transfer sovereign powers to the representation of the Third Estate. Rousseau's notion of the General Will gave Sieyès a concept with which to explain the sovereign power and authority of the Nation, but Sieyès's conceptualization of the Nation as a moral person, pre-existing any formal constitutional machinery or means of representation, was all his own and his ascription of the sovereign powers or the monarch to this entity was breathtakingly audacious. Keith Baker has expressed better than anyone the radical innovation inherent in Sieyès's formulation, though the claims he makes for it are possibly overstated,

The logic of *Qu'est-ce que le Tiers Etat?* threatened the entire standing order of international relations no less radically than it subverted the institutional order of the French monarchy. Once it was adopted, the history of humanity could be nothing but the story of national self-determination inflicted everywhere upon it in the two centuries since the French revolution.[7]

Though the importance and originality of Sieyès's work has long been acknowledged, one aspect of it has escaped notice. Sieyès's metaphorical tranposition of the powers of the monarch onto the nation through the assertion that the nation, and not the monarch, was the true sovereign, was an attempt to secularize what up to that point had been a notion grounded in political theology. Sovereignty in the French political tradition did not mean ultimate authority, it meant a particular type of ultimate authority, one that was undivided, absolute and analogous to the authority of God over creation. A comparison between the idea of sovereignty in the Anglophone tradition and that in the French tradition will help to illustrate this point.

The concept was invented by Bodin in his *Six Livres de la République* of 1576. Bodin came to this notion as part of his response to Catholic and Protestant resistance theories, particularly those of the Monarchomachs, which he held responsible for the civil wars.[8] Bodin developed the idea of a final authority out of a very old metaphor for the political community, that of the body politic, but he used that metaphor in a new way. Most previous uses of the body metaphor had used it to assert the interdependence of the elements of the commonwealth; Bodin instead used the analogy of the executive to the will to argue for the necessity for a single, absolute and indivisible final point of authority in the republic.[9] Bodin abandoned the intricate vocabulary of the natural law tradition in order to define the power of the Prince in a manner that could not be disputed or resisted. Absolute power, the essential element of sovereign power, demanded that,

the people or the lords of a republic give the sovereign and perpetual power to someone to dispose of their goods, persons and all of the state at his will. . . .[10]

Many commentators, following Carl Schmitt, have argued that Bodin's concept was, in essence, a secularized version of the Augustinian ideal of God as a universal law-giver.[11] This is difficult to prove, but what is undeniable is that it certainly acquired these characteristics in the seventeenth century. Both Hobbes and Bossuet, the major theorists of sovereignty in England and France respectively, had no hesitation in comparing kings to gods. In Hobbes's discussion of the illegitimacy of resistance to the Sovereign, for example, he explicitly endowed the sovereign with the powers of God,

And whereas some men have pretended for their disobedience to their Soveraign, a new Covenant, made, not with men, but with God; this also is unjust: for there is no Covenant with God but by the mediation of some body that representeth God's Person; which none doth but God's Lieutenant, who hath the Soveraignty under God.[12]

Bossuet went even further in his deification of the sovereign; while Hobbes's sovereign was only God's lieutenant on Earth, Bossuet flatly stated that kings were gods to men. In his most famous statement of the absolute power of the monarch, in Book IV of his *Politics Drawn from the Very Words of Holy Scripture*, Bossuet absorbed the entire state and all public life into the monarch through this analogy:

Majesty is the image of the greatness of God in a prince. God is infinite, God is all. The Prince, in his quality of Prince, is not considered as an individual; he is a public personage, all the state is comprised in him; the will of all the people is comprised in his own. Just as all virtue and excellence are united in God, so the strength of every individual is comprehended in the person of the Prince.[13]

Sovereignty may have been first posited in a secular, post-sceptical, as Richard Tuck puts it, frame, but it quickly acquired an explicitly religious gloss.[14]

The meaning of these theocratic statements was very different in the two contexts though. In both England and France the metaphor of the body politic was embedded in a doctrine of 'the King's two bodies', to use the phrase of Ernest Kantorwicz.[15] However, in England, during the seventeenth century the physical and mystical bodies of the King grew further away from one another, particularly in the rhetoric of the Common lawyers in the House of Commons.[16] Thus, through complicated political argument, British subjects might resist the actions of the physical monarch and leave the monarchy unstained. The long-term effect was the development of an entire constitutional legacy that organized the relationship of state and subject through a polarity of sovereign and natural right.[17]

Exactly the opposite occurred in France. There, constitutional doctrine and political practice tended to merge the two bodies of the King as the century progressed.[18] Sarah Hanley has argued persuasively that beginning with the minority of Louis XIII and culminating in the personal rule of Louis XIV the efficacy of any notion of public law or of the separation of the monarch from the monarchy was lost to a doctrine of total and absolute personal representation of the polity by the King.[19] The practice of this form of monarchy as the removal of the King from public sight to Versailles and the bureaucratization of rule is well known; what is less remarked on are the ideas which held this form of rule in place. The phoenix and sun images used to buttress the notion that the King never dies were supplementary to the idea of a Bourbon *mystique du sang*, the idea that sovereignty in the strict sense inhered in the actual blood that moved in the veins of the legitimate monarch. Thus Bossuet's claims for an absolute sovereign power, coeval with that of God over creation, were not made for the mystical body of the monarch which could in turn be transferred to and diluted in the mystical body of the Nation. Rather they were made for the actual physical body of the King. Ultimate power and religious authority were impacted in one sovereign body.

Moreover that ideal and practice of sovereignty were not seriously challenged right through the eighteenth century, despite the obvious political struggles that dominated the period after 1750.[20] The *parlements* never claimed to represent the sovereign nation, rather they claimed to represent the Estates-General in abeyance and that in turn was conceived of as a body that did not share in the King's sovereignty, but had the right of declaration of the interests of the *corps* that made up the country to the King.[21] Neither party in the great religious controversy between Jansenists and *Dévots* ever questioned the sovereign powers of the monarch, nor the extension of those powers to church organization.[22] No more vivid example of the seriousness with which the ideal of the sovereign monarch was taken could be found than the horrible execution of Damiens in 1757. As Reinhart Koselleck put it, the monarch's sovereignty was intact in 1789; it was the efficacy of that sovereignty that stood in question.[23] Indeed even in 1791 the Abbé Emery republished Bossuet's work on sovereignty as the most efficacious antidote to the radicalization of the revolution, and in the introduction asserted the traditional understanding of the nature of the sovereign:

This doctrine of popular sovereignty and of an originary contract with Kings is fallacious: and, understood in its vulgar interpretation, it is an erroneous and pestilential doctrine, capable of pitching every government into confusion and of inundating the world in tears and blood.[24]

In enunciating a doctrine of national sovereignty Sieyès was not simply performing a tactical manoeuvre of stunning brilliance which met with instant success, though he was doing that. He was also trying to secularize what remained a fundamentally theological concept, in the French context, and change its meaning all at once. Crucially, as Lucien Jaume has pointed out, the notion of the sovereign implied that of the subject, not that of the citizen. To be a subject meant submission to the sovereign, not participation in a free state, be the sovereign the King or the Nation.[25] The sovereign nation was potentially as much of an impediment to Sieyès's ideal of individual self realization in an empowered state as the monarchy had been.[26] To locate sovereignty in the Nation was to threaten the possibility of a representative system, organized by a constitution. Moreover, as hostile as Sieyès was to supernatural and theological concepts he could not by wishing it or writing it alone divorce the notion of sovereignty from that of religious authority.[27] To claim that the nation was sovereign was implicitly to grant it the right to reorganize the spiritual life of the country and to contribute to the fusion of the political and regenerative goals of the revolution. By positing that the goal of the revolution was the regeneration of the sovereign nation Sieyès unwittingly contributed to what early nineteenth-century historians like Michelet and Quinet recognized as a religious movement, the creation of a new man, embedded in a civic religion, itself supported and guaranteed by the state.[28] Sieyès and other reformers of his ilk faced the difficulty that the very tools they used to loosen the monarchy's grip on power threatened the project of creating a modern polity to which they were committed, by turning political questions into metaphysical or theological questions.[29]

Historians such as Ferenc Fehér and Ran Halévi have argued that this fusion of Regeneration and National Sovereignty was *the* logic of the revolution and eventually drove it to Terror.[30] Certainly the Terror was characterized by such a fusion of a desire to create a new civic religion with claims for the absolute power of the nation to impose that belief, the high point of which was of course Robespierre's creation of a Cult of the Supreme Being and his demand that atheism be declared a crime.[31] The revolution did not stop in July 1794 however and its subsequent history throws much light on the revolutionaries' attitudes to the uses to which the concept of national sovereignty had been put. Without retreating from any of their goals, neither regeneration nor political reform, the leadership of the Directory, particularly after Fructidor Year V, attempted to create a new ideal for the revolution, that of a commercial, modern republic. This drove them to review much of what they had inherited from the early years of the revolution, and in particular to develop a very new attitude to the concept of national sovereignty.

The Directorial elites wished to separate politics from regeneration. To achieve this they would have to disentangle the various strands of the revolution from the notion of national sovereignty. In pursuit of this goal they were aided, paradoxically, by the efforts of the counter-revolutionary theorists, particularly de Maistre. De Maistre recaptured the French concept of sovereignty for the counter-revolution by placing the revolution in the context of a providential history. His was the first solidly constructed theory of counter-revolution. He argued that the Revolution had been the result of the moral and religious decadence of France, it was the punishment for sin and was itself 'an event unique in history, because it is radically evil, [. . .], it is the highest form of corruption known, a pure impurity'.[32] The sin, in de Maistre's view, had been man's wilful disobedience of the authorities constituted by God; in Germany this had taken the form of the Reformation and Protestantism, in France the Enlightenment. De Maistre's jeremiad asserted that the national destiny of France was to be purged by the fires of revolution and so to become the theocratic magistrate of Europe, in alliance with the Pope. Even in the Terror he saw the force of providence working for religious renewal, 'the action of Providence is never more palpable than when it overwhelms the hand of man and acts for itself'.[33]

The emergence of a third vision of history raised the stakes of political conflict. Until de Maistre, there were essentially two relevant emplotments of history: the *philosophe* vision of the steady progress of enlightenment and Rousseau's narrative of decline and redemption through regeneration.[34] While Louis XVI had been personally pious, and the position of the Catholic clergy under the civil constitution clearly was important in motivating counter-revolutionary forces, before de Maistre's book the ideological defence of the monarchy had not been theocratic. Theorists of Monarchy, such as Mounier, had instead followed Montesquieu and argued that Monarchy was uniquely suited to modern, commercial societies.[35] The very existence of a theocratic idea served further to radicalize conflict and to destroy the possibility of any compromise among property-owners. Supporters of the Directory remarked on the tendency for all political conflicts to be organized by the framework of ideological polarization between theocratic royalist and directorial republican,

. . . if all the parties who have agitated the Republic have not directly attached themselves to royalism, royalism has co-opted them as auxiliaries from whom it could derive advantage.[36]

They were also in no doubt that the force of the royalists lay not in their social base, nor in what armed force they could raise but in their rhetoric,

The whole plan is executed without the government, the people or the army. The means of execution are a suite of epigrams and songs with devastating effect on public opinion.[37]

The direct response to the counter-revolutionary jeremiad was to offer an alternative history of the causes of the crimes of the revolution. Far from being an affliction sent by God to reprimand the French people for their sins, the revolution was the reconquest of their liberty by the French people. This republican rhetoric identified the destruction of the Huguenots, 'le parti le plus libre', by Richelieu as the occasion of decline in French history.[38] The decadence of the character of the French people dated from that era and its effects were nigh on total,

Cardinal Richelieu's despotism entirely destroyed the originality of the French character, its loyalty, its candour, its independence.[39]

The effect of the victory of Richelieu was to create the conditions where even as undivided a blessing as liberty could have dangerous possibilities. Given the degradation of the French people,

. . . the revolution, from which emerged a Republic innocent of our sins, was fertile in crime, because it was made by a people hardened and corrupted by a long arbitrary despotism.[40]

Terror was condemned as the consistent tactic of royalism. Indeed properly understood, Robespierre's power was royalism by other means and the return of the monarchy would entail the return of the Terror,

Royalism does not even fear that the new point of contact between it and anarchy will be noticed. The system taken up by it in those terrible times, is now carried on. . . .[41]

Supporters of the Directory aligned all practitioners of the politics of sovereignty with Terror. Their identification with the Huguenots was more than mere rhetoric designed to deflect blame for political violence. Rather it captured an essential understanding that the politics of the sovereign nation, understood in the specific French eighteenth-century context, could only ever be a continuation of the political practice of absolutism. The problem they faced as a consequence was that of disentangling the elements of the revolutionary project that had become impacted in that of the regeneration of the sovereign nation. How was political authority to be represented or the task of regeneration imagined?

Push came to shove for the Directory and its supporters during the summer of 1797 (Year V). In the face of a feared counter-revolution they staged a coup against the legislative majority on 18 Fructidor. The well-planned occupation of the strategic sites of Paris was undertaken by Augereau's troops. Arrests of deputies, journalists and even of one of the Directors, Barthelémy, followed, though the attempted arrest of Carnot and many others failed.[42] This initial act of purgation set the scene for the thoroughgoing overhaul of the administration. After some prompting from the remaining Directors, the councils passed the law of 19 Fructidor annulling election results in forty-nine departments and giving the Directors the powers to replace administrators in the departments as they saw fit.[43] So successful was this coup, and so total the defeat of the royalists that it would not be until 1814 that a significant royalist party would again emerge in France. Monarchy would reappear in France only in the aftermath of military defeat.

Such a coup was by definition an act of sovereignty, defined by Carl Schmidt as the right to define the exceptions to the rules, and opponents of the Directors were quick to denounce them as new terrorists.[44] The danger was that once forced to rely on the army to end a crisis the Directors would find themselves with no other tool of government. Their sense that endemic political warfare, civil war or terror, was a present danger for the republic can be read from the pamphlets they distributed. La Revellière-Lépeaux expressed the dangers of violence well,

. . . that is citizens, the danger of anarchy, if it triumphs it will tend toward monarchy across calamities and crimes, and that it only succumbs by creating an attitude more or less favorable to despotism among the public authorities.[45]

Violence was no solution to the political problems of France, it merely created a new, and possibly even more intractable, situation. The Directors had to find a legitimation for their rule and their actions.

Supporters of the Directory were not prepared to countenance a purely liberal, formal style of politics, indeed this had been the style of politics promoted by the authors of the Constitution of the Year III which the Directors felt had been a total failure.[46] Some sort of regenerative project had to be embraced; as de Moy put it:

> Without festivals we are only connected to one another by commercial relations, but these sorts of relations do not properly connect us. Left this way, circumscribed within our own social circles, and each one closed off within our own coterie, we will live strangers to one another, without knowing or esteeming one another.[47]

Neither were they prepared to institute a full-blown national civic religion. To do so would be to recreate the type of sovereign nation of which they were critical. The Directory and its supporters were to experiment with many routes between these conflicting imperatives; Theophilanthropy was the religious vehicle for their project.

Theophilanthropy had been founded only seven months before, its main sponsor was the ex-terrorist Valentin Hauy but its theorist, and the man most closely identified with the movement was Chemin-Depontès.[48] Theophilanthropy was the latest in a long line of forms of natural religion, however it was the first that explicitly tried to use Deist ideas as an antidote to the violence that had been created by the revolution. As Chemin-Depontès explained its goals,

> . . . The sole aim was to create a useful institution, which would heal the wounds of the revolution, resolve all hearts by preaching mutual understanding and the forgiveness of all grievances, which would unite all sects in universal tolerance, by giving morality, the sweetest ever professed, a sanction above all criticism, and which would unite the people in a genuine fraternity.[49]

Theophilanthropy was an attempt to define a moral stance based on a utilitarian ethic that retained the civic commitment of the Jacobin ideal by casting that utilitarian ethic in a religious frame. Happiness, rather than virtue, was seen as the highest good. Man's social nature, in the view of the Theophilanthropists meant that he rationally loved his country. Under their heavy rhetoric that commitment was imagined in two ways: the good citizen was a laborious citizen, who made his home a religious site, and that citizen was prepared to serve his country directly in case of war.[50] In the aftermath of Fructidor this rather vague and sentimental religious movement not only attracted the support of the Directors, and of La Revellière-Lépeaux in particular, and that of many republican theorists, like Thomas Paine, but also recruited a massive public following.[51] La Revellière-Lépeaux in particular saw in Theophilanthropy an institution that could produce the kinds of public religious ceremonies that would sacralize the affective and social relationships between human beings in society.[52] The affection of La Revellière for the new religion made of it a target for victims of 18 Fructidor such as Carnot. He denounced it and the Directory's religious policy as nothing more than a reworking of the Cult of the Supreme Being of 1794.[53] Nothing could have been further from the truth. The Directory colonized and supported Theophilanthropy precisely as a bulwark against a renewed total revolutionary religion, which at the same time could, hopefully, satisfy the desire for religious expression which was obvious in even the most republican departments.[54] This then was the place of Theophilanthropy in the politics of the Directory. It provided a locus within which the regenerative project of the revolution might be located. It operated as the second wing of their politics, the first of which was the foundation of a republican constitutional order. Theophilanthropy provided a means of sacralizing the republic without attributing to the republic the characteristics of sovereignty.

If we accept this argument, that the French revolution cannot be interpreted as the unproblematic transference of sovereignty from the monarch to the nation, then two consequences follow. Firstly we must reopen an old argument about the nature of the secularization of politics in France in the eighteenth century.[55] As David Bell has pointed out, though we are now well apprised of the structures of public communication in that period and about the secular forms of communication, such as the theatre, that informed the creation of public opinion as a political reality, we have not done such a good job of studying the specific intellectual and political debates on the nature of grace and salvation, representation and power. Possibly even more importantly we need to re-examine the commonplace that the transferrence of sovereignty in the revolution was a central feature in the creation of modern political culture.[56] The revolutionaries found sovereignty impossible to reconcile with a modern political order based on representation and legality. Nowhere can we find them transforming the concept, thus we are left with the question of just when and where it was made safe for modernity.

NOTES

1 François de Neufchâteau aux Commissaires du Directoire Exécutif près des Administrations Centrales et Municipales- Esprit Public, Paris, 25 Fructidor An V, in *Recueil des Lettres, Circulaires, Instructions, Programmes, Discours et autres Actes Publics, Volume 1*, p. xciii. All translations are my own, unless otherwise noted.
2 The hypothesis of a *discours révolutionnaire*, a formulation of Mona Ozouf, is derived from a structuralist view of culture and is inadequate as a representation of the possibilities of symbolic and communicative action in cultures as complex and various as eighteenth-century France.
3 The great exception to this charge is Jacques Guilhamou, see, *La Langue Politique et la Révolution Française* (Paris, 1989).
4 This was also the frame for the debate on public opinion between 1770 and 1789. Public opinion never claimed executive, or even legislative power, rather it claimed weak

rights of consultation in the formation of the royal will. Maurice Cranston adverts to these different positions, but, unfortunately, describes each of them as an account of sovereignty in, 'The Sovereignty of the Nation', in Colin Lucas ed., *The French Revolution and the Creation of Modern Political Culture. Volume 2, The Political Culture of the French Revolution* (Oxford, 1988) p. 97.

5   Keith Michael Baker, 'Sovereignty' in François Furet and Mona Ozouf eds. (Arthur Goldhammer trans.), *A Critical Dictionary of the French Revolution* (Cambridge MA, 1989) p. 850.

6   Of course this argument of Rousseau's is notoriously the knottiest point of his theory. For an explication of the difficulties involved in it see John B. Noone, *Rousseau's Social Contract: A Conceptual Analysis* (Athens GA, 1980), pp. 17–22.

7   Keith Michael Baker, *op. cit.*, p. 850.

8   J.H.M. Salmon, 'Bodin and the Monarchomachs' in *Renaissance and Revolt* (Cambridge, 1987), p. 121.

9   Jean Bodin, *Les Six Livres de la République, Livre Premier* (rev. ed., Paris, 1986), p. 179.

10 *Ibid.*, p. 187.

11 Carl Schmidt (George Schwab trans.), *Political Theology: Four Chapters on the Concept of Sovereignty* (Cambridge MA, 1985) p. 37.

12 Thomas Hobbes (Richard Tuck ed.), *Leviathan* (Cambridge, 1991), p. 122.

13 Jacques-Benigne Bossuet (Patrick Riley ed.), *Politics drawn from the Very Words of Holy Scripture*, (Cambridge, 1990) p. 160.

14 Richard Tuck, 'The "modern theory" of natural law' in Anthony Pagden ed., *The Languages of Political Theory in Early-Modern Europe* (Cambridge, 1987) pp. 110–11.

15 Ernst H. Kantorowicz, *The King's Two Bodies: A Study in Mediaeval Political Theology* (Princeton NJ, 1957).

16 Edmund S. Morgan, *Inventing the People: The Rise of Popular Sovereignty in England and America* (New York, 1985), p. 30.

17 Richard Tuck has long argued that the key figure in the development of this tradition was Selden, and that Matthew Hale popularized and deepened it in the eighteenth century, see, *Natural Rights Theories: Their Origin and Development*, (Cambridge, 1979) p. 94, and *Philosophy and Government 1572–1651* (Cambridge, 1993) pp. 205–40.

18 See Nannerl O. Keohane, *Philosophy and the State in France: The Renaissance to the Enlightenment* (Princeton NJ, 1980) pp. 153–74.

19 Sarah Hanley, *The Lit de Justice of the Kings of France: Constitutional Ideology in Legend, Ritual and Discourse* (Princeton, 1983), p. 319.

20 Ian Wilson argues that the Hobbesian view of sovereignty was more dominant in France than in England in the eighteenth century, introduced to general readership through Barbeyrac's work, see, Ian M. Wilson, 'The Influence of Hobbes and Locke in the shaping of the Concept of Sovereignty in eighteenth-century France', *Studies on Voltaire and the Eighteenth Century*, 101 (1973): 55.

21 Keith Michael Baker, 'Representation' in *The French Revolution and the Making of Modern Political Culture: Volume One, The Political Culture of the Old Regime* (Oxford, 1987) p. 476. Julian Swann's detailed account of the constitutional politics of the era fully supports this contention, see, *Politics and the Parlement of Paris under Louis XV* (Cambridge, 1995).

22 Monique Cottret, 'Aux Origines du Républicanisme Janseniste: Le Mythe de l'Eglise Primitive et le Primitivisme des Lumières', *Revue d'Histoire Moderne et Contemporaine*, Volume 31 (Janvier-Mars 1984), 100. Dale Van Kley, 'Church, State and the Ideological Origins of the French Revolution: The Debate over the General Assembly of the Gallican Clergy in 1765', *Journal of Modern History*, No. 59 (December, 1979) 641.

23 Reinhart Koselleck, *Critique and Crisis: Enlightenment and the Pathogenesis of Modern Society* (Cambridge MA, 1988), p. 8.

24 Abbé Emery, *Principes de Messieurs Bossuet et Fénélon sur la Souveraineté tiré du 5e Avertissement sur les Lettres de M. Jurieu, et d'un Essai sur le Gouvernement Civil* (Paris, 1791), p. iii.

25 Lucien Jaume, 'Citoyenneté et Souveraineté: le Poids de l'Absolutisme', in Baker, *op. cit.*, p. 517.
26 This reading of Sieyès and indeed of the goal of revolutionary culture, is Patrice Higonnet's, see, *Class Ideology and the Rights of Nobles in the French Revolution* (Oxford, 1981) and *Sister Republics: The Origins of French and American Republicanism* (Cambridge MA, 1988) pp. 224–6.
27 For Sieyès's attitude to all forms of political theology see Murray Forsyth, *Reason and Revolution: The Political Thought of the Abbé Sieyès* (Leicester, 1987), p. 33.
28 Claude Lefort, 'La Révolution comme Religion Nouvelle', in Baker, *op. cit*, p. 391. Mona Ozouf, 'Regeneration', in Furet and Ozouf, *op. cit.*, p. 781.
29 Pierre Rosenvallon, 'L'Utilitarisme français et les Ambiguités de la Culture politique prérevolutionnaire (position d'un problème)', in Baker, *op. cit.*, p. 438.
30 Ferenc Fehér, 'The Cult of the Supreme Being and the Limits of the Secularization of the Political', in *The French Revolution and the Birth of Modernity* (Berkeley CA, 1990), pp. 183–5. Ran Halévi, 'La Monarchie et les Elections: Position des Problèmes', in Baker, *op. cit.*, pp. 378–402.
31 Maxamilien Robespierre, 'Sur les Rapports des Idées Religieuses et Morales avec les Principes Républicains, et sur les Fêtes Nationales, Séance du 18 Floréal An II', in Marc Boiloiseau et Albert Soboul eds. *Oeuvres de Maximilien Robespierre, Tome X, Discours 27 Juillet 1793– 27 Juillet 1794* (Paris, 1967), pp. 442–64.
32 Joseph de Maistre, *Considérations sur la France* (re ed., Paris, 1980), p. 54.
33 *Ibid.*, p. 32.
34 Jean Starobinski, 'La Lance d'Achille', *Le Remède dans le Mal: Critique et Légitimation de l'Artifice à l'Age des Lumières* (Gallimard, Paris, 1989), pp. 165–208.
35 Roger Barny, 'L'Evolution idéologique de Jean-Joseph Mounier entre Rousseau et Montesquieu (1789–1801)', in, Michel Vovelle ed. *Bourgeoisies de Province et Révolution* (Grenoble, 1987), pp. 81–102.
36 Anonymous, *Liberté, Egalité, Fraternité: Journée du Dix-Huit Thermidor* (Paris, An VI), p. 6.
37 Lacratelle le Jeune, *Où faut-il s'arrêter?* (Paris, An V) p. 34.
38 Charles Theremin, *De la Situation Intérieure de la République* (Paris, An V), p. 7. An affection for a reformed Christianity had been evident earlier in the revolution as well, see Daubermesnils's comments on church organization in, *Sur le Bruit répandu, qu'il devoit être proposé à la Convention d'ordonner que les Ministres des Cultes seroient payés par leurs Sectateurs* (Paris, 1792), 5, 14.
39 Germaine de Staël, *Considérations sur la Révolution Française* re ed. (Paris, 1983), p. 75.
40 Theremin, *op. cit.*, p. 16.
41 Anonymous, *Liberté, Egalité . . .*, p. 16.
42 Lefebvre, *op. cit.*, p. 428.
43 Loi du 19 Fructidor in Victor Pierre ed., *18 Fructidor: Documents pour la plupart Inédits* (Paris, 1893), pp. 60–7.
44 L.N.M. Carnot, *Histoire du Directoire Constitutionnel, comparée à celle du Gouvernement qui lui a Succédé* (Paris, An VIII) p. 35.
45 La Revellière-Lépeaux, *Le Directoire Exécutif aux Français. Du 18 Fructidor An V de la République Une et Indivisible* (Paris, An V) p. 1.
46 Boissy d'Anglas, *Discours Préliminaire au Projet de Constitution pour la République Française* (Paris, 1795), 5.
47 De Moy, *Des Fêtes, ou quelques Idées d'un Citoyen Français relativement aux Fêtes publiques et d'un Culte national* (Paris, An VII), p. 1.
48 Chemin-Depontès, *Année religieuse des Théophilanthropes* (Paris, An V), pp. 5–7.
49 Chemin-Depontès, *Qu'est-ce que la Théophilanthropie? ou Mémoire contenant l'Origine et l'Histoire de cette Institution, ses Rapports avec le Christianisme, et l'Aperçu de l'Influence qu'elle peut avoir sur tous les Cultes* (Paris, An X) p. 9.

50 *Ibid.*, pp. 31–2.

51 Albert Mathiez, *La Théophilanthropie et le Culte Décadaire 1796–1801. Thèse pour le Doctorat ès Lettres présentée à la Faculté des Lettres de l'Université de Paris 1903* (Geneva, 1975) pp. 170, 244.

52 Louis-Marie La Révellière-Lépeaux, *Réflexions sur le Culte, sur les Cérémonies Civiles et sur les Fêtes Nationales* (Paris, An V) p. 34.

53 L.M.N. Carnot, *Réponse de L.M.N. Carnot, Citoyen Français, l'un des Fondateurs de la République, et Membre Constitutionnel du Directoire Exécutif, au Rapport fait sur la Conjuration du 18 Fructidor, au Conseil des Cinq Cents par J.Ch. Bailleul, au Nom d'une Commission Spéciale* (Paris, An VI) p. 47.

54 On this aspect of the revolutionary experience see Suzanne Desan, *Reclaiming the Sacred: Lay Religion and Popular Politics in Revolutionary France* (Ithaca NY, 1990).

55 For the old argument about Augustinianism and the Enlightenment see Carl Becker, *The Heavenly City of the Eighteenth-Century Philosophers* (New Haven, 1932), and Franco Venturi, *Utopia and Reform in the Enlightenment* (Cambridge, 1971).

56 See Anthony Giddens, *The Nation-State and Violence: Volume Two of a Contemporary Critique of Historical Materialism* (Cambridge, 1985), pp. 94–9. Rogers Brubaker, *Citizenship and Nationhood in France and Germany* (Cambridge MA, 1992) p. 35.

6   Religion, Radicalism and Rebellion in Nineteenth-Century Ireland: The Case of Thaddeus O'Malley

Fergus A. D'Arcy

In 1848, three days before the last great Chartist demonstration in London on 10 April, and three months before the abortive Irish rising at Ballingarry on 22–23 July, a gathering of workers and citizens of Dublin heard a Catholic priest, Thaddeus O'Malley, call upon working men to look to France. There the workers of Paris had bravely fought for their interests and had established the rights of labour. He went on to add that they were not, as in Ireland, exclusively Catholics and Protestants, but numbered many Jews and unbelievers as well; yet, regardless of their differences about the world of spirits they stood firmly together, 'comrades and brothers all'.[1] He then called upon the workers, Protestant and Catholic alike, to take a decisive part in the great movement for the establishment of a government in Ireland.

O'Malley's forthright speech did not come out of the blue. Already on 7 March 1848 he had written a letter on The Rights of Labour, published in the press three days later. In this he referred to a Workman's Bill of Rights which he had drafted and wished to see endorsed by an Irish parliament. This Bill aimed to secure justice for all labour, skilled and unskilled, male and female, rural and domestic.[2]

While his April speech, in professing admiration for the French workers, had not explicitly called on Irish workers to take up arms, O'Malley himself appears to have become caught up in the rapidly radicalizing situation that developed between then and Smith O'Brien's abortive rising in July 1848. In June, at a meeting in the Music Hall, Abbey Street, he came as close to calling for a revolution as one could do – he urged the continued growth of Confederate Clubs and would form one himself for the poor. One police report to the Castle had him stating the right of all to have arms, and that when a government acted with brute force it was only right to give it a strong dose of the same physic. Another police informant at the same meeting reported that 'priest O'Malley rose and made a long winded and determined speech telling the people they would get nothing but what they fight for and win and he called on the people above all to arm'.[3] This was on

21 June; two days later the Paris workers, however armed, felt what it was like to take on the state and the middle classes and to lose when they were slaughtered in the streets of Paris.

What happened to O'Malley in the immediate wake of the June days in Paris and the fiasco at Ballingarry in July is unclear. He may simply have remained in Dublin as chaplain to the nuns of the Presentation Order at George's Hill. However, he was to renew his public identification with the cause of labour three years later in a rather particular way. Before discussing this it may be useful at this point to offer some background as to why he should be of interest to students of Irish history in general and as to why he should be relevant within the particular thematic conjunction of radicalism, religion and rebellion.

Roy Foster has written that 'in the age of Fourier, Saint-Simon and the Spenceans there was little utopian or radical social theory in Ireland, though William Thompson should not be forgotten', and, he added, 'nor should Fintan Lalor, theoretician of a peasant revolution linked to national consciousness'.[4] Yet even in these cases the contribution was limited: Thompson's radicalism was forged in Britain and very largely worked itself out there, not in Ireland, while Foster himself admits of Lalor that he had little if any direct contact with the peasantry. In a landscape almost barren of radical theorists or social visionaries until the close of the nineteenth century, it is curious that the isolated figure of Thaddeus O'Malley has not been spotted or investigated before. In not a single survey or general history of nineteenth-century Ireland does his name appear in text or footnote, while in a few specialist monographs appearing in the last fifteen years he appears occasionally, in a passing reference and almost invariably it is an adversely critical or dismissive one.[5] That apart, he appeared as an entry in Alfred Webb's biographical dictionary of 1878, where the information was based on personal knowledge and hearsay and where what little was said was incorrect in a number of important particulars.[6]

At the time of his Rights of Labour letter in 1848, O'Malley, at fifty-one years of age, was already well known in the world of the working class and social politics. Born in Garryowen in Co. Limerick on 27 March 1797,[7] he was ordained to the priesthood in 1819 at twenty-two years of age.

From an early stage he entered the ranks of rebels and dissidents. In August 1822 he took up the pastoral care of the Catholics of Falmouth in England.[8] Twelve months later he went by invitation to the United States to serve the church in St Mary's, Philadelphia, where his Limerick friend Fr William Hogan ministered. At the time of O'Malley's arrival a virtual schism had developed between Fr Hogan and Bishop Conwell. This arose over the issue of control of church property and it led Hogan to set up an Independent Catholic Church in February 1821. He was excommunicated by Rome in August 1822. O'Malley arrived in October–November 1823. He began intervening to attempt a reconciliation of the opposing sides, only to be excommunicated in turn by Bishop Conwell. O'Malley left Philadelphia in April 1825, and went to Rome to plead the cause of the Philadelphian schismatics.[9] Here, however, in July–August 1825 he apparently retracted, and after suitable contrition and a promise never to return to Philadelphia[10] he recovered his priestly status but with a tarnished reputation. He went to Paris in 1827 and then to London where he appears to have made efforts to secure priestly employment. Having failed, he finally turned up in Dublin in the summer of 1830 where Archbishop Daniel Murray, having been given complete discretion by Rome, allowed him facilities to say Mass in the new Metropolitan Church.[11]

He soon became involved in public controversy on the questions of National Education and Poor Law. But the most remarkable and little known fact about the O'Malley of these years is that he was almost certainly the first man in modern Irish history to advocate a Federal solution to the Anglo-Irish problem. That he was active in the Federalist episode in the history of the Repeal Association in 1843–44 is known; that he was the editor of a journal called *The Federalist* over 1871–74 in support of Isaac Butt's Home Rule movement is also well known. That Butt should have acknowledged him as the Father of Federalism in Ireland is fact – but a curious one until it is realized that already from January 1831 he had begun to publish his paper, *The Federalist*.[12]

In this he laid down the principles that guided most of his public life thereafter – and one of the central ones was that of reconciling Orange and Green and of accommodating the interests of Protestant and Catholic Ireland. He argued that the simple Repeal advocated by Daniel O'Connell would lead to an *imperium in imperio,* and would be a recipe for conflict between two sovereign legislatures, and also could lead to the hegemony of a Catholic faction. His American experience convinced him of the superior harmony of a federal system and he specifically acknowledged the influence of Madison, Jay, Hamilton and *The Federalist Papers*.[13] It probably was critical also in his insistence that a prerequisite to prevent a Catholic ascendancy in a new Ireland was 'the complete and absolute divorce of the connection between the Irish Church and the Irish State'.

He never wavered in these views. In 1836 at a time when the Tory evangelical, Sir George Sinclair, was moving a bill in the House to abolish the Maynooth Grant, O'Malley, wrote, remarkably for his time and cloth:

There are very many Protestants in this country who, according to the lights that are given them, worship their God in spirit and in truth, in the unobtrusive quietness of a pure and placid conscience and in peace and charity with all mankind. These and their Catholic countrymen of a kindred spirit, though separated from each other by a slender partition, my mind delights to picture to itself as kneeling in reverend worship of our common faith in the same glorious temple of our common Christianity.[14]

He added:

We are only cementing the union of the two countries, and what if we were to try the best cement of all – the true cement of a union of the two Churches – so long as you continue to repel us so long we repel you: so long as love rejects love, so long does bigotry on your part beget bigotry on ours.[15]

He first gave serious thought to Federalism during the Catholic Emancipation struggle, which he regarded as 'squandering energies upon a partial sectarian question'.[16] He would insist that an 'Irish parliament would have no power touching the establishment of religion'. He advocated separate legislatures for England and Ireland but with a separate imperial legislature composed of representatives from these separate legislatures.

It was as early as 1831 within the pages of *The Federalist* that he first suggested the necessity of a national system of poor relief, funded in part by the transfer of tithe income and in part from progressive taxation. His social radicalism was here first evident in his remark that he was 'of such homely politics as to prefer that the rich should be deprived of some of their luxuries or even the middle classes of some of their comforts rather than that the poor should be debarred from the necessaries'.[17] His assertion of this anticipated the major conflict that arose between himself and Daniel O'Connell in 1837 which placed him strongly on the side of the workers and poor and O'Connell on the side of property. Here in 1831 he insisted that poor relief was not a question of moral obligation, as O'Connell suggested, but one of right. His incipient Christian Socialism came out in his remark at this point that 'until the lessons of the Gospel in reference to the relations of rich and poor are adopted as the preambles to our Christian legislation, Christianity shall have failed of its purpose'. He condemned O'Connell for saying charity was the solution to unequal distribution: 'I'm talking of rights, not charity'.[18] To deny the right of the poor to a poor law was to absolve the poor 'from whatever moral allegiance they owe to the laws of property'.

These sentiments, radical enough in 1831 by any Irish standards, let alone those of a Catholic priest of the Pro-Cathedral, were to be elaborated at great length six years later in O'Malley's pamphlet, *A Plan of a Poor Law for Ireland*. At the time of its serial publication over the winter of 1836–37, O'Malley had become a member of O'Connell's General Association which he hoped would become the embryo of an Irish parliament.[19] Seeking to move a series of resolutions embodying his concept of poor relief brought him into headlong collision with O'Connell in the public forum.[20] That division won O'Malley an extensive notice by and support from radicals in

Britain as well as workers in Ireland.[21] It brought out the fundamentally conflicting social philosophies of O'Connell's liberalism and O'Malley's collectivism. O'Connell's denial of any right of the poor to relief and his quite explicit support for the pre-eminent rights of property undoubtedly paved the way for the bitter conflict with the trade unions of Ireland which followed a few months later. Equally, it prepared O'Malley for the advance in his views which came a few years later when he delivered his *Address to Mechanics, Small Farmers and the Working Classes Generally*. Published in 1845 the address was actually delivered in 1844 in the Carpenters' Asylum, Gloucester Street. The date is interesting in the light of its contents. Basically it is a manifesto for co-operation as a salvation for the working classes and is based on the same principles as the Rochdale Pioneers were just then establishing.[22]

Space does not permit a detailed exposition of this work in the communitarian tradition. It shows the author familiar with the theories of Thomas Spence, Robert Owen, Henri St Simon and Charles Fourier and is the first and only publication in Irish history before 1880, to this writer's knowledge, that adverts to these major figures. That it should have been a theologically orthodox priest who introduced the working class of Dublin to these theories, if only to reject them, is in itself of some interest. His theory of Social Salvation involved the purchase of goods through, and communal living among, a Family Association or Family Community. It was published at a time when the Dublin working class was organizing itself into the Regular Trades Association, beginning to articulate a language of the rights of labour, and pressing for legislative protection against the rampages of an unbridled capitalism and industrialism. Since these workers themselves left few written records behind them we have no means of knowing how much influence O'Malley's pamphlet exerted on them, but there can be no question that he contributed something, perhaps something considerable to that growing articulation.

As the Famine descended upon the country and indeed affected the towns and capital as well, there was little scope for social engineering in the midst of economic catastrophe and it may well be that one of its effects was to have driven O'Malley to the extreme position the police appear to have discovered him in during the period March–June 1848. His efforts in 1847–48 to effect a reconciliation of the O'Connellites and the Young Irelanders had come to nothing.[23] By the following summer one source had him in the extraordinary position of being elected as delegate for Nottingham to the Chartist Convention of 1848.[24]

Some silence descended after 1848 – for three years. Then there appeared for at least six numbers, in November and December 1851, a Dublin newspaper called *The Christian Social Economist,* with O'Malley as founder, editor and main contributor.[25] The surviving copies reveal it to have been the only Christian Socialist journal produced in Ireland in the entirety of the last century.

One does not wish to overstate its socialism: it is very much the socialism of Frederick Maurice and John Malcolm Ludlow, though without Maurice's theological complexity. Nevertheless, with its masthead slogan 'The welfare of the people is the paramount law', its mere existence points to possibilities in Irish society that were available but of which it did not avail itself.

In setting out his 'mission' O'Malley identified sectarian religious strife as the primary woe and the religious press as a primary source of it. Equal rights for all was his alternative to it; he insisted that the cordial co-operation of the clergy with all classes was essential to achieving an effective amelioration 'of the condition of the masses'. Specifically he wanted a universal industrial education and a radical amendment of the useless poor law. He wanted to prevent the influence of a godless socialism upon the poor and to provide a practicable alternative. He insists on the solidarity, not of the working class, but of the interests of all classes.

Elsewhere in his first issue he wrote on socialism and how it had been disfigured by its charlatans. Defining socialism in terms of a large programme of practical reforms designed to improve greatly the social condition of the masses he added 'in this sense it is to be hoped that we are all socialists'. He also defined it as the working-class movement of co-operative development such as he had outlined in his 1844 address. Thirdly, there was the socialism which aspired to be a science, which he deplored for the reckless audacity of its logic. He insisted on the need for a Christian social philosophy – a Christian socialism – to posit against the 'atrocious political philosophy of the time which sacrificed hundreds of thousands of human victims'.[26] He urged the infusion into society of the practical social morality of the Gospel, as in the work of Thomas Arnold of Rugby.

Later issues of the journal called for legislative protection against sum-mary unfair dismissals from work, and a reform of the Poor Law system.[27] Here he recalled his early support for a poor law for Ireland, deplored the defects of the system as actually introduced in 1838 'under the thraldom of certain unproved dogmas of the political economists'. He insisted that it was a right, not a charity: since society currently allowed or recognized the right of accumulation, its inevitable correlative was destitution. He insisted that, as a law of security of life, a poor law ought to be as peremptory and important as the law of security of property. He further insisted that the poor rate should be a national not a local levy, and that the system should cease to punish the deserving and cease to defraud the poor of their rights.

In a separate and final surviving issue, on 27 December, he took up again the theme of federalism, arguing that Irish nationality and the British connection were not incompatible. He used the example of the Scots of whom there was no people in the world so alive to feelings of nationality yet no less attached to the British connection. He now urged the institution of English, Scottish and Irish parliaments and a High Imperial Parliament to deal with the international and colonial affairs of the three kingdoms.

Unfortunately for O'Malley, and perhaps for Ireland and its working people, the paper did not secure the support necessary to sustain its costs. Its failure silenced the radical priest for almost a decade and a half. In the middle of the 1860s he issued a third edition of his pamphlet *Tithe Rent, A Poor Rate, Radical Poor Law Reform*. If anything, while the characteristic theme remained unchanged, the tone was more radical still: he asked his readers to contrast what 'the legislature does for the security of property in favour of the upper ten thousand with what it does for securing the existence of the humbler masses'. In what was probably the first ever use of the word in Irish political discourse, he remarked of government that 'the right to live of the *prolétaire* it surrenders to the discretion of some half-dozen gentlemen (so called) 'guardians of the poor' who may too often be more truly called the guardians of their own pockets'.[28]

When at the end of the 1860s the Home Rule movement began to gather pace O'Malley re-emerged to support it, not surprisingly since it endorsed the position he had first advocated forty years before. It was typical of him that when he came now to promote the cause again it was for him inextricably linked to the cause of labour: speaking in Soho, London, in his seventy-fifth year in the winter of 1872, he indicated that as far as he was concerned, the object of Home Rule was 'the greater happiness for the greater number; labour and the dignity of labour is the question of the day'.[29]

Two years later he published the third edition of the substantial pamphlet *Home Rule on the Basis of Federalism* in which, incidentally, he urged that there should be a minister of labour in the national cabinets of the three kingdoms in a new federal system. It further urged the legislative institution of Courts of Arbitration with representatives of workers, employers and independent assessors. His work concluded with a plea to Fenians and Orangemen to drop their animosities and work together for the goal of a federal island.[30]

Five years later he died and has been little remembered since.[31] Yet his public life should serve to remind us that there was an alternative possible history for Ireland in the nineteenth century. That it was a path not followed, however, was clearly due to the strong attractions of the powerful and destructive dual carriageways of Irish nationalism and unionism which carried all before them in the end – federalism, religion and social radicalism included.

NOTES

1 *Freeman's Journal,* 7 April 1848.
2 *Ibid.,* 10 March 1848.
3 Trinity College Dublin Ms. S.3.5, *Police Reports of Confederate Clubs,* Report of 'C.D.',
   21 June 1848 and report of 'A.B.', 21 June 1848.
4 R. F. Foster, *Modern Ireland, 1600–1972* (London 1989) p. 314.
5 D.A. Kerr, *Peel, Priests and Politics* (Oxford 1982) pp. 148–9,165–70; A. Macauley,
   William Crolly, Archbishop of Armagh, 1835–49 (Dublin 1994) pp. 198–200, 209,
   370–1, D. Bowen, *Paul Cardinal Cullen and the Shaping of Modern Irish Catholicism*
   (Dublin 1983) pp. 80, 122, 273. The most recent reference is one of the few non-
   dismissive ones, see E. Larkin, *The Roman Catholic Church and the Home Rule Movement
   in Ireland, 1870–1874* (Chapel Hill and London 1990) pp. 100–2.
6 A. Webb, *A Compendium of Irish Biography* (Dublin 1878), pp. 403–4. Others followed
   Webb's errors, such as W.J. Fitzpatrick in *Dictionary of National Biography,* 1st ed.
   (London 1909), vol. 14, p. 1064, J.S. Crone, *A Concise Dictionary of Irish Biography*
   (Dublin 1928), p. 193, and F. Boase, *Modern English Biography,* (2nd impression)
   (London 1965), vol. 2, p. 1243. Other brief biographical entries with some errors
   include R. Herbert, *Worthies of Thomond,* first series (Limerick 1944) pp. 50–1. It
   appears the only brief and accurate account as far as it goes is G. Oliver, *Collections
   Illustrating the history of the Catholic Religion in the Counties of Cornwall, Devon, Dorset,
   Somerset, Wilts and Gloucester* (London 1857) p. 369.
7 Limerick Regional Archives, Parish Registers, St Michael's Roman Catholic Parish,
   Limerick City; this is the correct version of his date of birth which Webb and those who
   followed him presented incorrectly as the year 1796. He was the sixth child in the family
   of eight of John O'Malley and Bridget Behane.
8 Dublin Diocesan Archives, Murray Papers, Propaganda Fide to Murray, 9 Nov. 1830
   almost certainly to join his class-mate and friend, Fr. John McEnery, one of the founding
   fathers of anthropology who was ordained in Limerick City in June 1819 and spent the
   rest of his priestly life in Devonshire: see T. Sheehan, 'Fr John McEnery and palaeolithic
   man, 1796–1841', in *Studies,* vol. xxi, September 1932, pp. 471–9. See also G. Oliver,
   op.cit., p. 181.
9 F. Kenneally, O.F.M., ed., *United States Documents in the Propaganda Fidei,* 1st series
   (Washington 1967), vol. 3, pp. 299–300.
10 Dublin Diocesan Archives, Murray Papers, Propaganda Fide to Murray, 17 July 1830;
   Kenneally ed., *op. cit.,* pp. 304–9.
11 This account is based on *Records of the American Catholic Historical Society,* vol. xxviii,
   pp. 75–82; P. Guilday, *The Life and Times of John England, 1786–1842,* 2 vols (New
   York 1927), vol. 1, 421; W. Parsons, S.J., *Early Catholic Americana, 1729–1830* (New
   York, 1939); R. Herbert, *op. cit.,* pp. 50–1; J. Begley, *The Diocese of Limerick, from 1691
   to the Present Time* (Dublin 1938), pp. 520–1; Murray Papers, year 1830.
12 R.I.A., Haliday Tracts, vol. 1525, year 1831, *The Federalist, or, a series of papers showing
   how to Repeal the Union so as to avoid a violent crisis, and, at the same time secure and
   reconcile all interests. By a Minister of Peace* (Dublin 1831).
13 *The Federalist,* No. 1, Jan 1831, p. 29.
14 T. O'Malley, *A Letter to Sir George Sinclair, M.P., on his notice of motion touching
   Maynooth and its moralities, By a Roman Catholic Priest* (Dublin 1836) p. 30. See also,
   O'Malley to Archbishop Murray, 13 July 1836, enclosing the pamphlet and drawing
   Murray's attention specifically to this passage, 'which possibly Your Grace will not
   approve as implying too liberal an estimate of a Protestant's sincerity of faith . . .', Murray
   Papers, AB 3/31/5/7.
15 *Ibid.,* pp. 36–7.
16 *The Federalist,* No. 1, Jan 1831, p. 30.

17 *Ibid.*, No. 2, p. 75.

18 *Ibid.*, No. 3, p. 134.

19 *The Pilot,* 18 Nov. 1836.

20 G. Lyne, 'The General Association of Ireland, 1836–7', unpublished MA thesis, University College Dublin 1968, p. 43.

21 See for example *The Pilot,* 1, 15 Feb 1837 for votes of thanks from parishioners of St Michan's, Dublin, and from the Radicals of Hull, respectively.

22 S. Pollard, 'Nineteenth century co-operation: from community building to shopkeeping', in A. Briggs and J. Saville, eds., *Essays in Labour History* (London 1967), pp. 74–112.

23 National Library of Ireland, William Smith O'Brien Papers, Ms.438/1893, T O'Malley to Smith O'Brien, 22 May 1847, offering to mediate between John O'Connell and O'Brien as the leaders of the respective parties; likewise Ms 438/1908, 1910 and 1913, O'Malley to Smith O'Brien, 10,13 and 21 June 1847 respectively. See also, W.J. Fitzpatrick, *The Life, Times and Contemporaries of Lord Cloncurry* (Dublin, 1855), p. 514.

24 H.U. Faulkner, *Chartism and the Churches* (1st ed., New York, 1916 new imp. London, 1970), p. 113, citing R.G. Gammage, *History of the Chartist Movement, 1837–1854* (new ed., London, 1894), pp. 322, 324.

25 The only surviving copies known to this writer are in the newspaper collection of the British Library at Colindale.

26 *The Christian Social Economist,* 22 Nov. 1851.

27 *Ibid.,* 29 Nov. 1851.

28 T. O'Malley, *Tithe-Rent, A Poor Rate, Radical Poor Law Reform,* (3rd ed. Dublin 1865(?)), p. 4.

29 *Flag of Ireland,* 21 Dec. 1872.

30 T. O'Malley, *Home Rule on the Basis of Federalism,* (3rd ed. Dublin 1874) p. 67.

31 For obituary see *Freeman's Journal,* 3 Jan. 1877, which incidentally observes that in relation to his advocacy of federalism O'Malley was 'pardonably vain and conceited in proclaiming himself its "father"'. This writer is currently preparing a biography of O'Malley.

7 Our Lady of Marpingen: Marian Apparitions in Imperial Germany

David Blackbourn

I

The history of nineteenth-century Europe was punctuated by episodes in which scores of thousands, sometimes hundreds of thousands of people flocked to remote spots where the Virgin Mary had supposedly appeared. Likened by contemporaries to the crusades, these events were a very visible sign of the great religious revival of the period, a counterpoint to the more familiar political upheavals. The best known example is undoubtedly Lourdes, and most people who think about these events probably associate them with predominantly Catholic countries such as France, Italy and Ireland, where a number of nineteenth-century apparitions were given official church approval. But Marian apparitions also occurred in Germany, and the article that follows is mainly concerned with one of them.[1]

Modern apparitions have come in waves. One such wave occurred in the aftermath of the French Revolution, in France itself and in Italy and Germany under French occupation. There was a further set of apparitions in the 1830s and 1840s, this time particularly in France, most notably the visions of the novice nun Cathérine Labouré in Paris (1830) and of two young shepherds in the Alpine village of La Salette (1846). Then, following the celebrated visions of Bernadette Soubirous at Lourdes (1858), came the most extensive wave of European apparitions in the nineteenth century. In the following twenty years visions of the Virgin were reported in France, Italy, Ireland and Bohemia, as well as in Germany. By the twentieth century the idiom of the Marian apparition had established itself so firmly that it had eclipsed other kinds of religious vision still widely claimed a century earlier: burning crucifixes, bearded and ragged old men, plagues of caterpillars, or celestial omens – although the 'Virgin in the sky' at Pontmain (1871) showed that the new form could accommodate elements of the old.[2] It was the Virgin Mary who was at the centre of the interwar apparitions that followed Fatima in 1917, and of the apparitions that were claimed right across Europe on the second half of the 1940s, in Germany, France, Italy,

Hungary, Poland and Romania. The same was true of the new wave of apparitions during the 1980s in Yugoslavia, the Ukraine, Germany and Ireland, and outside Europe in Egypt and Uganda, the United States and Nicaragua. Beyond the primacy of the Virgin Mary, modern apparitions became more uniform in other respects. In the nineteenth century, for the first time, the visionaries were predominantly children or women; it also became customary for a 'message' to be disclosed by the apparition.[3] Growing uniformity can be linked in general to improved communications, and in particular to the growing standardization of devotional forms. Lourdes, above all, became a kind of template from which subsequent apparitions took their pattern.[4]

Modern apparitions are not explicable as the result of mere imitation, however, even though this demonstrably played a part. Nor are they susceptible simply of individual-psychological explanation. It is true that several recurrent motifs run through the lives of those who claimed apparitions. In the case of the young children and adolescent girls, who made up the largest number of seers, we can point to a common pattern of recent emotional upheaval – typically the loss of or neglect by a parent, often in conjunction with some other change in life, the crossing of a particular threshold. Sometimes this was a matter of being fostered out or sent to work away from home; sometimes it was associated with beginning school or being on the eve of confirmation. The children concerned were often coming into contact with stories of the Blessed Virgin and her visitations at a time when they were highly susceptible to the comforts and emotional consolations of a 'true mother' who would not desert or neglect them. Nor should we forget the fact that these children were frequently poor, or 'outsiders' of one kind or another. Many young seers were in farm or domestic service, others belonged to the 'dishonourable' profession of shepherd, still others had been forced to come to terms with a recent loss of family respectability, like the young Bernadette Soubirous, who picked rags and collected dirty hospital linen with her father, a bankrupt miller.[5]

The visions bestowed status and authority on the visionaries. In relaying the purported words of the Virgin, they determined who should approach the apparition site, how they should behave, and the procedures that would lead to a miraculous cure. They instructed that chapels be built, told of secrets they could not divulge, and prophesied woe for the sinful (along with the sceptical). The new status of the children also offered subversive possibilities. Eugène Barbedette, one of the Pontmain seers, was asked by a group of prominent Catholic laywomen and female religious in Fougères if the Virgin bore any resemblance to one of them. 'No', he replied, 'compared with the Blessed Virgin you are all ugly'.[6] If so many of the young seers had lived Cinderella lives before their apparitions, they now experienced that happy reversal of fortunes so characteristic of Cinderella and other folk tales, with the Mother of God cast in the role of Fairy Godmother.

Similar considerations apply to adult visionaries: the Romantic writer Clemens Brentano observed that the visionary Anna Katharina Emmerich had been 'abandoned by all and ill-treated like Cinderella'.[7] The women in question – they were almost always women – had commonly experienced recent illness and bereavement, and often occupied a marginal position within the family or community. Adult female seers, like their youthful counterparts, acquired a rare authority as the conduits through which divine dissatisfaction was expressed, and there are plenty of instances where it seems that they were revenging themselves, consciously or unconsciously, on a harsh world. Sometimes they were angry, lashing the mighty for their sins. An eighteen-year-old from Normandy, imprisoned for arson, returned to her village and recounted the dire predictions of the Blessed Virgin about what would happen if a chapel were not constructed in honour of Our Lady of La Salette. The strictures and warnings reported by the servant-visionary Estelle Faguette of Pellevoisin in the 1870s were matched by those of other young Frenchwomen of the period.[8] The notion of reversal was usually less apocalyptic and extravagant; yet it was always there by implication. The respect conferred by the apparitions gave women a chance normally denied them to slough off harsh responsibilities. Like illness, the status of visionary was a resource of the weak, a means of escape; it also offered a veiled means of protest against real or imagined ill-treatment.

Many of these elements were present in the apparitions that took place in the Bohemian village of Philippsdorf in 1866. Magdalena Kade was a thirty-year-old unmarried weaver's daughter with a long history of illness, including convulsions. Her father died when she was thirteen and her brother inherited the family home; her mother died in 1861, and in 1864 Magdalena moved out to live with another family, probably as a servant; in 1865 she was the victim of a series of cruel lampoons written by a fellow-villager. Admitted back by her brother because of illness, she lay in bed beneath a picture of the 'suffering mother', surrounded by her brother's lodgers. The apparitions began four weeks after she had returned home. 'Cured' as the Virgin Mary had promised, Magdalena Kade became the centre of medical attention and prompted a local cult of 'Mary the salvation of the Sick'. Thousands of pilgrims went to the village and the visionary was feted by visiting priests and persons of influence.[9]

There is value in this approach: it is surely better than presenting the visionaries as a bundle of clinical symptoms. But even if we interpret the individual experiences in this way, rather than reduce them to a category such as 'hysteria' in the manner of contemporaries like Charcot and Krafft-Ebing, our explanations remain limited.[10] For these were collective as well as individual phenomena. External pressure as well as emotional upheaval usually provide some indication why the apparitions took place when they did; and external stress of one sort or another certainly suggests why these events enjoyed the resonance they did. If we look at the waves of apparitions, some common elements stand out. One is the background of war and post-war anxiety, from Napoleonic Europe, through the visions that stalked the battlefields of Italian unification and the Franco-Prussian war, to the wave of apparitions after 1945. In content as well as timing, these were intercessions by the 'Queen of Peace'. It is also apparent that clusters of apparitions occurred at times of political turmoil, when Catholics felt themselves under threat from the civil power. This motif recurs from Cathérine Labouré's apparitions in the revolutionary France of 1830, through the wave of Marian visions during the secular state-building and anti-clerical decades of the 1860s and 1870s, to the explicitly anti-communist message of Fatima in 1917 and the 'Cold War apparitions' of the 1940s and 1950s.[11]

In this article I want to place the German apparitions of the 1870s in several contexts. Is there anything in the lives of the visionaries and their families that might suggest how these events came about? To what extent does economic and social crisis help to explain the popular resonance of the German apparitions, as it clearly does in La Salette, Lourdes, Knock and many other cases? What is the connection between the apparitions and larger changes in Catholic popular piety in this period, and what can we learn from such episodes about relations between clergy and laity? Finally, there is the question of politics. What do the the apparitions of the 1870s tell us about the position of Catholics within the newly-unified German state? Here I hope to address the question of religion and rebellion directly, while casting some light on Bismarck's Germany from an unfamiliar angle.

II

Apparitions of the Virgin Mary were widely reported in Germany during the 1870s, especially from the western and eastern margins of the new empire, including Alsace, the Palatinate, the Rhineland, Silesia and Posen. The three most publicised cases were in Mettenbuch (Lower Bavaria), Dittrichswalde (the Ermland), and Marpingen (the Saarland).[12] I shall concentrate on the last of these, not only because it has the richest and most varied archival evidence, but because it also acquired the largest public and political resonance.

Marpingen was a large village with about 1600 inhabitants situated in the hill country of the northern Saarland, solidly Catholic and largely unremarkable.[13] It was in the diocese and the Prussian administrative district of Trier, part of the Rhine Province to which that area of the Saarland had belonged since 1834. Marpingen was some miles from the nearest railhead in St Wendel and it was, as one contemporary put it, 'not marked on normal maps'.[14] True, the village was not quite the isolated community some later depicted. A growing proportion of village men earned their living in the Saar coalfield to the south, peasants conducted business in nearby market towns, figures as various as the rural postman, notaries, money-lenders, knife-grinders and travelling musicians passed through with news. At the beginning of July 1876, however, attention in Marpingen was centred on haymaking, which had an important place in the annual agricul-tural cycle. Work began at dawn, with all available hands pressed into service. Children were no exception, and the village school had a 'haymaking-holiday'.[15] Those too young to take part or to help with the care of farm animals were given the task of gathering berries or other fruits of the forest.

It was in order to gather bilberries that, on the hot Monday of 3 July, a number of young girls found themselves in the Härtelwald, a hilly wooded area with many rocky gullies a few minutes away from Marpingen. There were five girls in all. Three were eight-year-olds and fast friends: Katharina Hubertus, Susanna Leist and Margaretha Kunz. With them in the woods were Katharina's six-year-old sister Lischen and another six-year-old, Anna Meisberger. The girls had separated to look for berries, and were not together when the Angelus sounded and they started to make their way home. Between the wood and the village was an area of wild meadow with thick bushes around it. It was here that Susanna Leist suddenly called out, bringing Katharina and Margaretha hurrying to her, and drew her friends' attention to a 'figure in white'. When the girls reached home, agitated and frightened, all three described seeing a woman in white with a child in her arms. The reactions of parents and neighbours are disputed, but it is clear that the girls remained in a state of excitement. Margaretha slept badly and prayed a lot, Katharina dreamed of the woman in white, Susanna was reluc-tant to go to bed at all. The following day they returned to the spot and knelt down to pray. According to their account, after they had recited the Lord's Prayer three times the apparition appeared again to Margaretha and Katharina – although not to Susanna, the original seer. 'Who are you?', they asked the figure in local dialect, and received the reply: 'I am the Immaculately Conceived'.[16]

The apparitions continued. The figure, now confidently identified by adults as the Blessed Virgin, instructed that a chapel be built, encouraged the sick to come, and asked that water be taken from a nearby spring. Soon there were reports of miraculous healings, and within less than a week thou-sands of pilgrims were streaming to Marpingen. Reports spoke of 20,000 in the village, with up to 4000 at the apparition site, singing, praying and taking away foliage or handfuls of earth. In the words of the parish priest, Lourdes was 'feeble compared with the mighty current that here is breaking through all barriers'.[17] The three seers subsequently claimed visions in other parts of the village – in their homes, in barns and stables, in the school, in the graveyard and the church – and what they described became more luxuriant. The Virgin appeared with and without the Christ-child, sometimes accompanied by angels. She was dressed now in white, now in gold or azure. The apparitions also took on darker tones. On one occasion the girls reported seeing the Virgin clad in black, on another they described a celestial procession passing over the graveyard. The devil also made several appearances. The apparitions were to last for fourteen months.

Marpingen became a *cause célèbre*. Journalists, priests and the sellers of pious memorabilia descended on the village, along with pilgrims from Germany and abroad.[18] Supporters and opponents dubbed Marpingen 'the German Lourdes', even 'the Bethlehem of Germany'.[19] 'It is an undeniable fact that the whole world is talking about Marpingen', wrote one sympathetic commentator. 'Marpingen has become the centre of events that have shaken the world', suggested another.[20] The hyperbole was forgivable. One newspaper, linking the themes of the apparitions and the Eastern crisis that was dominating the press, ran an editorial under the headline 'Marpingen and Stambul'.[21] Bismarck himself made slighting remarks about Marpingen, and his interest reflected another element of the village's new celebrity (or notoriety).[22] The apparition movement collided with the machinery of state. The result was a lengthy struggle that was to extend from Marpingen and the surrounding areas of the Saarland to the courtrooms of the Rhine Province and the Prussian parliament in Berlin.

In trying to unpick the beginning of these events, let us start with the visionaries. By common consent, Margaretha ('Gretchen') Kunz was the dominant figure among the three seers. The word that seemed to occur to everyone who met her was *geweckt* – bright or sharp.[23] Her father had died in a mill accident five months before her birth, and it would be surprising if she did not experience some resentment from her brothers and sisters, as the last-born of a large family, another mouth to feed in suddenly straitened circumstances. We know that the life of the family changed after the death of Jacob Kunz. He had owned a share in the Alsweiler mill, and the family belonged to the solid middle peasantry ('cattle-peasants') of Marpingen: one of Margaretha's uncles was a village notable.[24] But the mill was subject to forced sale, his widow was unsuccessful when she challenged this in the courts, and Jacob Kunz left debts. Gretchen's elder brothers went down the pit; her sister Magdalena became a servant girl in the village.[25] It is worth noting the parallels here with the fourteen-year-old Mathilde Sack, a tailor's daughter who was the central figure in the Mettenbuch apparitions.[26] She also had to come to terms with a fractured family and a loss of family respectability: her mother had died when Mathilde was eleven, her father had been gaoled, and she disliked her stepmother. After leaving to work variously for a gold-beater, a confectioner and in domestic service (she was dismissed by one dissatisfied mistress), Mathilde finally departed an unhappy family home when her brother went into the army, going as a farm servant to her aunt in Mettenbuch, where apparitions were reported soon afterwards.[27] There are echoes in both cases of Bernadette Soubirous, bankrupted miller's daughter and unhappy farm servant.[28]

There is no doubt that the German visionaries felt guilt, fear and uncertainty in their new roles; but there was also awareness of the new attention they commanded. They jealously guarded the apparition sites, issuing warnings to the parish priests and indicating with a shake of the head that certain individuals should not approach. They spoke of secrets, told pilgrims that a celestial omen would be explained and – in Marpingen – 'prophesied' the death of a sick child. Katharina Hubertus said that she had been told to become a nun.[29] The Mettenbuch seers fashioned for themselves, from devotional scraps and fragments, the image of a better world. They described Mary wearing 'gold shoes and white stockings' and 'angels, as they ate grilled fish from a golden table'; the Virgin reportedly gave instructions that they make up and drink daily from a concoction that sounds like a rustic ambrosia.[30] The Madonna of Marpingen was more domesticated, as the seers described her appearances in particular houses and other village landmarks. There was doubtless a reassuring element to this: a Blessed Virgin who could be associated with Schäfer's meadow, or with the round stone that stood at the end of the upper village, was rendered benign, placed firmly within a bounded world. Their message that Mary had graced these everyday spots also cast the places themselves in a new light and enhanced the status of the messengers, for through their privileged position the children placed their own stamp vicariously on places and properties that were normally an adult preserve. Indeed, we can go further: the behaviour of the Marpingen seers was often puckish and pert to the point of childish malice, especially in the case of Gretchen Kunz.[31]

At the same time, the story told by the girls was shaped by adults. Pious accounts later emphasized that the parents had used carrot and stick to try to force the children to back down. Frau Kunz supposedly told Gretchen that if she continued to tell lies her brother Peter would 'beat her half to death' when he came back from work.[32] But the later testimony of the seers makes it clear that they were prompted and encouraged almost from the beginning, as adults topped and tailed the story of a 'woman in white' into a recognizable apparition narrative.[33] It is possible to reconstruct how support for the apparitions spread outwards from the upper village where the visionaries lived into the rest of Marpingen, via family clans and friendship networks – predominantly female clans and networks. Village women played a major role in nurturing the apparition movement, although the evidence also suggests that attitudes towards the apparitions were decisively influenced when village notables and other 'men of good character' gave their support.[34]

A micro-level analysis of how the apparitions were taken up in Marpingen tells us much about the lines of authority in the village: about the relations of adults and children, men and women, notables and village poor. I have been able to give only the briefest sketch here. The positive local reception of the apparitions is revealing in other ways, too. The ease with which a 'woman in white' could be transformed into Mary Immaculate casts light on religious change in Marpingen during the third quarter of the nineteenth century. The zeal with which Mary's intercession was greeted tells us something about Catholic anxiety, even desperation, in the 1870s. And the eagerness with which villagers exploited pilgrims commercially indicates the economic plight of Marpingen in the same decade. In following up these points we need to turn to Marpingen's relations with a larger world, particularly to the ways in which external pressures affected the village and made it more receptive to the apparition story.

III

Villagers faced pressures, in the first place, simply by virtue of being Catholics. In 1834, the small Principality of Lichtenberg to which Marpingen belonged was sold by the Duke of Saxe-Coburg-Gotha to the King of Prussia.[35] The area became an object of Prussian state-building under the aegis of a Protestant dynasty, a Protestant state church, a Protestant field administration, and a Protestant officer corps.[36] Many in Berlin also believed that Prussia had a Protestant mission, although few went as far as foreign minister Ancillon, who called in 1832 for a 'Protestantization of the Catholic Rhineland'.[37] Anti-Catholic discrimination was endemic: one Catholic priest declared that he would sooner live under the Turks.[38] Where, as in the case of state forestry or mine officials, the lines of denominational and social conflict coincided, the potential for Catholic alienation and discontent was multiplied. There were countless signs of this in the decades prior to German unification on Protestant-Prussian terms. The third quarter of the nineteenth century also saw mounting communal tension. The historical patchwork quilt of Protestant and Catholic communities on the western border of Germany, and the further intermingling of the denominations through new demographic patterns, made this tension especially severe in the Saarland. Marpingen's miners experienced it in the coalfield.[39] All villagers witnessed the fierce denominational struggles (over shared churches, the construction of new buildings, the ringing of church bells) that erupted in villages throughout the area – in Offenbach, Kappeln, Weierbach, Oberreidenbach, Sien.[40] One of these disputes, beginning in 1863–64 and resurfacing in the 1870s, occurred in Berschweiler, an immediately neighbouring village and the birthplace of Margaretha Kunz's mother.[41]

What sharpened Catholic feelings in the 1870s was the harshness of the Prussian Kulturkampf, a conflict in which 1800 priests were gaoled or exiled, wanted notices were issued for bishops, homes were searched and 16 million Marks of church property was seized.[42] The diocese of Trier was seriously affected. In December 1873 the diocesan seminary was closed down and in March 1874 Matthias Eberhard became the second Prussian bishop to be arrested, receiving a fine of 130,000 marks and a nine-months' prison sentence.[43] He died six months after his release from gaol, exactly one month before the Marpingen events began. The diocese was, in the emotive phrase of the time, 'orphaned'. Marpingen was directly affected by the so-called 'bread-basket law', which removed state subsidies from priests who refused (as virtually all did) to declare support for the government's measures. There is evidence of the strains this produced in the village.[44] Indirectly, Marpingen watched priests in other Saarland parishes being arrested, particularly in neighbouring Namborn, where the hunting down and arrest of Jakob Isbert in July 1874 resulted in one of the most violent episodes of the Kulturkampf. Namborn was in the same deanery as Marpingen, and the crowds that stormed the railway station at St Wendel in an attempt to free Father Isbert included many from surrounding rural areas. The rural mayor who arrested the priest, the anticlerical Wilhelm Woytt, also had responsibility for Marpingen, where he was deeply unpopular. It is a measure of local sentiment that he was known as 'the Devil of St Wendel'.[45] In the wake of official repression there was heightened Catholic feeling, part militant, part mystical. With each new onslaught, the sense of panic and desperation brought reports of stigmatists and prophets, signs of a collective longing for some kind of supernatural intercession and deliverance.[46]

The Kulturkampf was not the only source of pressure and anxiety in Marpingen. Historians disagree about many aspects of the 'Great Depression', but no-one disputes that 1873 saw the advent of agricultural crisis and industrial recession.[47] Marpingen was hit by both. Land prices had collapsed after earlier speculation, leaving high levels of debt; prices were low, credit was short, and – in the words of one writer – the moneylenders were active 'from 3 o'clock in the morning until 10 o'clock at night'.[48] (Villagers would later show a certain insolent pride in parading the visionaries before these same moneylenders and cattle-dealers, in Tholey.) Bailiffs serving distraint orders and the itinerant poor crowding the highroads testified to the crisis.[49] We are dealing, in short, with a period of agrarian distress, a European-wide phenomenon that also formed an important part of the background to the

Knock apparitions of 1879. At the same time, Marpingen was severely affected by industrial recession in the Saarland. By the mid-1870s half of the employed population worked away from the village in the southern Saar coalfield, which developed so fast in the 1850s and 1860s that it was dubbed 'black California'.[50] The loss or reduction of their income had a demon-strably adverse effect on Marpingen.[51] That is not the only significance of this first generation of miner-peasants. Their new way of life marked a significant break in the life of the whole village. The miner-peasants walked to work early on Monday morning and returned late on Saturday night, living effectively as *Gastarbeiter* for six days a week in poor accommodation, subjected to quasi-military discipline by mine officials and distrusted by many indigenous miners as rate-busting rustics (and 'backward' Catholics). They lived in two worlds, at home in neither. For those they left behind, central aspects of life were also transformed: the organization of farm work, relationships between husband, wife and children, family marriage strate-gies.[52] The Marpingen seers had brothers and other family members who earned a living in this way; many of the 'rival children' who later claimed apparitions also had absent fathers and brothers; miners' wives and children were to be prominent in reporting 'miraculous' cures.[53] These circumstances are surely significant, especially when we put them together with other pieces of evidence. Broken families were, as we have seen, a motif in many appari-tions. We also know something about the strains that arose in comparable German commuting villages in Württemberg, and in other communities where adult males were regularly away seeking employment, such as the 'village without men' (*Weiberdorf*) in the Eifel depicted in Clara Viebig's novel of that name.[54] We have the evidence, finally, of a curious parallel to the Marpingen events two years later in the Friuli, when an outbreak of 'collective hysteria' arose among the women of Verzegnis at a time when most of the village men were absent as migrant seasonal labourers.[55] These examples suggest that we take seriously the social-psychological dimension involved at Marpingen, where the strains of economic and social dislocation were borne by families.

This angle of approach also requires that we look at the place occupied by women and children in the changing devotional forms and popular piety of the decades before the 1870s. The word 'changing' needs to be empha-sized. It would be wrong to regard what happened in Marpingen simply as the 'traditional' response of a pious community to the threats posed by a 'modern' state and economy. The history of Marpingen earlier in the cen-tury shows how misleading that would be. In the 1840s the village was still being described in the most unflattering terms by its parish priest. Lack of interest in church services, card playing, enthusiasm for the tavern, dancing through the night on feast days, unruly young people, the negligent upbringing of children, crude sensuality – these were 'quite general' in the parish.[56] Even by the standards of contemporary clerical disapproval, the village seems to have stood out, and events in the first half of the nineteenth century suggest an unusual degree of spite and hostility towards successive parish priests. Father Licht had his windows broken; Father Hoff had serious differences with his flock over dancing and standards in the local school; Father Bicking, in the 1840s, had problems over almost everything, meeting verbal and physical abuse that may have led him eventually to leave Marpingen.[57]

The transformation that occurred in the following generation is essential to an understanding of what happened later. The changes were similar to those described by Jonathan Sperber in his study of popular Catholicism in the Rhineland and Westphalia – and by Emmett Larkin in his work on Ireland in the same period.[58] In Marpingen, as elsewhere, there was a purposive renewal of piety and reassertion of clerical control. Religious brotherhoods and sodalities were founded; a well and shrine linked to the legend of a miraculous image of the Virgin were restored; church attendance improved, and illegitimacy rates fell.[59] The parish priest in 1876 (he had been there since 1864) was Father Jacob Neureuter, one of the new breed of intensely Mariolatrous clergy produced by the more independent seminaries of the 1850s and 1860s, and the cult of the Virgin Mary was central to the religious revival in Marpingen, as it was across Europe. It touched everything – sodalities, hymnals, statuary, even the liturgy – and formed the centrepiece of a recharged, emotionally laden piety.[60] This change was paralleled by two others. One was the 'feminization' of Catholicism (much less studied in the German case than in some others).[61] The second was the growing emphasis on the child as a symbol of purity and simple faith – what might be called 'infantilization'. Children, for their part, grew up in a world increasingly suffused with the songs, flowers, perfumes and images of the Virgin Mary. They were also being prepared for communion at a younger age, something that may have influenced several German seers of the 1870s.[62] These changes were reinforced by the great popular missions held in Germany in the 1850s and 1860s, and they received the warmest encouragement from Pope Pius IX, for whom the cult of the Virgin Mary in general and the doctrine of the Immaculate Conception in particular were central concerns.[63]

IV

All of this might suggest a substratum of truth to the charge levelled by officials and liberals that clerical inspiration was at work on susceptible women ('madwomen', 'hysterical women') and children ('the maids favoured by the deity').[64] In Marpingen we have young girls who had just begun study of the catechism at school, instructed by a parish priest who had placed his own oil painting of the Virgin and child in the local church and sermonized about Lourdes, and by a teacher who had also related the story of Bernadette.[65] Moreover, the apparitions began on the very day – 3 July 1876 – that 35 bishops, 5000 priests and 100,000 lay Catholics were gathered for a major ceremony at Lourdes.[66] It was a time when details about the Pyrenean apparitions were widely reported in the Catholic press, when Catholics in Marpingen (as elsewhere in Germany) would certainly have been voicing the common lament that the Virgin had not yet graced German soil. Lourdes had an obvious impact on German Catholics. Where such apparitions had been approved as exemplary, the church threw its formidable institutional weight behind them. It showed great organizational flair in promoting the apparitions as official cults, sending in religious orders to run sites like the Lourdes Domain as specialists, learning from the great exhibitions of the period when it came to the transportation of pilgrims by railway or the use of lighting for dramatic effect. Through sermons, popular pamphlets and the word-of-mouth accounts of those who had been on major 'national pilgrimages' (which began in the 1870s), expectations were aroused and the faithful everywhere learnt what the Blessed Virgin 'ought' to look like.[67] The effects of this can be seen at Marpingen, where a routinely familiar story about a woman in white was reshaped by local crisis and the longing for deliverance, by the contingencies of time and place, and not least by the agency of particular adults, into a rather different story about Mary the Immaculately Conceived.

At the beginning the responsibility of the clergy was indirect: they followed popular sentiment more than they led it. This remained true as the apparitions continued, although the degree of clerical enthusiasm should not be underestimated. Very large numbers of priests visited Marpingen. Of the five hundred pilgrims in the village on 28 August 1877, around 40 were members of the clergy. The exceptionally large crowd six days later included 'hundreds' of priests from Germany and abroad.[68] Some idea of the geographical spread can be gleaned from the unlucky twenty who were caught and prosecuted for the illegal celebration of mass in Marpingen. They came not only from the Rhine Province and the nearby Palatinate, but from Baden, Westphalia and East Prussia.[69] There was clearly widespread clerical belief in the apparitions: priests wept when the three girls told their story, accompanied triumphant processions of the 'miraculously' cured to the visionaries' homes, took Marpingen water away with them.[70] This is not surprising, given their training and the circumstances of the 1870s. The apparitions must have represented a solace for many, a sign of grace in a cold, hard world 'sunk in materialism', and an intercession of such potency that it would jolt the progress-mongers out of their complacency.[71] In the words of one: 'I firmly hope and believe that things are still to happen here at which the *Kulturkämpfer* will marvel, as once did Columbus and his fellows when they discovered America'.[72] Priests with notebooks became a familiar sight in Marpingen; and by prompting the visionaries (however innocently), as they certainly did, by recording the events and by publicizing them in the press and in cheap pamphlets, many priests helped to legitimate events that they saw as a great cause.[73]

Yet there were clerical sceptics too, and with good reason. Among visiting priests and those who corresponded with Father Neureuter there was concern at aspects of the visionaries' accounts, particularly the descriptions of the devil: 'dark points', in the words of one, 'curious matters which make an extremely unfavourable impression', in the opinion of another.[74] There were further disquieting elements. Pilgrims streamed there without their parish priests in a manner that seemed dangerously spontaneous. These large unofficial movements of the faithful ran directly counter to the clerical tendency to encourage more organized and controlled pilgrimages. The pilgrims attracted to the 'miraculous' children also showed some inclination to neglect the official site of Marian devotion in the village (the well and shrine near the church) in favour of the new site in the wood, which lay on the opposite side of the village. In Marpingen, as elsewhere, there is a local topography of apparitions that we should not neglect. Popular faith in the curative powers of water and 'the place' itself was strongly tinged with animistic beliefs. At the same time, the commercial opportunities presented by the pilgrimage trade presented the spectre of that intermingling of the sacred and profane so often criticized by clergy – although, it should be said, this problem was touched on by clerical critics of Marpingen less than one might expect.[75]

The two central issues were undoubtedly 'superstition' and clerical control. The emotional drama surrounding the apparitions released popular sentiments that could hardly fail to alarm the clergy. Pilgrims saw processions 'floating through the air'; others believed they had been guided to their goal by the 'miraculous star of Marpingen'. There were reports of imminent plague from which only those who partook of the water would be spared, of heaven and hell opening and demons roaming abroad.[76] The Marpingen apparitions also triggered numerous imitations. Within the village itself a score of 'rival children' claimed increasingly extravagant visions.[77] Further local apparitions were reported from Gronig, Wemmetsweiler, Münchwies and Berschweiler. In Münchwies a group of children worked themselves into a religious ecstasy: at one point a group burst in on Father Neureuter at Marpingen 'bathed in sweat' and asking to take communion. Children and adults saw the devil standing next to the Virgin and dancing around her in the shape of a dog, a donkey and a cow.[78] In Berschweiler a group of a dozen children, mainly girls, fought violent struggles with the devil in front of large crowds. We are told how 'eleven girls rolled on a bed with convulsive twitches and improper movements, while screaming and shouting about the apparitions they were witnessing', performances that commonly went on beyond midnight.[79] A little further afield, the 'Virgin in a bottle' at the Gappenach mill, over which the miller, his wife, an impoverished tailor and a woman known as 'the nun of Naunheim' were prosecuted, attracted 5000 pilgrims a day. There was another Virgin in a bottle at Mülheim.[80]

Many of these cases, especially the ones involving nocturnal activities, were an explicit challenge to clerical authority, sometimes accompanied by threats. In Münchwies the local priest criticized the 'night-time mischief' of local youth in terms remarkably similar to those applied in earlier decades to 'unruly' Marpingen.[81] Even the original Marpingen apparitions alarmed some local priests sufficiently that they sermonized against them and warned their parishioners off, without conspicuous success.[82] While many liberal and Protestant observers argued that the Catholic clergy should somehow have nipped matters in the bud, a sardonic reporter in the *Gartenlaube* was more realistic: the clergy was 'simply not master of a movement over which it has long lost any control'.[83] This verdict applies, in more complicated ways, to the parish priests of Marpingen and Mettenbuch. Both were overwhelmed, in the first place, by the new demands on them: correspondents who wanted information and 'miraculous' water, pilgrims requiring masses to be said and confessions to be heard, clerical visitors who 'tortured' the parish priests with their questions – not to mention abusive mail and inquisitive officials.[84] Neureuter in Marpingen and Father Anglhuber in Mettenbuch were racked by personal doubts about the authenticity of the apparitions, troubled by the possibility of childish mischief or diabolical inspiration, although it is clear that both came privately to believe in them. However, given the formal obligation on any parish priest in this position to maintain a prudent reserve, both came under enormous pressure from their parishioners and others to embrace the apparitions wholeheartedly. The phrases 'keep under control' and 'don't encourage' echo poignantly through their correspondence, along with 'what should I do?' and 'I don't know where to turn'. Neureuter came close to cracking under the strain.[85]

Whenever claims of apparitions and miraculous cures arose, canon law laid down that a formal ecclesiastical enquiry be held. Marpingen, Mettenbuch and Dittrichswalde were subject to such enquiries, and in each case a negative judgment was the result. But the church faced difficulties in conducting the investigations and in getting its judgments to stick. In the case of Marpingen, the Kulturkampf had deprived Trier of a bishop: the diocese was being run by members of the cathedral chapter acting as papal legates and using Latin code-names.[86] The chain of command in the diocese had been weakened (this was one of Neureuter's problems) and a canonical enquiry was hard to organize. Eventually the task was entrusted to an octogenarian Luxemburg cleric with strong German connections, Titular Bishop Laurent of Chersones. In 1878 he deemed the account of the Marpingen seers 'unseemly', 'unworthy and sacrilegious' and the apparitions themselves inauthentic.[87] However, the interplay of piety and politics made it difficult for the improvised hierarchy in Trier to come out openly against the apparitions. This would have given a weapon to anticlericals and bitterly disappointed the faithful. As a result, the church sat on the Marpingen findings. By doing so it stored up future trouble from frustrated advocates of the 'German Lourdes': in the twentieth century the policy of masterly inactivity backfired, as Marpingen flared up again in the Nazi 1930s and the Cold War 1950s, amid accusations that the clerical authorities had 'betrayed' the cause of Our Lady.[88] In the short-term, though, the decision in Trier may have represented prudent calculation, for in the Mettenbuch case, where Bishop Senestrey of Regensburg was free to conduct a textbook enquiry, the pastoral letter rejecting the apparitions failed to quell widespread belief in their authenticity. Regensburg continued to be troubled by the issue through the 1880s.[89] The 'silent Kulturkampf' in Bavaria, like the open Kulturkampf in Prussia, heightened the popular Catholic propensity to believe in the intercession of the Blessed Virgin, whatever its clergy said.

Max Weber – who else? – once wrote that the 'machinery' of the Catholic church was at odds with the forces of popular piety, a struggle it was bound in the long run to win.[90] Perhaps; but the example of Marpingen suggests a more complex dialectic. On the one hand, the impressive reconstruction of clerical authority in Marpingen and in thousands of parishes like it, elsewhere in Germany and Europe, owed much to the willingness of the church to go with the grain of popular belief. The attachment of the faithful to animistic beliefs and women in white was not driven out, it was driven underground – that was what the Marianization of devotional forms often meant in practice. But this, in turn, could cause problems for clerical authority. Marpingen offers a good example. The events of the 1870s and later showed the damage that could be caused when grit got into the cogs of Weber's machinery. And what looked like an all-powerful organization to officials and liberal anticlericals looked rather different if you were a harassed parish priest or vicar-general faced with the 'miracle of Marpingen'.

V

Reactions to the apparitions not only revealed divisions among the lower clergy, and between clergy and laity; they also revealed divisions within the laity itself. These had a clear sociological dimension. The miraculous sites attracted large numbers of visitors from the Catholic aristocracy, German and non-German. Spees, Stolbergs, Löwensteins – all the great families were represented in Marpingen.[91] The Princess Helene of Thurn und Taxis patronized both Mettenbuch and Marpingen, travelling to the latter with a retinue of seventeen servants.[92] At the bottom of the social scale, the apparition sites attracted peasants, agricultural labourers, farm and domestic servants, significant numbers of small tradespeople and – above all in Marpingen – workers. Marpingen became something of a miners' pilgrimage.[93] Conspicuously absent among pilgrims and other supporters of the apparitions were members of the Catholic bourgeoisie, certainly bourgeois men. It is true that we encounter theologians and publicists who were enthusiastic, and a handful of businessmen appear in the record as having visited Marpingen (although not always with any great faith).[94] But in the extensive sources, official and unofficial, hostile and friendly, there is not a single reference to pilgrims who were industrialists or managers, no mention at all of any pilgrim from the middle or higher ranks of the bureaucracy, no pilgrim engaged in the exercise of law, medicine, engineering or architecture. The social composition of those who went to Marpingen reflected the skewed distribution of Catholics in the overall population. But the striking under-representation of the propertied and educated middle classes also said something about Catholics who belonged to those classes. For there were, of course, Catholic doctors, lawyers, officials and businessmen, but they were precisely the Catholics of whom it was complained that they were 'too close to the Protestants and lukewarm', that they led worldly lives and read novels.[95] These were the Catholics who distrusted 'excessive' mariolatry and found episodes like Marpingen more embarrassing than inspirational. From the austere academic Franz-Xaver Kraus, who regarded Marpingen, like Lourdes, as an ultramontane nonsense, to the factory owner who expressed himself scandalized by the affair, these attitudes were widespread.[96] They were especially prevalent in the educated middle class, and they extended to figures prominent in Catholic public life. Thus Julius Bachem, lawyer, publicist and leading Centre Party politician, did everything possible to distance himself from the supernatural claims on which Marpingen rested.[97]

Yet Bachem defended the inhabitants of Marpingen, in parliament and in the courts, against charges that arose from events there. This combination of personal scepticism and public defence was not hypocrisy, but another telling sign of the times. It was the great – involuntary – achievement of the Prussian state and its liberal allies that they did so much to paper over the real divisions among German Catholics. The very reasons that made it difficult for the church to win popular support for its rejection of the apparitions were the same ones that tended to bring German Catholics together – for all were tarred with the same brush.[98] To understand this, we have to appreciate the scale of the political and bureaucratic offensive faced by Catholics in the 1870s. Liberals were in many ways the pacemakers here. It was, after all, a left liberal – the doctor, pathologist and scientific popularizer Rudolf Virchow – who coined the phrase Kulturkampf. And the fierceness with which liberals supported this 'struggle of civilizations' demonstrates their heady belief in Progress, defined above all against the 'dead hand' of the church and Catholic 'backwardness'.[99] The reactions of liberal politicians and press to Marpingen reveal a boundless contempt and hostility. The apparitions were painted as an example of deception and credulity – the 'Marpingen miracle swindle', the 'crassest stupidity', 'mindless superstition', 'a colossal swindle based on stupidity', a product of the 'credulous bigoted masses'.[100] A darker, pseudo-scientific language also coloured these denunciations. Apparition sites were habitually described as a *Sumpf*, or swamp; believers (especially women) were the victims of 'mania' or 'hysteria'; the episodes were a form of collective pathology, an 'epidemic popular disease'.[101] The apparitions were also, in the view of many liberals, an attempt to foster 'hatred' against the Reich and inflame the 'fanatical mob' into 'revolutionary upheaval'.[102]

Contempt, dehumanizing language, fears for public order: all made it easier for liberals to support repressive measures, urging the government to 'proceed with maximum energy against this anti-state and treasonable agitation'.[103] For National Liberals, who identified themselves strongly with Bismarck, 'energetic measures' were constantly invoked. Energy, strength, endurance, lack of sentimentality – this was the catalogue of manly virtues, the self-image with which National Liberals warmed themselves as they 'struggled' (or backed the struggle of the state) against the clerical enemy.[104] Left liberals such as Virchow, and newspapers like the *Frankfurter Zeitung*, had greater misgivings about the methods employed in the Kulturkampf. The latter argued that Marpingen was a swindle that would have been better dealt with by 'a manly and honourable word and open discussion' than by repression.[105] Yet they were also committed by the logic of their position to a firm prosecution of the anticlerical struggle in which they so passionately believed. Marpingen provides a perfect instance of the way that progressive liberals allowed Bismarck to wage 'proxy wars' on their behalf.[106] As a result, the state which had censored liberal newspapers and dismissed liberal officials in the 1850s and 1860s was now cast in the role of progressive cultural steamroller. The price paid by liberals was acquiescence in the repressive measures taken in places like Marpingen.

How, then, did the Prussian state act in Marpingen? The authorities remained ignorant of what was happening for a week. The local gendarme was in gaol on an immorality charge, and the only state-appointed official in the village, the Ortsvorsteher, provided no information to his superiors.[107] The local Landrat, the decisive figure in the Prussian field administration, was on holiday. When his deputy, district secretary Hugo Besser, and the local rural mayor, Wilhelm Woytt, first heard about Marpingen and the size of the crowds gathering there, they over-reacted. Besser panicked, and Woytt seems to have used the opportunity to revenge himself on a community that resented his vigorous support of the Kulturkampf, and was also in dispute over his salary. The result was a half-hearted effort by the two men and a group of gendarmes to read the riot act to 4000 singing and praying pilgrims, followed by a telegram to the nearest garrison in Saarlouis requesting assistance.[108] Shortly after noon on 13 July, ten days after the apparitions began, the eighty-strong Eighth Company of the Fourth Rhenish Infantry Regiment, under Captain von Fragstein-Riemsdorff, arrived in St Wendel to be briefed by the district secretary. They set off for Marpingen soon after 6 p.m., going cross-country and using forestry tracks. They approached the woods at about 8 p.m., sounded a drum-roll that caused confusion even among the soldiers (some mistook it for the order to load rifles), and proceeded to disperse the crowd with fixed bayonets. The company was then billeted on Marpingen at the village's expense, starting by requisitioning beds, food, hay and other provisions (including wine) in the early hours of the morning.[109] The commanding officer later observed laconically that 'the inhabitants of Marpingen showed themselves to be slack and grudging in the lodging of men and the procuring of necessary provisions, etc, so that energetic action and blunt measures were necessary on my part to regularize the circumstances of the case'.[110] Writing in the *Kölnische Volkszeitung*, Matthias Scheeben suggested that the behaviour of the military was no better than might have been expected of troops in an occupied country.[111] Writer and newspaper were later prosecuted for this slur.

The civilian authorities now pursued a dual-track policy, the first part of which aimed to discover the 'instigators' of the whole affair. The local Landrat, the District Governor from Trier, examining magistrates and public prosecutors descended on the village and began a lengthy round of enquiries and disciplinary measures. Neureuter and two neighbouring parish priests had their homes searched and their correspondence seized; all three priests were then arrested and removed from their posts as school inspectors. Two village schoolteachers were transferred away from the village, and further arrests were made. All the women in the village aged between twenty-five and fifty were subject to a mass identification parade to discover who had placed a cross at the apparition site. There were numerous interrogations, especially of the three girls and their parents (Margaretha Kunz was questioned twenty-eight times) and the children were removed from their homes and placed under surveillance in an orphanage in Saarbrücken designed for Protestants.[112] One of the key figures in all of this activity was a senior Berlin detective dispatched to Marpingen by the Ministry of the Interior at the beginning of October.[113] The name of this detective, appropriately enough, was Marlow. It was not his real name, of course. He was actually called

Leopold Friedrich Wilhelm Freiherr von Meerscheidt-Hüllessem, and he later played a major part in the surveillance of socialist activities in the 1880s, and in compiling the list of suspected homosexuals maintained by the criminal police in Wilhelmine Germany.[114] But he operated in Marpingen under the name Marlow, passing himself off (not altogether successfully) as a sympathetic Irish-American journalist with the *New York Herald*, for which role he had been provided with appropriate papers. His activities in the village recall the dirty tricks practised by the Prussian criminal police in the era of Hinckeldey and Stieber during the 1850s: Marpingen was the apprenticeship of an *agent provocateur*.[115] Eventually the efforts of 'Marlow' and others led to charges being brought against twenty adults for fraud, aiding and abetting fraud, and public order offences.[116]

The second part of the authorities' actions was aimed at preventing inhabitants of Marpingen or visitors from turning the Härtelwald into a pilgrimage site. This was to be achieved by heavy policing. Access to the woods was periodically restricted, or denied altogether, and they were regularly patrolled, first by the infantry company (withdrawn two weeks later), then by gendarmes and a company of the Eighth Rifle Battalion posted to the village in February 1877.[117] More than a hundred villagers were fined for entering the woods, even when they went to cut straw, reach their meadows or take a short-cut to the railway station in St Wendel. On one occasion gendarmes seized the heavily pregnant Katharina Meisberger, the only one of a group of fourteen or fifteen women who had failed to flee, and she was 'harassed' to reveal the names of her companions; on other occasions gendarmes surprised people by jumping out from behind bushes. Numerous villagers were also interrogated, and subsequently fined, over the illegal provision of bed and board to pilgrims, an activity that could lead to a late-night knock on the door even for someone whose barn accommodated, say, a knife-grinder who visited the village every year.[118]

How to explain this heavy-handed arrogance? That the Prussian state should have acted more repressively than its Bavarian counterpart did over Mettenbuch comes as no great surprise, certainly given the circumstances of the 1870s.[119] What might seem more surprising is the severity of the actions in Marpingen compared with Dittrichswalde, where the visionary children were actually Poles. The difference serves as a salutary reminder that the western border was in some ways more sensitive than the eastern border, because more recently digested into Prussian administration, and because the Franco-Prussian war was so fresh in the memory. Coercion in Marpingen was partly fuelled by overheated fears of French plots, in which villagers were cast as the enemy within.[120] Circumstances explain much of the rest. If the local gendarme had not been in gaol, if the Landrat had not been on holiday, if the rural mayor had been less than a bigot, if the District Governor had been less of a 'rigid Protestant' . . . who knows?[121] But, as the Russian proverb has it: if my grandmother had a beard, my grandmother would be my grandfather. Contingency played its part, but this was no chapter of accidents. Poor police intelligence, inflexible military response, innate distrust of Catholics – all were deep-wired in a Prussian state that was simultaneously authoritarian, cheapskate and brittle.[122] And once the mailed fist had been used, the bureaucracy found itself committed to a position from which it was difficult to withdraw without loss of face.

Distinctions should nevertheless be made. The gendarmes and the field administration, with the Ministry of the Interior ultimately behind it, took a harder line than the legal bureaucracy. This had something to do with professional pique among judicial officials in the Saarland that bureaucrats in Trier, Koblenz and Berlin were interfering in their sphere of competence (the arrival of 'Marlow' is a case in point). It may also be related to the larger proportion of Catholics in the judicial branch than in the field adminis-tration. In the end, however, there was another distinction: between a Ministry of the Interior and field administration that pressed for cases to be made, even where (as in Marpingen) it was an uphill struggle, and judicial officials who recognized that it was an uphill struggle, and resented the misuse of their time.[123] Marpingen reveals some of these tensions. It also shows how arbitrary bureaucratic actions could be checked by the rule of law. Almost from the beginning, the state's position in Marpingen began to unravel in the courts, as priests, publicists and pilgrims were acquitted. In the major trial that arose out of the affair and took place in 1879, every defendant was acquitted on every charge.[124]

Moreover, like the notorious Zabern case in 1913, when the Prussian army ran amok in an Alsatian garrison town, a case that offers some par-allels, Marpingen became a *cause célèbre* not least because public opinion and political exposure made it one.[125] Leading Catholic publicists like Georg Dasbach and Edmund Prince Radziwill wrote about the affair, papers like the *Kölnische Volkszeitung* highlighted the abuses that had taken place, and the conduct of the authorities was the subject of a full-scale debate in the Prussian parliament on a motion tabled by the Catholic Centre Party.[126] Over-reaction and high-handedness there certainly were; but we should recognize that in the Prussian state of the 1870s there were also limits imposed by the rule of law and political embarrassment.[127]

VI

There is a final point that needs to be made, one that addresses the overall theme of this volume. A striking features of events in Marpingen was the difficulty faced by the Prussian state in successfully exercising its authority. It is clear that a whole range of nominal state officials – the parish priest, schoolteachers, successive local Ortsvorsteher, the village watchman, the communal forester – failed, sometimes spectacularly, to cooperate with the gendarmes and investigating authorities.[128] Prudential considerations no doubt account for some of this. In other communities the lives of those branded as 'Judases' were made very uncomfortable.[129] In Marpingen, the evasive and contradictory statements made by the schoolteacher Magdalene André probably owed something to nervousness of this sort.[130] For the most part, however, non-cooperation resulted from sympathy with local opinion against 'outside' authority. Harsh and arbitrary measures predictably served only to feed the sympathy. Conversely, one reason for the brusque interrogations and petty harassment of local people by some officials and gendarmes was undoubtedly frustration caused by the wall of silence they encountered, as the tight-lipped solidarity of villagers compounded the lack of cooperation from minor local officials.[131] Much the same happened in other areas during the Kulturkampf, and it raises a larger set of questions about the nature of Catholic resistance to the Kulturkampf.

The most obvious sign of Catholic resistance was organizational. At the head of the organizations that defended Catholics during the 1870s stood the Centre Party, which secured four-fifths of all Catholic votes at the high-point of the Kulturkampf.[132] We should not pass over this fact too lightly, given that pious Catholics in newly-unified Italy boycotted politics. It matters that in Germany the ballot-box was chosen over the boycott (or banditry) by so many Catholics. The Centre Party rested, in turn, on a sub-structure of associations through which Catholic identity was articulated. These included the clubs, or *Casinos*, of middle-class Catholics, Catholic peasant and journeymen associations, and a host of religious and charitable organizations: Pius associations, Boniface associations, and so on. Bourgeois Catholics played an important leadership role in many of these. Organizations of this kind also gave priests and aristocrats a series of 'modern' public roles to bolster the ties of deference that still bound many lower-class Catholics to them. The clergy played an equally crucial role in the development of the Catholic press. The organized Catholic response to the Kulturkampf through these channels is fairly well known to German historians.[133] Less familiar, but no less important, were the countless examples, large and small, of what contemporaries referred to as 'passive resistance'.[134] These included hiding priests on the run or trying to block their arrest, bringing pressure to bear on those (locksmiths, for example) who 'collaborated' with the authorities, and secreting church records or funds before state commissioners could seize them.[135]

Both forms of response can be found in Marpingen. In an area where formal organization was thin on the ground, village notables worked together with prominent outsiders to publicize what had happened in Marpingen and seek redress. Well-known priest-publicists like Edmund Radziwill and

Paul Majunke helped villagers to use all the available channels of public life to make their case: petitions to the authorities, legal action, press coverage. Both of these men were also members of the Reichstag, and Radziwill in particular used this position to work for the release of the three girls. Advice was sought from other Centre Party figures. In the long run these initiatives brought success, although it is fair to say that until a relatively late stage Marpingen did more for the local fortunes of the Centre Party than the party did for Marpingen.[136]

Meanwhile, in the village itself, a different kind of everyday resistance was being practised. Occasionally it was violent; mostly it fell into the category of 'passive resistance'.[137] Gendarmes were frozen out or mocked; a public prosecutor complained wearily that the population 'performed spying duties on every corner and path, in order to bring the activity of the authorities to a standstill'; house-searches had to be undertaken with locksmiths from outside the village; and villagers worked with the sexton and members of the parish council to spirit away money donated by pilgrims, just as elsewhere church funds were secreted.[138] When Father Neureuter was released from gaol at the beginning of December 1876, he received a festive welcome home as the young men of Marpingen rode out to meet him on the St Wendel road and provide a guard of honour.[139] The circumstances turned these declarations of faith into implicit acts of defiance. The emblems of the apparition movement – the cross that marked 'the place' and the flowers that adorned it, the lighted candles and pictures, the Marian hymns – became potent symbols of non-compliance with the dictates of the state. Again and again, Marpingen Catholics placed the representatives of authority in a vulnerable, or laughable, position. Officials painted themselves into the position of treating the flowers left at 'the place' as evidence of law-breaking, just as eleven girls in Schweich were imprisoned for being caught in possession of garlands after celebrating the release of their priest.[140] The refusal of villagers to accept the closing of the woods is particularly interesting. It recalls earlier, bitter disputes with Prussian forestry officials over rights to former communal woodland, and it indicates a stubborn reluctance to concede that the state had a right to dictate where Catholics should go and how they should behave.[141] It was, in short, a defence of 'public space' and its uses that had less dramatic counterparts elsewhere during the Kulturkampf. In Münster, for example, efforts to open a narrow road near the bishop's palace to wheeled vehicles were resisted, the papal flag was defiantly flown in the woods, and – following a ban on flags during a papal jubilee – a young woman climbed up to place a garland of yellow and white flowers on a prominent statue in the Domplatz.[142]

In Marpingen, as in Münster, we are dealing with a particular kind of social movement, one that generally employed moral rather than physical force and proved very difficult to break. It had its own icons and symbols, in the form of rosaries, candles and the ubiquitous flowers (the symbolic use of flowers during the Kulturkampf warrants an article to itself.) In its pattern and texture, this kind of Catholic movement clearly drew on the revived popular piety and devotional forms of previous decades. Yet we should not exaggerate the element of clerical inspiration. The clergy often had to restrain frustrated parishioners, and much of the resistance in Marpingen flowed around a struggling parish priest. Like the enthusiastic popular response to the apparitions themselves, the movements of communal self-defence I have been describing were hybrids. They owed something to the clergy, but could also outrun clerical control. They show a Catholic populace willing to be impressed by rank – by aristocratic pilgrims distributing favours, or by a Prince Radziwill taking up their cause – but hardly deferential in the customary sense. They indicate finally, if Marpingen is any guide, that we should recognize the roles played both by male notables and by women, children and youth.

VII

The fact that the German apparitions of the 1870s have received so little attention is itself revealing. There are several reasons why Marpingen, say, is less familiar than Lourdes, Knock or Fatima, not least the fact that it was never officially recognized by the church and persisted as an unofficial cult. But one reason is that this is simply not what we expect of *German* Catholics. We think of nineteenth-century German Catholicism as somehow more 'modern' – as, in many respects (such as theology) it was. When German Catholics faced external pressure and threats, we expect them – like German workers – to form organizations. And this, of course, they did. Germany was indeed, as Hubert Jedin has said, the 'classic land' of Catholic associational life.[143] Formal organizations are not everything, however. There is another history of German Catholics that deserves attention: a history of mentalities, of popular piety, and of the ways that these interlocked with migration and social change, the relations between men, women and children, the attempt to reconstruct clerical authority. Only in the last decade has it started to receive the attention it deserves. Redirecting attention to this other history can also, and not least, throw new light on political and legal structures. For it would be as wrong to exclude questions of power and politics as it would be to view them too narrowly. In the present article I have tried to show that there is no reason at all why this sort of research should lead us to neglect politics. Our histories can, and perhaps they should, bring together the history of mentalities and organizations, everyday life and politics.

NOTES

1 See also David Blackbourn, *Marpingen: Apparitions of the Virgin Mary in Bismarckian Germany* (Oxford, 1993). In some of the notes below readers are referred to chapters of the book for evidence and further details. The present article also draws on material previously published in G. Eley ed., *Society, Culture, and the State in Germany, 1870–1930* (Ann Arbor, Mich., 1995). I am grateful to the University of Michigan Press for permission to use it here.

2 R. Laurentin and A. Durand, *Pontmain: histoire authentique*, vol. 1: *Un signe dans le ciel* (Paris, 1970).

3 M. L. Nolan and S. Nolan, *Christian Pilgrimage in Modern Western Europe* (Chapel Hill, 1989) pp. 266–89; V. Turner and E. Turner, *Image and Pilgrimage in Christian Culture* (Oxford, 1978); V. Turner and E. Turner, 'Postindustrial Marian Pilgrimage', in J. Preston ed., *Mother Worship* (Chapel Hill, 1982) pp. 145–73.

4 See Blackbourn, *Marpingen*, ch. 1; also H. Thurston, *Beauraing and Other Apparitions* (London, 1934); B. Billet et al. eds, *Vraies et fausses apparitions dans l'Eglise* (Paris, 1973); M. P. Carroll, *The Cult of the Virgin Mary* (Princeton, 1986) pp. 115 ff.

5 On Lourdes, R. Laurentin and B. Billet, *Lourdes. Dossiers des documents authentiques*, 7 vols (Paris, 1958–66) vol. 1, pp. 75 ff, 131–5; Carroll, *Cult of the Virgin*, pp. 158–9. Generally, Blackbourn, *Marpingen*, ch. 1.

6 R. Laurentin and A. Durand, *Un Signe dans le ciel*, p. 65.

7 J. Hellé *Miracles* (London, 1953) p. 191. On Brentano and Emmerich, see H. Graef, *Mary. A history of doctrine and devotion*, 2 vols (London, 1963), vol. 2, p. 386.

8 J. Devlin, *The Superstitious Mind. French Peasants and the Supernatural in the Nineteenth Century* (London and New Haven, 1987), pp. 152–3; R. Ernst, *Maria redet zu uns. Marienerscheinungen seit 1830* (Eupen, 1949) pp. 39–41; T. de Cauzons, *La Magie et la sorcellerie en France* (Paris, 1911) vol. 4, pp. 597– 617.

9 F. Storch, *Maria, das Heil der Kranken. Darstellung der ausserordentlichen Vorfälle und wunderbaren Heilungen, welche im Jahre 1866 zu Philippsdorf in Böhmen sich ereignet haben* (Georgswalde, n.d.); P. Sausseret, *Erscheinungen und Offenbarungen der allerseligsten Jungfrau Maria* (Regensburg, 1878), vol. 2, pp. 244–9; W.J. Walsh, *The Apparitions and Shrines of Heaven's Bright Queen*, 4 vols (New York, 1904), vol. 4, pp. 59–70.

10 Examples in R. Krafft-Ebing, *Lehrbuch der gerichtlichen Psychopathologie* (Stuttgart, 1875), pp. 200–2, and *Lehrbuch der Psychiatrie auf klinischer Grundlage*, 3 vols (Stuttgart, 1879–80), vol. 2, pp. 90–3, 116–17, vol. 3, pp. 87–90. Compare Carroll, *Cult of the Virgin*; M. Oraison, 'Le point de vue du médecin psychiatre clinicien sur les apparitions', in Billet et al. eds, *Vraies et fausses apparitions*, pp. 123–47.

11 Detailed argument and references in Blackbourn, *Marpingen*, ch.1. T. Kselman, *Miracles and Prophecies in Nineteenth-Century France* (New Brunswick, 1983) and N. Perry and L. Echeverría, *Under the Heel of Mary* (London, 1988) deal extensively with the political context.

12 The extensive printed sources on these cases include, on Marpingen: A. F. von Berg [=Adam Fauth], *Marpingen und das Evangelium* (Saarbrücken, 1877); W. Cramer, *Die Erscheinungen und Heilungen in Marpingen* (Würzburg, 1876); F. von Lama, *Die Muttergottes-Erscheinungen in Marpingen* (Saar) (Altötting, n.d); *Marpingen – Wahrheit oder Lüge?* (Münster, 1877); *Die Marpinger Muttergottes-Erscheinungen und wunderbaren Heilungen* (Paderborn, 1877); *Marpingen und seine Gnadenmonate* (Münster, 1877); J. Rebbert, *Marpingen und seine Gegner* (Paderborn, 1877); N. Thoemes, *Die Erscheinungen in Marpingen* (Stuttgart, 1877); on Mettenbuch, B. Braunmüller, *Kurzer Bericht über die Erscheinungen U. L. Frau bei Mettenbuch* (Deggendorf, 1878); on Dittrichswalde, 'Die Erscheinungen der unbefleckt Empfangenen in Dittrichswalde', *Der Sendbote des*

göttlichen Herzens Jesu, 14 (1878) pp. 56–62; 'Die Erscheinungen zu Dittrichswalde', *St-Bonifatius-Kalender für das Jahr 1879*, pp. 147–59; on Alsace, 'Wunder in Elsaß', *St-Bonifatius-Kalender für das Jahr 1893*, pp. 89–104; Berg, *Marpingen*, pp. 26–7; on Silesia, *Deutsche Allgemeine Zeitung*, 29 August 1876; on Posen, *Kölnische Zeitung*, 6 September 1876.

13 On topography: W. Bungert, *Heimatbuch Marpingen* (Marpingen, 1980); K. Höppstadter and H.–W. Herrmann, *Geschichtliche Landeskunde des Saarlandes* (Saarbrücken, 1960), pp. 5–16.

14 Cramer, *Die Erscheinungen*, p. 6.

15 Landesarchiv Saarbrücken, Einzelstücke 107, Zusammenstellung des wesentlichen Inhalts der Untersuchungsacten betreffend die Mutter-Gottes-Erscheinungen in Marpingen. Saarbrücken den 9. August 1878. Kleber Untersuchungsrichter [LASB, E 107], 293.

16 Accounts of the apparitions can be found in LASB, E 107, 1–14; Bistumsarchiv Trier [BAT], B III, 11, 14/3, 1–49; also the published sources in n.11.

17 LASB, E 107, 424: Jacob Neureuter, notebook entry of 11 July 1876.

18 See Blackbourn, *Marpingen*, ch. 4.

19 LASB, E 107, 484; 'An der Gnadenstätte von Marpingen', *Die Gartenlaube* (1877), p. 669; *Marpingen und seine Gnadenmonate*, p. 16.

20 *Marpingen – Wahrheit oder Lüge?*, p. 4; *Die Marpinger Mutter-Gottes-Erscheinungen und wunderbaren Heilungen*, p. 13.

21 *Breslauer Zeitung*, cited in *Germania*, 13 January 1877.

22 Rebbert, *Marpingen und seine Gegner*, p. 9.

23 LASB, E 107, 87, 99; E. Radziwill, *Ein Besuch in Marpingen* (Berlin, 1877), pp. 3–4. Kunz also had her mother's heavy physical build (see LASB, E 107, 325), and a photograph of the three shows her dominating the group: Lama, *Die Muttergottes-Erscheinungen*, p. 36; Bungert, *Heimatbuch*, p. 229.

24 The uncle was Stephan Kunz IV, a substantial peasant and auxiliary field-guard (*Gehilfs-Feldhüter*): LASB, E 107, 79, 431–2; BAT, B III, 11, 14/4, 117.

25 LASB, E 107, 75, 307; the notary Hess to Edmund Radziwill, 28 November 1876, cited in *Marpingen – Wahrheit oder Lüge?*, pp. 13–15.

26 The other (younger) children were 'under her influence', said the teacher Mayr: Staatsarchiv Landshut [SAL], 164/2, 1162, Besprechung mit Lehrer Mayr von Berg vom 7. Mai 1877. This general view is borne out by the evidence.

27 Details drawn from Bischöfliches Zentralarchiv Regensburg, Generalia F 115 [BZAR, F 115], Fasc. IV, Untersuchung der Angaben der Mettenbucher Mädchen in Waldsassen – 1878 u. 1879, esp. the Protokoll aufgenommen im Kloster der Cisterzianerinnen zu Waldsassen am 7. November 1878; and the unnumbered folder labelled Mettenbuch. Mathilde Sack in Waldsassen. Additional material in Fasc. I, Bericht des Pfarramtes Metten (23 July 1877), and Fasc. I, Beilage 1, Protokoll der Vernehmung der Mathilde Sack, Schneiderstochter, 14 J. alt (25 December 1876).

28 On female farm servants, see R. Schulte, 'Dienstmädchen im herrschaftlichen Haushalt. Zur Genese ihrer Sozialpsychologie', *Zeitschrift für bayerische Landesgeschichte*, 41 (1978), pp. 879–920.

29 LASB, E 107, 6, 64–5, 184, 129–30, 446; BAT, B III, 11, 14/3, 9–42; *Die Erscheinungen in Marpingen*, pp. 54, 81.

30 SAL, 164/2, 1162, Besprechung mit Lehrer Mayr von Berg vom 7. Mai 1877; BZAR, F 115, Fasc. V, Vernehmung des Fr. Xav. Kraus in Regensburg. Nov. 1878. Weitere Vernehmungen in Metten. Dezbr. 1878.

31 Examples and analysis of all these points in Blackbourn, *Marpingen*, ch. 4.

32 BAT, B III, 11, 14/3, 5; LASB, E 107, 301–4, 322; Cramer, *Die Erscheinungen*, p. 9; Thoemes, *Die Erscheinungen in Marpingen*, p. 23.

33 BAT, B III, 11, 14/3, 59–65: Margaretha Kunz's 'confession', 26 January 1889. Frau Leist told the girls on the first evening: 'Go back into the woods tomorrow, pray, and if you see her again ask who she is, if she says she is the Immaculately Conceived, then she is the Blessed Virgin'. Susanna Leist, asked who had suggested they return to the woods, was silent for fifteen minutes, then replied: 'It was *not* my mother': LASB, E 107, 60–1: Leist interrogation on 31 October 1876. On apparitions as 'fictions', see J. Kent, 'A Renovation of Images: Nineteenth-Century Protestant "Lives of Jesus" and Roman Catholic Alleged Apparitions of the Blessed Virgin Mary', in D. Jasper and T.R. Wright eds, *The Critical Spirit and the Will to Believe* (Basingstoke, 1989) pp. 37–52.
34 Details and references in Blackbourn, *Marpingen*, ch. 4.
35 On this background – six changes of sovereignty between the 1760s and 1834 – see Bungert, *Heimatbuch*, pp. 94–113, 195–205; M. Müller, *Die Geschichte der Stadt St Wendel* (St Wendel, 1927) pp. 189–91, 229; O. Beck, *Beschreibung des Regierungsbezirks Trier*, 3 vols (Trier, 1868–71) vol. 2, pp. 66–73.
36 Müller, *St Wendel*, pp. 239–44; R. Vierhaus, 'Preussen und die Rheinlande 1815–1915', *Rheinische Vierteljahrsblätter*, 30 (1965), pp. 152–75.
37 F. E. Heitjan, *Die Saar-Zeitung und die Entwicklung des politischen Katholizismus an der Saar von 1872–1888* (Saarlouis, 1931), p. 17.
38 H. Klein, 'Die Saarlande im Zeitalter der Industrialisierung', *Zeitschrift für die Geschichte der Saargegend*, 29 (1981), p. 99.
39 W. Laufer, 'Bevölkerungs- und siedlungsgeschichtliche Aspekte der Industrialisierung an der Saar', *Zeitschrift für die Geschichte der Saargegend*, 29 (1981) pp. 154–5; K. J. Rivinius, 'Die sozialpolitische und volkswirthschaftliche Tätigkeit von Georg Friedrich Dasbach' , in *Soziale Frage und Kirche im Saarrevier* (Saarbrücken, 1984) pp. 121–2; K.–M. Mallmann, '"Aus des Tages Last machen sie ein Kreuz des Herrn"? Bergarbeiter, Religion und sozialer Protest im Saarrevier des 19. Jahrhunderts', in W. Schieder ed., *Volksreligiosität in der modernen Sozialgeschichte* (Göttingen, 1986) pp. 155–6.
40 Landeshauptarchiv Koblenz [LHAK], 403/10611, 251–358, 429–58, 573–715; LHAK, 403/10612, 11–26.
41 LHAK, 403/10611, 517–52.
42 On the repressive aspects of the Kulturkampf, M. Scholle, *Die Preußische Strafjustiz im Kulturkampf 1873–1880* (Marburg, 1974).
43 F. R. Reichert, 'Das Trierer Priesterseminar im Kulturkampf (1873–1886)', *Archiv für mittelrheinische Kirchengeschichte*, 25 (1973) pp. 65–105; *Bericht über die Gefangennehmung des Herrn Bischofs Dr. Matthias Eberhard sowie über die Austreibung der Professoren aus dem bischöflichen Priesterseminar zu Trier* (Trier, 1874).
44 The law generally hit poorer, left-bank Rhenish parishes harder. On Marpingen clerical income, see BAT, 70/3676, 43–6, 81–4; on the tensions that resulted, BAT, 70/3676a, 158–9: Father Jacob Neureuter to vicar-general Trier, 30 October 1893.
45 On Namborn, LHAK, 403/15716, 12–13; BAT, B III, 11, 14/6[1], 96–9; K. Kammer, *Trierer Kulturkampfpriester* (Trier, 1926), p. 156; Müller, *St Wendel*, pp. 270–3; J. Bellot, *Hundert Jahre politisches Leben an der Saar unter preußischer Herrschaft (1815–1918)* (Bonn, 1954); K.–M. Mallmann, 'Volksfrömmigkeit, Proletarisierung und preußischer Obrigkeitsstaat. Sozialgeschichtliche Aspekte des Kulturkampfes an der Saar', in *Sozialfrage und Kirche im Saar-Revier*, pp. 211–12.
46 On Elisabeth Flesch, the 'blood-sweater' of nearby Eppelborn, and other cases, see Blackbourn, *Marpingen*, ch. 3.
47 H. Rosenberg, *Grosse Depression und Bismarckzeit* (Berlin, 1967); G. Eley, 'Hans Rosenberg and the Great Depression of 1873–96', in Eley, *From Unification to Nazism* (London, 1986) pp. 23–41.
48 J.J. Kartels, 'Die wirthschaftliche Lage des Bauernstandes in den Gebirgsdistricten des Kreises Merzig', *Schriften des Vereins für Sozialpolitik*, 22 (1883) p. 208; also H. Horch,

Der Wandel der Gesellschafts- und Herrschaftsstrukturen in der Saarregion während der Industrialisierung (1740–1914) (St Ingbert, 1985), pp. 234–8 and Müller, *St Wendel*, p. 212, on moneylenders and cattle dealers in the area. On earlier speculation by peasant-miners, O. Beck, *Die ländliche Kreditnoth und die Darlehenskassen im Regierungsbezirk Trier* (Trier, 1875) p. 112; J. Müller, *Die Landwirtschaft im Saarland* (Saarbrücken, 1976) pp. 24–7.

49 Testimony of gendarme Hentschel in G. Dasbach ed. *Der Marpinger Prozess vor dem Zuchtpolizeigericht in Saarbrücken* (Trier, 1879) p. 163; Müller, *St Wendel*, p. 276.

50 Bungert, *Heimatbuch*, p. 301; Laufer, 'Aspekte', p. 154.

51 LASB, E 107, 434.

52 K. Fehn, 'Das saarländische Arbeiterbauerntum im 19. und 20. Jahrhundert' in H. Kellenbenz ed., *Agrarisches Nebengewerbe und Formen der Reagrarisierung* (Stuttgart, 1975), pp. 195–214; M. Zenner, 'Probleme des Ubergangs von der Agrar- zur Industrie- und Arbeiterkultur im Saarland', in *Soziale Frage und Kirche im Saarrevier*, pp. 70–1; Bungert, *Heimatbuch*, p. 303; Steffens, 'Einer für alle, alle für einen? Bergarbeiter-familien in der 2. Hälfte des 19. Jahrhunderts', in T. Pierenkemper ed., *Haushalt und Verbrauch in historischer Perspektive* (St Katharinen, 1987) pp. 187–226; K. Hoppstädter, '"Eine Stunde nach der Schicht muß jeder gewaschen sein". Die alten Schlafhäuser und die Ranzenmänner', *Saarbrücker Bergmannskalender* (1963) 77–9.

53 Details in Blackbourn, *Marpingen*, chs. 4–5.

54 J. Kuczynski, *Geschichte des Alltags des Deutschen Volkes*, vol. 4, *1871–1918* (Berlin, 1982), pp. 414–15; C. Viebig, *Das Weiberdorf. Roman aus der Eifel* (7th ed., Berlin, 1901). On *Weiberdörfer* in the Saarland, N. Fox, *Saarländische Volkskunde* (Bonn, 1927) p. 389; Kartels, 'Die wirthschaftliche Lage', p. 197; Steffens, 'Einer für alle', pp. 214–16; and for an Austrian example, E. Viethen, 'Tradition und Realitätseignung – Bergarbeiterfrauen im industriellen Wandel', in H. Fielhauer and O. Bockhorn eds., *Die andere Kultur. Volkskunde, Sozialwissenschaften und Arbeiterkultur* (Vienna, Munich and Zurich, 1982) pp. 241–59.

55 L. Petit, 'Une Epidémie d'Hystéro-Démonopathie, en 1878, à Verzegnis, province de Frioul, Italie', *Revue Scientifique*, 10 Apr. 1880, 974A–5A. On the dislocation of worker-peasantries in Friuli, see D.R. Holmes, *Cultural Disenchantments: Worker Peasantries in Northern Italy* (Princeton, 1989).

56 Parish priest Father Bicking: H. Derr, 'Geschichte der Pfarrei Marpingen', dissertation (Trier, 1935) pp. 27–9.

57 Derr, 'Pfarrei Marpingen', pp. 11–12, 20–9, 35. Bicking had a further problem with irregular church book-keeping, a 'hateful business': BAT, 70/3676, 20: Bicking to vicar-general Trier, 25 October 1847. Also *ibid.*, 22–5, 30, 34–7.

58 J. Sperber, *Popular Catholicism in Nineteenth Century Germany* (Princeton, 1984).

59 Derr, 'Pfarrei Marpingen', pp. 30–4, 54–63, and table on illegitimacy rates; Thoemes, *Erscheinungen*, pp. 9–12; *Marpinger Mutter-Gottes-Erscheinungen*, pp. 12–13.

60 Marpingen was 'teeming with images of the Virgin' said a hostile observer in 1876: police commissar von Meerscheidt-Hüllessem, cited in *Saar- und Mosel-Zeitung*, 20 December 1876. On 'Marianization' in the Trier diocese, see A. Heinz, 'Im Banne der römischen Einheitsliturgie. Die Romanisierung der Trierer Bistumsliturgie in der zweiten Hälfte des 19. Jahrhunderts', *Römische Quartalschrift*, 79 (1984), pp. 37–92; *idem*, 'Marienlieder des 19. Jahrhunderts und ihre Liturgiefähigkeit', *Trierer Theologische Zeitschrift*, 97 (1988), pp. 106–34; B. Schneider, 'Die Trauben- und Johannesweinsegnung in der Trierer Bistumsliturgie vom Spätmittelalter bis zum ausgehenden 19. Jahrhundert', *Archiv für mittelrheinische Kirchengeschichte*, 37 (1985), pp. 57–74; K. Küppers, 'Die Maiandacht als Beispiel volksnaher Frömmigkeit', *Römische Quartalschrift*, 81 (1986), pp. 102–12.

61 H. McLeod, *Religion and the People of Western Europe 1789–1970* (Oxford, 1981) pp. 28–35; R. Gibson, *A Social History of French Catholicism 1789–1914* (London, 1989)

pp. 104 ff; F. Lannon, *Privilege, Persecution and Prophecy. The Catholic Church in Spain 1875–1975* (Oxford, 1987); B. Pope, 'Immaculate and Powerful: The Marian Revival in the Nineteenth Century', in C.W. Atkinson, C. H. Buchanan and M. R. Miles eds., *Immaculate and Powerful: The Female in Sacred Image and Social Reality* (Cambridge Mass., 1985), pp. 193–4.

62 On this unexplored subject, H. Jedin, *Handbuch der Kirchengeschichte*, vol. 6/2: *Die Kirche zwischen Revolution und Restauration* (Freiburg i. B., 1971), pp. 664–5.

63 On missions in the Saarland, LHAK, 442/6438, 171, 179–83, 241–3, 247–8, 277–80, 307–11, 331–4, 349–50, 399–407, 427–30, 449–64. On Pius IX, R. Aubert, *Le Pontificat de Pie IX* (1846–1878) (Paris, 1950), pp. 466–9.

64 *Saar-und Mosel-Zeitung*, 18 July 1876; *Nahe-Blies-Zeitung*, 21 October 1876.

65 Radziwill, *Besuch*, p. 7; Derr, 'Pfarrei Marpingen', p. 43; BAT, B III, 11, 14/3, 55; LASB, E 107, 75–6, 84, 102–4.

66 Cramer, *Die Erscheinungen*, p. 8.

67 Kselman, *Miracles and Prophecies*; Pope, 'Immaculate and Powerful', pp. 185–6; J. Hellé, *Miracles* (London, 1953), pp. 83–4; G. Korff, 'Formierung der Frömmigkeit', *Geschichte und Gesellschaft*, 3 (1977), pp. 356–7.

68 LASB, E 107, 165; *Marpingen und seine Gnadenmonate*, p. 41.

69 LHAK, 403/15716, 130–1, 134–9, 144–7, 154–5, 158–61. On the difficulty of apprehending them, see LASB, E 107, 168–9.

70 LASB, E 107, 372–3; P. Sausseret, *Erscheinungen und Offenbarungen* (Regensburg, 1878) vol. 2 p. 230; *Saar- und Mosel-Zeitung*, 30 March 1877.

71 Quotation from LASB, E 107, 359–61: Father Klotz to Father Schneider, 19 August 1876. Konrad Schneider was parish priest in Alsweiler, near Marpingen, and spent long periods in the village after the apparitions.

72 *Ibid.*, 364: Father Schneider to Father Bollig of Mertesdorf, 10 October 1876.

73 BAT, B III, 11, 14/3, 59–65.

74 *Die Marpinger Mutter-Gottes-Erscheinungen*, p. 24; LASB, E 107, 118–19.

75 On the pilgrims and their conduct, and on commercialization, see Blackbourn, *Marpingen*, ch. 5.

76 *Kölnische Zeitung*, 23 August 1876; *Die Erscheinungen in Marpingen*, pp. 8–81; Berg, *Marpingen*, p. 44; *Saar- und Mosel-Zeitung*, 6 February 1877; Müller, *St Wendel*, p. 274.

77 LASB, E 107, 126–8, 163, 189, 444, 494; *Prozess*, pp. 171–2, 193–6; *Die Marpinger Mutter-Gottes-Erscheinungen*, p. 17; *Marpingen – Wahrheit oder Lüge?*, pp. 84–5; *Marpingen und seine Gnadenmonate*, pp. 32, 42–3.

78 *Prozess*, p. 157 (Neureuter's testimony); LHAK, 442/6442, 73–80: Father Göller to Landrat of Ottweiler, 22 July 1877, teacher Kill to Landrat of Ottweiler, 22 July 1877, Landrat of Ottweiler to District Governor Trier, 25 July 1877.

79 *Der Marpinger Prozess vor dem Richterstuhle der Vernunft von einem Unparteiischen* (Vienna, 1881), p. 29; also LASB, E 107, 127, 160; *Saar- und Mosel-Zeitung*, 12 January 1878; *St-Paulinus-Blatt*, 20 January 1878; *Vossische Zeitung*, 16 January 1878.

80 Berg, *Marpingen*, pp. 29–30; *Saar- und Mosel-Zeitung*, 27 March, 30 March, 1 April, 5 April, 7 April 1877; *Kölnische Zeitung*, 1 July 1877.

81 LHAK, 442/6442, 76–80: Father Göller to Landrat of Ottweiler, 22 July 1877.

82 Examples include priests in Tholey, Bliesen, St Wendel, Illingen and Hasborn: LASB, E 107, 75, 201; BAT, B III, 11, 14/5, 126; *Kölnische Zeitung*, 26 July and 3 August 1876.

83 'An der Gnadenstätte von Marpingen', 667.

84 It was the visiting Father Wolf who 'tortured me with his questions': *Prozess*, p. 153. On the abusive mail, *Die Marpinger Mutter-Gottes-Erscheinungen*, p. 21.

85 Details and references in Blackbourn, *Marpingen*, ch. 6.

86 C. Weber, *Kirchliche Politik zwischen Rom, Berlin und Trier 1876–1888* (Mainz, 1970) pp. 20–7.

87 BAT, B III, 11, 14/3, 43–9. On Laurent: K. Möller, *Leben und Briefe von Johannes Theodor Laurent*, 3 vols (Trier, 1887–89); O. Foesser, 'Johann Theodor Laurent und seine Verdienste um die katholische Kirche', *Frankfurter zeitgemäße Broschüren Neue Folge* (1890), pp. 11, 153–84; J. Goedert, *Jean-Théodore Laurent. Vicaire apostolique de Luxembourg 1804–1884* (Luxemburg, 1957).

88 See Blackbourn, *Marpingen*, ch. 11.

89 Details of the enquiry in BZAR, F 115, Fasc. I, Akten der bischöfl. Commission, vom 21. Sept. bis 14. Nov. 1877, with further materials in supplements and in Fasc. II; the judgment is in Fasc. VI: Gutacten über die Sache. Entscheidung durch den Hirtenbrief v. 23. Jan. 1879. On the problems that arose, see Fasc.VII: Vollzug der Entscheidung 1879–81, and the unnumbered files, Mettenbuch 1881–84, Mettenbuch 1885, Mettenbuch 1887–88, Mettenbuch 1886–90.

90 '. . . the specific Catholic form of piety in all of its richness, is quite a different thing from what I have designated above as the "machinery" of the church – in truth it is antagonistic to this machinery, and has only a meagre chance for the future': Max Weber to Frau Gnauck-Kühne, 15 July 1909 [?], cited in W. J. Mommsen, *Max Weber and German Politics* (Chicago, 1985) p. 123 n 134.

91 Müller, *St Wendel*, p. 275; LASB, E 107, 162, 166, 361–2; *Prozess*, p. 84; *Marpingen und seine Gnadenmonate*, p. 46; *Marpingen – Wahrheit oder Lüge?*, pp. 44–5.

92 Fürst Thurn und Taxis Zentralarchiv, HMA 2699, Nr. 2974–8, 3211–17, 2803, 2809–10; HMA 2700, Nr. 3031: bills for trips to Marpingen and Mettenbuch in 1877–78.

93 Blackbourn, *Marpingen*, ch. 4 has a detailed sociological break-down of pilgrims to both Marpingen and Mettenbuch. See also Mallmann, 'Aus des Tages Last'.

94 LASB, E 107, 86–92, 236.

95 E. Gatz, *Rheinische Volksmission im 19. Jahrhundert* (Düsseldorf, 1963), pp. 97–8. Conversely, the scepticism about Marpingen among 'thinking' Catholics was exploited by Protestant writers: Berg, *Marpingen*, p. 40.

96 F.-X. Kraus, *Tagebücher*, ed. H. Schiel (Cologne, 1957), p. 381: entry of 23 September 1877; *Germania*, 9 February 1877.

97 J. Bachem, *Lose Blätter aus meinem Leben* (Freiburg i. B., 1910), pp. 65–75, and *Erinnerungen eines alten Publizisten und Politikers* (Cologne, 1913), pp. 133–42. The same attitude coloured Bachem's discussions of Marpingen in court (see *Prozess*) and in parliament: *Sten. Berichte über die Verhandlungen der durch die Allerhöchste Verordnung vom 3. Oktober 1877 einberufenen beiden Häuser des Landtages. Haus der Abgeordneten* (Berlin, 1878), vol. 2, 46 Sitting, 16 January 1878, pp. 1151–59.

98 See D. Blackbourn, 'Progress and Piety: Liberals, Catholics and the State in Bismarck's Germany', in *Populists and Patricians* (London, 1987), pp. 143–67, here 155.

99 Blackbourn, 'Progress and Piety'.

100 Ludwig Seyffardt, *Sten. Berichte*, 30 November 1877, reprinted in *Erinnerungen* (Leipzig, 1900) pp. 195–6; *Saar- und Mosel-Zeitung*, 16 July 1876; *Nahe-Blies-Zeitung*, 24 August, 5 September and 28 October 1876; *Kölnische Zeitung*, 20 October 1876.

101 For detailed examination of this language, see Blackbourn, *Marpingen*, ch. 9.

102 *Nahe-Blies-Zeitung*, 7 September 1876. Cf. *Saar- und Mosel-Zeitung*, 24 August 1876; *Kölnische Zeitung*, 26 August, 3 November 1876; *National-Zeitung*, 17 January 1878; *Deutsche Allgemeine Zeitung*, 17 August 1876.

103 *Nahe-Blies-Zeitung*, 7 September 1876. This was entirely typical of National Liberal newspapers.

104 The trope of 'manliness' is explored in Blackbourn, *Marpingen*, ch. 9.

105 *Frankfurter Zeitung*, 16 January 1878.

106 R. Aldenhoff, *Schulze-Delitzsch. Ein Beitrag zur Geschichte des Liberalismus zwischen Revolution und Reichsgründung* (Baden-Baden, 1984) p. 233. Cf. O. Klein-Hattingen, *Die Geschichte des deutschen Liberalismus* (Berlin, 1912) vol. 2, pp. 49–55.

107 LASB, E 107, 428.

108 LHAK, 442/6442, 17–20, 133–4; *Prozess*, pp. 14–15, 149–50; BAT, B III, 11, 14/4, 10.

109 LASB, E 107, 15–19, 31–45; BAT, B III, 11, 14/4, 27; LHAK, 442/6442, 135–41. See also Cramer, *Die Erscheinungen*, pp. 19–21; Bachem, *Erinnerungen*, pp. 135–7; *Marpingen – Wahrheit oder Lüge?*, pp. 40–1.

110 LASB, E 107, 437.

111 *Kölnische Volkszeitung*, 26 September 1876.

112 Details and references in Blackbourn, *Marpingen*, ch. 7.

113 LHAK, 442/6442, 27: Minister of Interior Berlin to District Governor Wolff Trier, 30 September 1876.

114 D. Fricke, *Bismarcks Prätorianer. Die Berliner Politische Polizei im Kampf gegen die deutsche Arbeiterbewegung (1871–1878)* (Berlin, 1962) pp. 68–71; J. Haller, *Geschichte der Frankfurter Zeitung* (Frankfurt, 1911) p. 800.

115 On Stieber and Hinckeldey, A. Funk, *Polizei und Rechtsstaat: die Entwicklung des staatlichen Gewaltmonopols in Preussen 1848–1918* (Frankfurt, 1986) p. 60–70.

116 Full details in Blackbourn, *Marpingen*, ch. 7.

117 Stadtarchiv St Wendel, Abt. C, 2/56, 134–44, 165–73; LASB, Best. Landratsamt Saarbrücken, 1, 739; LASB, E 107, 156, 350. On the costs, see LHAK, 442/6442, 61–5.

118 These examples (out of many) in BAT, B III, 11, 14/4, 71, 174–5, 178.

119 The handling of Mettenbuch by district officials in Deggendorf, Regen and Viechtach, and the responses from provincial authority in Landshut, can be followed in SAL, 164/2, 1161–4; 164/15, 814; and 164/18, 697.

120 The soldiers who intervened were initially briefed that insurrection was afoot: LASB, E 107, 425. Belief in, and rumours about, a French 'plot' coloured many subsequent actions: *ibid.*, 29, 150–2, 155, 198.

121 The senior Prussian legal official Karl Schorn singles out the mishandling of Marpingen by particular individuals in his highly critical account: *Lebenserinnerungen* (Bonn, 1898) vol. 2, pp. 259–62.

122 A. Lüdtke, *'Gemeinwohl', Polizei und 'Festungspraxis'. Staatliche Gewaltsamkeit und innere Verwaltung in Preußen, 1815–1850* (Göttingen, 1982); R. Koselleck, 'Die Auflösung des Hauses als ständischer Herrschaftseinheit', in N. Bulst, J. Goy and J. Hoock eds, *Familie zwischen Tradition und Moderne* (Göttingen, 1981) pp. 120–1; R. Tilly, 'Popular Disorders in Nineteenth-century Germany', *Journal of Social History*, 4 (1971), 14, 21.

123 See, for example, LHAK, 442/6442, 113–14: report by examining magistrate Kleber on the state of the Marpingen enquiry, 17 September 1877. Kleber's summary of evidence in LASB, E 107 is larded with sceptical notes, especially where the role of Meerscheidt-Hüllessem was concerned.

124 On the trial of Matthias Scheeben and the *Kölnische Volkszeitung*, whose acquittal was upheld on appeal, see LASB, E 107, 17; BAT, B III, 11, 14/4, 27; LHAK, 442/6442, 135–41; Bachem, *Erinnerungen*, p. 136; *Frankfurter Zeitung*, 30 May 1877. On the major trial in 1879, at Saarbrücken, see *Prozess*. Details of other legal cases in Blackbourn, *Marpingen*, ch. 10.

125 D. Schoenbaum, *Zabern 1913. Consensus Politics in Imperial Germany* (London, 1982).

126 Parliamentary debate in *Sten. Berichte*, sitting of 16 January 1878.

127 On the rule of law, see D. Merten, *Rechtsstaat und Gewaltmonopol* (Tübingen, 1975); Funk, *Polizei und Rechtsstaat*; H.-J. Strauch, 'Rechtsstaat und Verwaltungsgerichtsbarkeit', in M. Tohidipur ed., *Der bürgerliche Rechtsstaat* (Frankfurt, 1978) vol. 2, pp. 525–47. More generally, R. J. Ross, 'Enforcing the Kulturkampf in the Bismarckian State and the Limits of Coercion in Imperial Germany', *Journal of Modern History*, 56 (1984), 456–82.

128 Examples in LASB, E 107, 129, 142–4, 260–3, 265, 382; BAT, B III, 11, 14/4, 27, 42; *Prozess*, pp. 13–17.

129 See LHAK, 442/10419, 175–77; Kammer, *Trierer Kulturkampfpriester*, pp. 36, 75.
130 LASB, E 107, 104, 279–83.
131 On these frustrations, see Blackbourn, *Marpingen*, ch. 7.
132 J. Schauff, *Die deutschen Katholiken und die Zentrumspartei* (Cologne, 1928) p. 75.
133 Sperber, *Popular Catholicism*, pp. 207 ff; Blackbourn, 'Progress and Piety'.
134 Pius IX, in an encyclical of February 1875, declared the May Laws 'null and void' and
     called on Catholics to practise 'passive resistance': K. Bachem, *Vorgeschichte, Geschichte und
     Politik der Deutschen Zentrumspartei*, 9 vols (Cologne, 1927–32) vol. 3, pp. 299–300.
135 Examples in Kammer, *Trierer Kulturkampfpriester*; H. Schiffers, *Der Kulturkampf in
     Stadt und Regierungsbezirk Aachen* (Aachen, 1929); L. Ficker, *Der Kulturkampf in
     Münster*, ed. O. Hellinghaus (Münster, 1928); W. Jestaedt, *Der Kulturkampf im Fuldaer
     Land* (Fulda, 1960).
136 Details in Blackbourn, *Marpingen*, ch. 8.
137 LASB, E 107, 18, 38–45, 156–7; LHAK, 442/6442, 157–8; *Kölnische Zeitung*, 24
     November 1876; *Nahe-Blies-Zeitung*, 1 February 1877; *Saarbrücker Zeitung*, 2 February
     1877; *Saar- und Mosel-Zeitung*, 6 February 1877. Klaus-Michael Mallmann ('Volks-
     frömmigkeit', pp. 218–19) exaggerates the degree of violence.
138 LASB, E 107, 166–9, 224 ff, 431–2; Radziwill, *Besuch*, p. 4; LHAK, 442/6442, 117
     (quotation from public prosecutor Petershof, 20 September 1877).
139 LASB, E 107, 375; *Germania*, 6 December 1876.
140 On the Schweich incident, Kammer, *Kulturkampfpriester*, p. 94.
141 On earlier disputes, see Horch, *Wandel*, pp. 57–64, 93–8, 145–6, 232–4; O. Beck, *Die
     Waldschutzfrage in Preussen* (Berlin, 1860); *idem, Land- und volkswirthschaftliche
     Tagesfragen für den Regierungsbezirk Trier* (Trier, 1866), pp. 48–61, 72–6.
142 Ficker, *Kulturkampf in Münster*, pp. 221–6, 234–5, 241–4.
143 Jedin, *Handbuch der Kirchengeschichte*, vol. 6/2, p. 220.

8   A Vision to the Dispossessed? Popular Piety and Revolutionary Politics in the Irish Land War, 1879–82

Paul Bew

'Our Lady of Knock, the strange intrusion of the supernatural in Ireland . . .
  Here was a vision to the dispossessed, inaccessible to the practitioners of the dismal science.'

Sheridan Gilley, 'The background to Knock',
The Tablet, 18 September 1979.

'So you are admitting that the saints and the miracles were inventions to strengthen the Church's hold on ignorant people?
  No, I am not admitting anything of the kind, and you, Evans, are talking like an Ulster Orangeman. I am putting forward the idea that if civilization was to advance, it needed such aids and the Church was the only civilizing element in a very rough time.'

Robertson Davies, *The Cunning Man*,
London 1994, p. 80.

The relationship between nationality and religion is one of the most vexed questions in modern Irish historiography; indeed it is one of the most vexed questions in modern Irish political debate.[1] In certain moods Irish nationalists like to claim that the cause of Irish nationality transcends that of Irish Catholicism, at other moments it is starkly acknowledged that this can not really be so. Yet this debate tends to go on without any precise reference to the real interplay between Catholic popular piety and the political practice of radical nationalist movements. In particular, it is surprising that historians have paid, until recently, little attention to a remarkable coincidence. In the summer of 1879, County Mayo saw two simultaneous developments of great importance – the outbreak of the decisive phase of the Irish land war and the appearance of the most celebrated of all Irish Marian apparitions in the County Mayo village of Knock. Scholars have had surprisingly little to say about the relationship between the two events. I exempt from this criticism Professor James Donnelly's brilliant and prize-winning essay: 'The Marian Shrine at Knock: The First Decade' which appeared in *Eire-Ireland*, vol. 28, no. 2, 1993, which is now the standard account. Professor Donnelly ably demonstrates the support for the Knock phenomenon by mainstream 'centrist' constitutionalist Land Leaguers, such as the pious T. D. Sullivan whose newspaper *The Nation* gave it much favourable coverage. Professor Donnelly's essay – which is in other respects so authoritative – does not, however, deal with the problem of the relationship between the miracle cure phenomenon at Knock and the specifically revolutionary wing of the Land League which is at the centre of this essay. In this effort, I am trying to 'rectify' a weakness in my own *Land and the National Question in Ireland, 1858–82* (Dublin and Atlantic Highlands, New Jersey, 1978) which does not mention the events surrounding the apparition at Knock, in the course of a lengthy discussion of the outbreak of the land war in Mayo in 1879.

The land war of 1879–82 decisively restructured Anglo-Irish relations; its effect was to make a Dublin parliament of some type an inevitability. The Knock apparition may be placed alongside those of Lourdes and Marpingen as amongst the most significant such events in nineteenth-century Europe. The importance of both events is, in fact, widely appreciated in, as it were, rather separate Irish histories; but as the non-debate in Ireland at the time of their joint centenary in 1979 showed, there is no real sense of their interconnection. There are, it is true, a number of scattered and conflicting notions to be found at the level of popular culture. Some believed that the appearance of the Virgin was a sign of divine support for the Land League. In 1986, the nationalist author, Michael Ó Cuinneagain, complained that the Irish hierarchy – regrettably being composed of West British elements – had celebrated the centenary of the Knock apparition but had not pointed to it as proof that God supported the land war and (by extension) the Provisional IRA.[2] Others held that it was an attempt by a conservative Catholic clergy – possibly aided by the local policemen – to lead the people away from the path of social conflict. Yet despite these speculations there has yet to be a full analysis of the relationships between the religious and revolutionary impulse. To begin this task it is necessary to start not with the apparition of 21 August 1879 itself, but with the preceding political context, the development of a mass land agitation in the west of Ireland.

The broad socio-economic context is clear. The years 1877–9 in Ireland saw poor harvests, decreasing demand for agricultural produce and falling prices; this established some of the necessary preconditions for an agrarian agitation. But there was also a rather specific political dimension: an apparent combination of the radical wing of constitutional nationalism, led by Charles Stewart Parnell, MP for Meath, with the most pragmatic and activist sections of the Irish Republican Brotherhood, a body which had launched an unsuccessful insurrection in 1867. In October 1878 John Devoy, speaking for the Irish American wing of this movement, offered Parnell support on the following conditions.[3]

(1) Abandonment of the federal demand and substitution of a general declaration in favour of self-government.
(2) Vigorous agitation of the land question on the basis of a peasant proprietary, while accepting concessions tending to abolish arbitrary eviction.
(3) Exclusion of all sectarian issues from the platform.
(4) Party members to vote together on all imperial and home questions, adopt an aggressive policy and energetically resist coercive legislation.
(5) Advocacy of all struggling nationalities in the British Empire or elsewhere.

The key element here was the notion of a new land agitation; as Tory and Unionist critics were to note it actually predates by a full year the onset of serious primary distress in the west of Ireland. As a further development of this project, a secret meeting was held at Claremorris in County Mayo in March 1879 at which the neo-fenians resolved to support a land agitation provided that they could nominate its provincial officials and recruit freely at meetings. In April 1879, the first land meeting of the new campaign – openly martialled by Fenians – was held at Irishtown. In his later testimony before the Special Commission arising out of allegations in *The Times* against Parnell, Michael Davitt contended that the Fenians did not participate in the land movement as members of the IRB but as farmers and farmers' sons.[4] This, quite simply, is not the truth;[5] nearer to the mark is Davitt's own later acknowledgement that the 'extreme men' brought to the land movement 'an advanced nationalist spirit and revolutionary purpose'[6] as well as organizational experience and an intact network of immeasurable value.

These generalities about 'spirit and purpose' do, however, require some concrete refinement. Arms on a large scale were imported into the west of Ireland. It is clear that a particular political calculation was at work here – many radicals believed that the British Parliament would always support the interests of Irish landlords; in consequence, a land agitation would inevitably challenge the constitutional link with London. At that point, some looked to a withdrawal of Irish MPs from Westminster in protest; but others hoped to see a successful insurrection with – this time – the peasant support which was so visibly lacking in 1867. But the arms also played a role in a more purely local context; they gave the local secret society militants – for example, a key figure, P. J. Gordon of Claremorris[7] – a much greater capacity for intimidation of those who resisted the progress of the new movement. Amongst those who fell into this category were Archdeacon Bartholomew Cavanagh of Knock parish, County Mayo; possibly influenced by his young curate, a member of a conservative Catholic gentry family, Cavanagh resolutely denounced the new agitation. This was in line with the view of the highly popular and strongly nationalist Archbishop McHale of Tuam; but McHale was popularly believed to be on the verge of death and easily manipulated by his conservative clerical nephew. Cavanagh was a different matter;

a respected and visible local priest who in May 1879 signalled out Fenian
leaders for special vilification. Most Catholic clerics in Mayo were prepared
to sanction publicly the new movement – if only to retain a measure of control – but Cavanagh decisively rejected it, drawing on a substantial Catholic
tradition which insisted that such movements merely led young men into
the path of crime. In reaction, on 1 June 1879 the Fenians sponsored a
meeting at Knock where 20,000–30,000 people reportedly met to enter a
'solemn and emphatic' protest against Archdeacon Cavanagh's condemna-
tions – delivered from the altar – of the new land movement.[8] But the
calling of this meeting was not the end of the matter. Local traditions claim
that it was decided to pressurise Cavanagh in a more direct and blunt fashion.
According to Cavanagh's biographer, W. D. Coyne writing in the 1940s:

> At a special secret meeting, therefore, the subject was fully discussed. Various sug-
> gestions were offered but rejected. The extreme penalty was considered fitting to
> meet the menace of a dangerous priest who talked of the moral law . . . At length, it
> was resolved that a lesser punishment than death would meet the position in the
> district. It would probably be sufficient warning to other parishes, especially when
> the 'heads' had reached the conclusion that milder punishments were, at this stage,
> the correct procedure. The proposal was made and carried that the appropriate
> punishment for Archdeacon Cavanagh was to have him subjected to a course of
> suitable treatment finally to have his ears cut off.[9]

This account of Coyne's is perhaps a little overwritten. While mutilation
of cattle, for example, was a relatively commonplace feature of the Irish land
war the mutilation of people in general – still less of Catholic priests in
particular – was not. Direct assassination of landlords, agents or peasantry
who failed to support the popular will were frequent occurrences, but in no
instance was a Catholic priest done to death in this fashion. In short, none
of the 863 agrarian outrages committed in 1879 in Ireland – or indeed the
2,585 of 1880 provides us with an example of this sort. Nevertheless, it is
clear that a policy of intimidation was decided upon even if we may doubt
the likelihood of any final drastic sanction. But, at this point events took a
surprising turn. As Coyne put it: 'before the date fixed for the sacrilegious
act, the extraordinary events of 21 August 1879 had occurred at Knock'.[10]

On the evening of that rainy summer day a small crowd clustered in great
excitement around the gable wall of the church at Knock. In his book, *The
Apparition at Knock: A Survey of Facts and Evidence* (Tuam 1959), the Rev
Michael Walsh asks 'What did they see?'[11] and gives a precise answer:

> According to their own evidence they saw three figures standing at the gable wall of
> the Church, about eighteen inches or two feet above the ground. The central figure
> was recognized as that of Our Lady. She was wearing a large white cloak fastened at
> the neck and on her head was a brilliant crown. She held her hands raised to the
> level of her shoulders and facing each other. Her eyes were raised towards Heaven,
> as if in prayer. She was raised slightly above the other two figures. On Our Lady's

right was a figure recognized as that of St Joseph. His hands were joined, his head was slightly bowed and his body slightly bent towards Our Lady, as if paying her his respects. On Our Lady's left was a figure considered by one witness to be St John the Evangelist. He was dressed like a bishop. He held an open book in his left hand, and he had his right hand raised with the index and middle fingers pointing upwards, as if he were preaching and emphasizing some special point. On St John's left was an altar, full sized, and on it was a lamb, which was facing towards the figures. Just behind the lamb was a cross. St John was standing in such a position that his back was turned neither to Our Lady nor to the altar, and he was partly facing towards the altar as would a priest celebrating the Tridentine Rite of Mass. The altar was in the centre of the gable just under the window on a higher level than the figures; its position was to the east of the figures but in a line slightly behind them. The figures were 'full and round as if they had a body and life', but they spoke no words, and no words were addressed to them. When people approached them, they moved backwards towards the gable. An old woman tried to kiss the feet of Our Lady, but she found nothing in her embrace but the wall. One witness saw a rose on Our Lady's brow and angels hovering round the head of the lamb. Another said she saw around the lamb a number of stars in the form of a halo. The apparition lasted for about two hours. It was still daylight when it was first seen, but half an hour afterwards darkness had fallen. The three figures and the altar and lamb were surrounded by a soft brilliant light which covered the whole gable of the Church.

The vision has been subject to much deconstruction. The sociologist, Eugene Hynes, has argued that the figure originally perceived to be 'the Bishop' and later recast as St John the Evangelist reflected Archbishop McHale's key position 'in the consciousness of the witnesses'.[12] Sceptics insist that it was a magic lantern fraud, perpetuated, according to taste, by the local police or priest anxious to direct the people away from the land war and towards more spiritual concerns. (This theory was examined at the time and dismissed by Dr Lennon, the professor of science at Maynooth.) In fact, the Archdeacon reacted in the first instance by rejecting the story relayed by his housekeeper, Mary McLaughlin. Gradually, however, he moved over the next few days towards an acceptance of the vision. Perhaps more importantly so did those of his parishioners who belonged to the secret society which had been at loggerheads with the local priests. Coyne describes how the local Fenian activists responded. According to his informants, the militant activists had second thoughts:

There was a complete change. The few who belonged to the vicinity of the parish and were aware of the dreadful decision now appeared to have received new courage. They denounced the whole proceedings. They called together their friends in the parish and proclaimed they would rally round the pastor regardless of consequences to themselves, and challenge any man to touch them.

The story of the Apparition had so impressed even the hardest of hearts that they regarded it as a direct sign through Our Lady that a crime of the kind contemplated was desecration of the basest sort and one that would assuredly cry to heaven.[13]

Knock became the centre of intense religious enthusiasm. The first organized pilgrimage to Knock Shrine came from Limerick in March 1880. It consisted of fifty members of the Holy Name Confraternity, a very large and famous Confraternity, attached to the Redemptorist Church – but soon there were pilgrims from all over the world. These pilgrims frequently made claims of cures – these were noted by the Archdeacon in his diary. By the end of 1880, the list included some three hundred cases. The Knock Shrine earned itself a central place in Irish Catholicism, a place which it retains to this day.

Some, though not all the Mayo nationalist press reported on Knock with some warmth and detail: only two national papers did so – one was the *Nation* edited by the strongly catholic T. D. Sullivan, a Home Rule MP of a solid but not radical hue. The reporter who covered the story so sympathetically for the *Weekly News* of Dublin in January and February 1880 is worthy of some note. He was Thomas Sexton, who in April 1880 was to be elected to parliament for Waterford in the Home Rule interest; he was to become one of Parnell's most intellectually gifted and eloquent lieutenants. His critical speech on the introduction of coercion in 1881 was a highly influential classic. T. P. O'Connor described him in later years as 'vice-leader of the House of Commons' claiming that 'he had an extraordinary mastery of figures and in mental arithmetic he was far beyond any man in the House'.[14] Nor is this simply the amiable partisan version of a friend; John Morley told Edward Hamilton, a very senior Treasury official that 'nobody could be better in counsel: he (Sexton) had a mind as sharp as a knife'.[15] Sexton's articles were of particular significance because the major national journal of Catholic Ireland, the *Freeman's Journal* stayed clear of the Knock story – perhaps reflecting the close friendship between the sceptical Archbishop McCabe of Dublin and the Gray family who owned the newspaper. The *Freeman's Journal* gave some brief news story mention in February 1880 and thereafter refrained from comment. The *Freeman* ironically had William O'Brien, also to join the ranks of Parnellite MPs in late 1882, as its special commissioner reporting on agrarian distress in the west a few miles from the site of the Knock apparitions. O'Brien was a devout, even mystic Catholic, but he seems to have received no editorial encouragement to cover the story. For this reason alone, the failure of later historians to link the events at Knock into the political crisis is perhaps made rather more explicable.

Nevertheless, many pilgrims made their way to Knock. The personnel seems to have been markedly similar to those attending a typical Land League meeting. 'Some of them decently-clad peasantry, men and women; but others, and these the majority, the most wretched looking creatures that it is possible to conceive'.[16] Many may have been attracted by Thomas

Sexton's reportage. Sexton was always careful to avoid a firm commitment; 'if' Thomas Nerney of Tulsk, County Sligo was blind he is now 'cured' is a typical phrase.[17] But he wrote nothing which supported a sceptical view. Others, especially the London press, describe events in a more pained way, the *Daily News*, for example, recorded instances of what it perceived to be hopes cruelly raised:

One delicate looking youth, seemingly in consumption, knelt in the mud for it was mud everywhere around the stone cross already alluded to. He did not move the whole time I was there, and it was obvious that the mode of relief which the poor lad was feeling was too likely to end in accelerating his descent into the grave.[18]

The same correspondent continues:

One distressing scene I witnessed, that of a father and mother leading a paralysed youth of about seventeen. They brought him up to the windows on which one of the broken images was placed. The mother took hold of it, kissed it and made the sign of the cross. The father followed her example. It was then handed to the son, but he seemed reluctant to do anything and then said querulously to the father 'What do you want me to do with it?' They succeeded, however, in reconciling him, and with a great effort he raised the broken image to his lips, kissed it and then replaced it on the window ledge, the boy anxiously watching them the while, and praying fervently, as did the parents.[19]

Then there is the case of a rather famous cure – that of a 'gentlewoman'. The *Weekly News* (dated 2 February) carried this report:

On Saturday last, a lady of property, Miss Bourke of Curraleigh, sister of Mr Walter Bourke JP and surgeon – Major Bourke, of the Indian Army, was driven into Knock from her residence a few miles distant, in her carriage. She had long been an invalid and was helpless as an infant for some time past. Four people – including Archdeacon Cavanagh – assisted her into the church. She prayed for a while before the altar and then to the amazement of the congregation walked out with only the assistance of her mother.

Miss Bourke of Curraleigh is listed in Archdeacon Cavanagh's Diary (Ad Majorem Dei Gloriam) as cured in January 1880. This claim is repeated, for example, in Coyne's biography of Cavanagh.[20] By the end of February, however, Father Cavanagh had to respond to an enquiry as to Miss Bourke: 'Ah poor thing she is dead since' Father Cavanagh added. 'When a portion of the cement off the wall is put into water, the water becomes muddy and there is a sediment in it: but when it stands for some time the water becomes beautifully clear, just like the purest spring water. Before Miss Bourke was brought to the chapel, some of this water was sent to her, and she drank it and she felt much better next day, but she is dead now, poor thing'.[21]

There was one rather striking development at the Knock shrine; many pilgrims in search of cures left their crutches behind at the church. As

Professor James Donnelly notes: 'By no means all of those who left their limb supports at Knock had been cured there; many pilgrims did so in anticipation of a cure or an act of faith that one would be forthcoming. But the common assumption was that the power of God in the intercession of the Mother, Our Lady of Knock, had rendered these supports perfectly worthless'.[22] There is, however, one source which is not mentioned by Professor Donnelly. It is Andrew Dunlop's memoir *Fifty Years of Irish Journalism* published in Dublin and London in 1911. Dunlop, was a Fellow and past Vice-President of the Institute of Journalists, who prided himself on his professionalism. In his memoirs he observes in passing: 'The "miracles" did not long survive the publication of my four articles'[23] but does not actually outline the content of these articles. At the time in 1911, the Knock phenomenon was at rather a discount in Ireland and Dunlop did not feel it necessary to expand any further. It is necessary, therefore, to turn to Dunlop's texts in the *Daily News* of London which appeared initially on 27 February 1880. Dunlop's account does not contradict that of Donnelly but it implies that some of the pilgrims also had a rather pragmatic insurance policy in place. Dunlop reported:

As I was leaving the hotel door this morning a man with a circular shaped foot, slightly lame, and having a stick in his hands, asked me for alms. He said he had come from the Kings county. I asked him what had brought him to Claremorris. He said, the same as has brought other people, to visit Knock. I said he did not appear to have been very successful. 'Oh' he said 'I left one stick there and brought one with me.

Another 'well dressed' man from Limerick, told Dunlop later that day:

I just said to my family before I left home that come what might I would not return with my crutch; and even if I should need one when I return I can get a new one; they don't cost so much.[24]

Much in all this naturally depended on the first cure; the *sine qua non* of later such events. As Professor Donnelly points out: 'The first cure was Delia Gordon, when a small particle of cement from the apparition gable of Knock Church was placed in her ear'.[25] Delia, in fact, on 2 February 1880 gave an interview to the sympathetic special correspondent of *The Nation* on the subject:

I met, soon after, in the enclosure, Mr P. J. Gordon, of Claremorris, his wife, and his daughter Delia, a pretty and most engaging child of twelve. She is now the picture of health and spirits. Up to August last she suffered intensely from attacks of violent pain in her left ear. 'Sometimes' said Mr Gordon, 'we had to get up in the night to get flannel, hot whiskey and different other remedies, to try and relieve her of the pain. This needed to happen perhaps, two or three times a week'. Mrs Gordon then told the story of the cure. 'On the Sunday next but one' she said, 'after the first of the apparitions, I brought Delia here to Knock with me to Mass. While we were in the church the pain attacked her so violently that she began to cry. I brought her out to the gable, and bade her pray. I took the pin of my shawl, picked out a little of the cement, made the sign of the cross on it and put it into her ear. At that moment a friend came up and spoke to me. She went away in a few minutes; I turned back and asked the child, "Well, Delia how is the pain?" She said, "It's gone, mamma." She never had a pain to trouble her since.' Delia lifting her timid eyes in reply to a question from me, confirmed her mother's account with a happy smile.[26]

It is an interesting story: it begs the question who precisely were Delia's resourceful parents, Mr and Mrs P. J. Gordon? In later life, Delia became the head cashier of a furniture store known as 'City of Paris' in Cincinnati.[27] It is said that she always retained the piece of cement taken from the gable wall by her mother. The unsentimental Andrew Dunlop could not resist one wry – some would say sly – comment on Delia's cure; one which after all opened the way for the arrival of a flood of pilgrims to Knock. Dunlop seems to have felt that this had positive business implications for P. J. Gordon, Delia's father. 'Hotelkeepers and carowners doing a brisk trade. I find in the *Weekly News* of the current week an advertisement announcing that Mr P. J. Gordon is prepared to provide cars to convey visitors from Claremorris to Knock'.[28]

But, of course, P. J. Gordon's significance as a local political figure by far outstripped his significance as a businessman. Gordon was one of the key Fenian Land Leaguers in Mayo;[29] a paid Land League organizer he was important enough to be named as 'traverser' alongside Parnell at the abortive state trial of Land League leaders which collapsed on 25 January 1881 when the jury failed to agree.[30] P. J. Gordon was also considered by the local police to be the figure behind several murders of those opposed to the Land League and he was eventually imprisoned for intimation.[31] It is not difficult to see why, when one looks at Gordon's platform rhetoric. For example, on 20 June 1880, P. J. Gordon said at Shrule, County Mayo:

It is better for you to lose your blood as Allen, Larkin and O'Brien did and we are determined to do the same . . . I repeat the name of Allen, Larkin and O'Brien. They have walked to the scaffold and the last prayer they uttered from their lips was 'God save Ireland'. Pass them (landgrabbers) by with scorn, and I will tell you, my people, that like Castlereagh when he sold his country to the Government, he may go and buy a razor and cut his throat. If they are treated with contempt, they will come on their bended knees and ask forgiveness of their country. But, I say, don't forgive them. They have sold their nationality and away with them.[31]

Even by Land League standards, P. J. Gordon was an astonishingly brazen public figure: on another occasion he publicly approved, for example, of the murder of Lord Mountnorres.[32] The Shrule speech was given nine days before the murder in Ballinrobe of David Feerick, a land agent: Shrule is ten or twelve miles from Ballinrobe. A few days later P. J. Gordon referred to the reaction of the authorities to the death of Feerick:

I will sketch over the attempt at Ballinrobe. They have run over to Claremorris and took one man from amongst us. But they wanted to have some bird in the nest. They knew he had nothing to do with the murder . . . The police went as far as Queenstown, and arrested . . . men on their way to America. I stole away five of them and before a week elapses the other two will be away too. If there was a crime committed against this man, let them find out the guilty party, and the guilty party is his own heart. He has evicted a poor widow and her orphans and left them to starve.[33]

This is strong stuff – an impudent suggestion that the murdered man had committed suicide. Not surprisingly the local police were unimpressed. In fact, the man they arrested was 'a notoriously bad character', T. J. Quinn, (brother of J. P. Quinn, the Land League Secretary) a close friend of Gordon's, who was also later interned alongside Gordon under the Protection of Person and Property Act on 10 March 1881. It is thanks to a later letter of T. J. Quinn's to William O'Brien, that we know that Mrs P. J. Gordon embroidered the original 'Land for the People' banner displayed at the inaugural Land League meeting at Irishtown.[34]

Mr and Mrs Gordon were clearly an interesting couple and they can not be excused of any lack of initiative. Later following the foundation of the Ladies Land League, Mrs Gordon took over the duties of Mrs Pat Sheridan because of the latter's alcoholism, establishing a close link with Sheridan, one of the most celebrated Land League militants. The Gordons lived in Claremorris but did not normally attend mass at Knock but they decided to do so on the second Sunday after the apparition. Lack of knowledge probably explains Father Cavanagh's claim in his diary of cures that Delia 'had been stone deaf and for years used deaf and dumb alphabet' – it is certainly not a claim made by Delia's parents in any of their interviews with journalists. Nevertheless, with Delia's cure, an entirely new relationship opens up between the Archdeacon and secret societies. It is not simply that all threats were dropped. According to Coyne, Father Cavanagh, one of the leading anti Land-League priests in Mayo, was transformed into a kind of patron saint of those being sought by the authorities for involvement in acts of agrarian violence. As Coyne puts it on 'many occasions':

Young men, on the run, hastened to the Archdeacon late at night seeking Confession and the Sacraments. These young men on their way, afoot, via Cobh to America frequently took in Knock on the route, asking Our Lady's blessing and protection on a hazardous journey.

Writing home some time ago one of them related how one night, he with others called at the Archdeacon's house. It was necessary to travel by dark because they were marked down for arrest under the Coercion Act dealing with the land agitation.

They knocked at the house, and although there was no one resident there, except the Archdeacon, the door was opened by a stranger who appeared to know of their mission without an explanation.

They were told the priest had a strenuous day and was resting for the night and were asked to return early next morning when he would hear their confessions and give them Holy Communion. Next morning they had an interview with Archdeacon Cavanagh and told them of their experience in his cottage; of the peace and holy joy that filled them while the stranger was speaking and giving them directions as regards their journey etc. The Archdeacon asked them not to speak of this until after his death and they faithfully kept that promise.

It was freely believed that the stranger was some heavenly visitor; an event that people accepted as quite a common happening at the Archdeacon's house.[35]

The events at Knock in 1876 bear a marked resemblance to those of Marpingen in 1876; on 3 July 1876 some girls from the Saarland village of Marpingen saw an image of the Virgin Mary.[36] Within a week, tens of thousands of pilgrims were pouring into this backwoods village, to pray and seek miraculous cures by drinking the sacred water 'of the spring where the images had appeared'. Both events occurred at moments of intense crisis for the communities involved; the Kulturkampf in Germany and the Land League in Ireland.

There are marked similarities between the two priests. Both were intense Marians – from his student days Bartholomew Cavanagh was known to practise special devotion to the Mother of God,[37] whilst Jacob Neureuter, although rather more intellectual than Cavanagh, showed an intense devotion to the Virgin Mary.[38] Both were told by their housekeepers of the respective apparition;[39] both were initially sceptical. Both later became convinced believers; in this, they followed the earlier pattern established by Father Peyremale at Lourdes. Like Neureuter, Cavanagh was not at the start an 'instigator'[40] but in numerous ways he lent legitimacy to the apparition. Cavanagh indeed convinced himself later that he had seen apparitions. The Catholic church authorities in both countries were rather cautious in their reaction. The similarities should not be pushed too far – young girls play the key role in the Marpingen vision whilst it is older women and some men who are involved in Knock. The state in Germany responded in a heavy-handed way whilst the UK state was largely indifferent. But there is one absolutely central lesson to be learnt from both cases; it is, as David Blackbourn notes, 'the power of religion in nineteenth century Europe, something that still receives too little attention in general textbooks on the period'.[41] Professor Blackbourn refers to a 'sort of popular religion that surfaced at Marpingen, where orthodox faith mingled with animistic and quasi-magical folk beliefs'.[42] Professor Donnelly makes precisely the same point about Knock. It is certainly the case that any history which does not pay attention to these factors is an impoverished one. Sheridan Gilley was right to argue at the time of the centenary of Knock that to do so is to give us history with 'the passion left out and that leaves out half of Irish history'[43] though it might be added that if it was a vision to the dispossessed, it was also a vision to the Catholic gentry,[44] strong or respectable peasantry as well as Fenian opportunists and local small businessmen – categories which sometimes overlapped. But how does it affect our conceptualization of the agrarian crisis? It certainly makes it more difficult to see the land war as above all an anti-millenarian modernizing phenomenon.[45] It is clear too that despite the League's initial appeal to a significant section of the protestant tenantry in the north[46] that it was easier to marginalize religious passions by rhetoric – as in the original New Departure protocols – than it was to do so in practice.

It is evident too that it was not only mainstream constitutional nationalists who supported and boosted the Knock phenomenon – as Professor Donnelly has already shown – but that the revolutionaries were also deeply involved in the same project. Indeed, their skill in appropriating it is all the more remarkable, given Archdeacon Cavanagh's profound original hostility to their objectives. Cavanagh himself became integrated in a sense within the revolutionary project. There is no sense in which, as some have fondly imagined – a radical secular republican project stood outside of, and opposed to, a more mainstream Catholic nationalist project.

Indeed, as Andrew Dunlop indicates, no Protestants in the Knock locality believed in the authenticity of the original apparition of August 1879 – but none dared say so. This is more likely to be due to the pressures operated by men like Gordon than the warm-hearted and peace loving Archdeacon Cavanagh. This did not, of course, prevent a tradition of rather coarse protestant sneering about these events from a safe distance; for example, the satirical passages in *Tenant Right in Tipperary; Being Humourous Letters from Tague O'Flannigan to Mike Collins.*

Teddy M'Ginn had a short leg and a shorter one; but before going to Knock, he did six weeks' penance and said any quantity of 'Hail Mary's'; and when he arrived he was so pure and easily performed on that in twenty-four hours the short leg was four inches longer than the other, and he had to be carried out of the locality before he could stop the growth. Dan Doran has been bald-headed for twenty years. You may know he's not troubled with much hair, for his wife says he has combed his head with a towel ever since she knew him. Well, he just went round the chapel twice on his knees, and had his head rubbed with a holy spittle by Father Tom, and the next morning he had to tie up the hair with a rope before he could get his trousers on. And it's reported he has to cut it twice a day to keep it from blinding him; but it's not only the Christians that's getting the benefit; the brute beasts are coming in for a share. A lazy lump of a heretic came through the country last week with a dancing bear, and he happened to tie the poor creature up to the rails of the chapel; and when he came back to take it away, he found it on its knees, a completely altered beast, and ever since it has refused to dance for the amusement of the vulgar. And no matter where it's up at night, the creature is sure to be on its knees at the chapel in the morning, groaning responses to Father Cavanagh like a trained priest. Now, dear Mike, although we have a deal of trouble with the Land Question, and things are getting worse every day, if the Land League would just give over the whole case to the church, there's as much miraculous power going waste as would settle the matter while you would wink. And nothing but a miracle can settle it, for our boys have determined to pay no rint, and when convenient, to shoot the landlords; and the landlords are determined to collect the rints and stay where bullets will not catch them. Now, can anything short of a miracle of the very first order satisfy both? – and will it not take a miracle to please landlords with tenants that pay no rints? And it will take another – aye, and a thumper too – to enable the tenants to avoid paying rints and make an honest living by shooting landlords. Indeed, some people say one miracle would settle the whole question if Mr Parnell would submit himself to the Church and have a small miracle performed on himself – that of infusing into him a little common sense, patriotism, and dacency.[47]

This is a ferocious burlesque and in a rather brutal way does outline the differences between two world-views. It makes it clear in a perverse way that for Unionists too there was a connection between the events at Knock and the revolutionary aims of the Land League movement. The group of neo-Fenian revolutionaries – amongst whom P. J. Gordon was to be a key figure – disintegrated after the Phoenix Park murders of Thomas Burke and Lord Frederick Cavandish. Key figures like Thomas Brennan, T. J. Quinn, Patrick Egan, and P. J. Sheridan fled to America; it appears that such a flight was in part necessitated by the need to protect Parnellism from any contamination through any association whatever with the Phoenix Park murders, the most traumatic political assassinations in nineteenth-century British political history. Yet it can be said that some of the links between Parnellism and crime were also links between Parnellism and the miracle cures at Knock in 1879/80; this is so whether we can consider the case of the revolutionary agrarian Mr and Mrs P. J. Gordon and the cure of their daughter, Delia, or the sad failure of efficacy in the case of Miss Bourke, sister of Colonel Bourke, Catholic landlord later to be assassinated by the Land League in April 1882 – a rather 'curious coincidence' indeed.[48] The story of Knock is no simple sense a contrast to the conflicts of the land war; indeed, 'Knock' seems to replay them in a particularly intimate way.

NOTES

1 C. C. O'Brien, *Ancestral Voices* (Dublin, 1994); P. Maume, *D. P. Moran* (Dublin, 1995). I am much indebted to Dr Maume for comments on this essay.
2 Michael Ó Cuinneagain, *Partition from Michael Collins to Bobby Sands* (Tantallon: Donegal Town, 1986).

3 P. Bew, *Land and the National Question in Ireland, 1858–82* (Dublin and Atlantic Highlands NJ, 1978) p. 49. See P. Bew, *C. S. Parnell* (Dublin, 1980), for Parnell's rather different priorities.

4 Donald E. Jordan, *Land and Popular Politics in Ireland: County Mayo from the Plantation to the Land War* (Cambridge, 1994), p. 219.

5 Paul Bew, 'The Nature of Irish Political Biography' in J. Noonan ed., *Biography and Autobiography: Essays on Irish and Canadian History and Literature* (Ottawa, 1994) pp. 19–27.

6 M. Davitt, *Fall of Feudalism* (New York, 1904), p. 125.

7 An active Fenian leader and bitter anticlerical, see Gerard Moran, *A Radical Priest in Mayo* (Dublin, 1994), p. 147.

8 Donald E. Jordan, *op. cit.*, p. 224.

9 Liam Ua Cathain (William D Coyne), *Venerable Archdeacon Cavanagh* (Dublin, 1953) pp. 72–3.

10 Coyne, *ibid.*

11 Michael Walsh, *op. cit.*, pp. 6–7.

12 Eugene Hynes, 'Why Knock? Why 1879? A Sociology of Supernatural Apparition'. Paper read to ACIS Conference, Belfast 1995.

13 Coyne, *op. cit.*

14 T. P. O'Connor, *Memoirs of an Old Parliamentarian* (London, 1929) vol. 1, p. 157.

15 D. W. R. Bahlman ed., *The Diary of Sir Edward Hamilton 1885–1906* (Hull, 1993) 6 July 1893, p. 206.

16 *Daily News*, (London), 27 February 1880.

17 *Weekly News*, (Dublin), 2 February 1880.

18 *Daily News*, 27 February 1880.

19 'The Alleged Miracles in Ireland', *Daily News*, 28 February 1880.

20 Coyne, *op. cit.*, p. 95.

21 *Daily News*, 1 March 1880.

22 Donnelly, *op. cit.*, p. 80.

23 A. Dunlop, *Fifty Years of Irish Journalism* (Dublin, London, 1911), p. 240.

24 *Daily News*, 28 February 1880.

25 Donnelly, *op. cit.*

26 The special correspondent of the *Nation* reprinted in *The Galway Vindicator and Connaught Advertiser*, 7 February 1880.

27 Coyne, *op. cit.*, p. 95.

28 *Daily News*, 2 March 1880.

29 P. Maume, 'Parnell and the IRB Oath', in *Irish Historical Studies*, vol. XXXIX, no. 115, 1995, p. 366.

30 T. W. Moody, *Davitt and Irish Revolution 1846–82* (Oxford, 1981) p. 361, 427–8.

31 Sir Henry James, *The Work of the Irish League, The Speech: replying in the Parnell Commission Inquiry* (London, 1890), p. 242.

32. James, *op. cit.*, p. 253.

33 James, *op. cit.*, p. 243.

34 Maume, *op. cit.*

35 Coyne, *op. cit.*, pp. 109–10.

36 For a superb treatment, see David Blackbourn, *The Marpingen Visions: Rationalism, Religion and the Rise of Modern Germany* (Oxford, 1993). In his brief reference to Knock, Professor Blackbourn cites the view of some that pellagra played a role by inducing hallucinatory symptoms; but it is worth noting Dr George Sigerson's analysis in his *Final Report for the Mansion House Relief Committee on Destitution – Diseases in the West* (p. 166, n 1) Dublin 1881, which states that only 'one case of an adult near Killalla presented some symptoms which resembled those of the first stage of the pellagra.' This

in the course of a wide survey but Sigerson did add: 'The subject is one that requires continued observation'. Professor Donnelly says maize was not given out in Mayo until *after* the apparition, and that the visionaries' social status was mostly too high for them to have to rely on famine relief.

37 Coyne, *op. cit.,* p. 21.
38 Blackbourn, *Marpingen*, p. 89.
39 *Ibid*, p. 217; *Weekly News*, 14 February 1880.
40 Even the sceptical Dunlop fully accepted this, unlike later polemicists such as Michael McCarthy, *Priests and People in Ireland* (Dublin, 1902) p. 228.
41 Blackbourn, *op, cit.*, p. 406.
42 *Ibid.*
43 'The background to Knock', *The Tablet*, 18 September 1979.
44 As Dunlop notes *Fifty Years*, p. 240–1.
45 J. Lee, *The Modernisation of Irish Society, 1848–1918* (Dublin 1973) p. 63.
46 Paul Bew and Frank Wright, 'The Agrarian Opposition in Ulster 1848–87' in S. Clark and J. Donnelly eds. *Irish Peasants* (Madison, 1983).
47 *Tenant Right in Tipperary: Being Humourous Letters from Tague O'Flannigan, Ballinamuck, to Mike Collins, Renfrewshire, entered at Stationers' Hall,* (1910) p. 107–8. This was first published in 1881 as a Tory attack on Gladstone's land legislation.
48 Dunlop, *Fifty Years*, p. 240–1. Perhaps even more of a coincidence than Dunlop realized, P.J. Gordon (National Archives: Irish Crime Records 1881–2, vol. 1, p. 40) was charged in July 1881 at the Castlebar Crown Court that 'he did encourage others to kill Walter Bourke' (*Connaught Telegraph*, 23 July 1881). One final interesting coincidence – Dr Zimmer, Professor of Celtic Languages at the University of Berlin, was present both at Marpingen and Knock (*Sinn Féin*, 23 November 1907).

9 Gender and the Sexual Politics of Pilgrimage to Lourdes

Ruth Harris

The idea of a national pilgrimage to Lourdes only took shape in the aftermath of defeat and civil war in 1870–71, as part of an attempt to encapsulate and channel a mood of national soul-searching. This spiritual enterprise was inseparable from the wider political attempt to restore the Bourbon Monarchy,[1] release the Pope from his Vatican prison and re-establish the alliance between throne and altar.[2] Bernadette Soubirous's apparitions had occurred in 1858 and, while they transformed the grotto into an important Marian shrine, pilgrimage to Lourdes throughout the 1860s lacked any coherent organization.[3] Everything commonly associated in the popular imagination – the removal of the stretchers from the famous white trains, the crippled and dying escorted to the grotto by nuns and lay helpers, the massive eucharistic processions – had not yet evolved. Indeed, it was only in the 1870s that Lourdes triumphed over other sanctuaries, and its special vocation as the pilgrimage of the sick emerged later still at the very end of the decade.

In this paper, I want to examine the way the intimate, the institutional and the spiritual were all linked in this story. This investigation will involve an understanding of gender relations and the 'spiritual politics' behind the movement, a term which I will use to designate the way organizers of national pilgrimage saw an indissoluble bond between their spiritual aspirations and political vision. Moreover, I will analyse how these conjunctions impinged on the rituals surrounding bodily suffering and healing, as well as the spiritual dynamics which underpinned Marian devotion.

But before attacking these broader themes, I must begin by querying the so-called 'feminization of religion' in the nineteenth century, a thesis crucial towards understanding not only changing church structures and devotional practices, but also providing the interpretative schema which has formed our conception of religion in the 'age of secularization'. The factual basis for this argument is epitomized by Charles Langlois's compendious work on women religious who, by 1880, comprised three-fifths of Church personnel and supplied an army of welfare and educational workers,[4] confirming a long-term trend that really began with the seventeenth century.[5] In essence, by the end of the nineteenth century, the Catholic Church in France was a women's institution, despite the continued leadership of male prelates and spiritual directors.

The second element in this thesis focuses on devotional shifts: the explosion of the Cult of the Virgin, and the apparent increase in the 'maudlin', 'meretricious' and 'emotive' practices such as the cult of the Sacred Heart, the adoration of the Infant Jesus, the multiplication of societies of the Children of Mary. This aspect has led historians to make more controversial suggestions, which are often unconsciously infused by the clichés of Republican anti-clericalism, and concentrate on women's rejection of the principles of the Revolution.[6] Links are made between the defensive stance of Catholicism and the multitude of seemingly ill-educated, often superstitious, and above all 'anti-modern' women who, through their alliances with priests, posed an obstacle to enlightenment and progress.[7] In this narrative, the priests are seductive devils and the women victims of an obscurantism which led them away from the central currents of Republicanism, positivism and the nation state which offered true freedom and emancipation.[8] The thesis of the 'feminization of religion', apparently designed to bring women's beliefs back onto the historical stage has, therefore, strangely had the opposite effect: women are once again seen as merely manipulated, their spiritual concerns and political aspirations condemned as outmoded relics awaiting final extermination.

I will not argue against the 'feminization of religion' either in its institutional or devotional guise; rather, I wish to reassess it in such a way as to question the prejudicial and anti-feminist overtones which infuse it. Pilgrimage to Lourdes was an enterprise jointly imagined by priests and women, and its distinguishing feature – the care of the sick and dying – was the brainchild of the female participants. In essence, the mood of national repentance was enough to launch the movement, but in itself was insufficient to keep it going; rather the rituals surrounding the sick and their care made Lourdes unique, conferred its powers of endurance and turned it into a model to be emulated.

I will begin by examining the relations between priests and women and argue that Jules Michelet was half-right, albeit for the wrong reasons, and that his anti-clerical stereotypes require re-examination. In his *Le Prêtre, la femme et la famille* (1845), the republican historian and ideologue painted a fantastic and enduring portrait of the interaction between spiritual directors and unsuspecting women, the sensual nature of which increased the latter's religious fervour and often destroyed conjugal intimacy. In Michelet's view, women were often their husbands' enemies as much as they were enemies of republican enlightenment. Although the documents cannot confirm whether or not the women of Notre-Dame de Salut were estranged from their spouses, I will be able to show how women's feelings towards priests *were* passionate, and that these emotions promoted the success of the pilgrimage movement. However, women were hardly victims, but rather willing agents who deserted the

Republic for warmly-felt reasons, and their special connection to the Church
and its ministers was often central for defining their identity. Moreover, I will
suggest that for all its limitations, the church offered these women at least as
many, if not greater, outlets for their energies than did the modern, secular
republic which is so often seen as the only credible agent of emancipation.

Next, I will examine the gendered division of labour which developed
within the mature pilgrimage movement. At Lourdes, new rituals of devotion and care expressed a certain vision of the hoped-for society. In this
highly choreographed – if often frenetic – week, men, women and children
took on their roles in an effort to be chivalrous, nurturing, or directed
according to their place in the pre-ordained hierarchy. Everyone took up
various positions *vis-à-vis* the diseased bodies under their care, often crossing
boundaries of human contact which usually underpinned social and gender
relations. In this unusual and emotive context, greater subordination
conferred greater power, and it is this paradox which I will explore.

Finally, I will examine the rituals and beliefs that were key to the spirituality
of the miraculous at Lourdes. The massive eucharistic processions introduced
by priests to sacramentalize proceedings forty years after the apparitions appear
to suggest the imposition of an aggressive Christocentrism designed to balance
Marian fervour. Once again, appearances deceive. I will suggest that the
spirituality of Lourdes, while highly inflected by considerations of gender and
hierarchy, did not proceed along simple and predictable lines.

To understand the national pilgrimage, we must know better the men and
women who animated the movement. The key figures were the Assumptionists, a new order founded in the 1840s by the charismatic Père d'Alzon.
A Catholic 'homme de combat', d'Alzon was shaped by his upbringing in
the Protestant Gard, his hatred of the Camisard schismatics only matched
by his detestation of the other evils of revolution and materialism.[9] His
spirituality was rigorous and explicitly militant, a 'virile' Catholicism manifested not only in the way he trained the boys at his collège in Nîmes and
clothed them in the uniforms of the papal Zouaves,[10] but also in the rigour
of the physical and spiritual exercises that he demanded from his novices. He
was an eloquent and sophisticated mouthpiece for many of the major theological and devotional shifts of the nineteenth century, a fervent supporter of
Marian and eucharistic devotion as well as a champion of papal infallibility.[11]

D'Alzon was a conservative legitimist who believed absolutely in the cause
of the counter-revolution. His hatred of the principles of 1789, however, did
not mean that he endorsed a return to the *ancien régime*. While he and the
Assumptionists revelled in the iconography and romantic legacy of the middle
ages, D'Alzon saw himself as a Christian progressive. Mixing the doctrines of
de Maistre, de Bonald and the radical Lammenais, he refused to countenance

the subordination of spiritual to temporal authority and set his face against the secularizing desire to privatize religion.[12] What he envisaged was a hierarchical society based on tradition in which the ligatures of social cohesion were strengthened by mutual obligations and duties. The vision of moral order, however, was humanized by his belief in the equality of all before God, an aspect which gained full expression in the national pilgrimage to Lourdes. D'Alzon and his disciples were ardent proponents of Christian charity, and increasingly of social-catholic measures. For the Assumptionists, the succession of disasters wrought by republican experimentation was an obvious divine sign of the iniquities of secularism and materialism. D'Alzon hoped once again to found a harmonious society that was divinely sanctioned and in which religion recovered its pre-eminent role in rituals of authority and power.

In this way, he intended to defend the *droits de Dieu* against the *droits de l'homme,* and urged the faithful to assemble in the thousands to fight militantly against liberalism and socialism.[13] Pilgrimage was important in this programme because it manifested *public* repentance. While his left-wing opponents sought to establish their political and cultural legitimacy through a range of symbols and rituals – from Marianne to Bastille Day[14] – d'Alzon and the Assumptionists used similar methods and focused on prayer, procession, and Marian adoration. They were just as concerned with the mobilization of crowds in the public arena, and sought to conquer that domain through the mass media, the train lines, and the public square.[15]

The young men who translated his ideas into practice hailed from all ranks, from pious peasant stock and Catholic elite, directing the Assumption from their headquarters in the eighth arrondissement in Paris. There they established the network of charitable *œuvres* and the press empire which the Assumptionists controlled, with *La Croix,* the largest Catholic daily in France, the jewel in the media crown. The actual direction of their activities – which led to a precipitous expulsion from France in 1900 after years of anti-Dreyfusard activism – was not determined, however, until the galvanizing experience of the defeat and Commune. The two most important men, François Picard and Vincent de Paul Bailly,[16] lived with the indelible imprint of the personal and national humiliation which the war and the Commune produced. The Commune in particular, which made priests go out in disguise for fear of attack, left them bitter and enraged. They felt like martyrs and saw a terrifying re-living of the days of the Revolutionary Terror.

The letters they wrote as they fled for their lives define their enemies. Although the *gardes nationaux* threatened them with capture, they gave special attention to the working women of Paris, who were portrayed as ferocious harpies, willing to dispatch unpopular priests without ceremony.[17] They seemed almost to relish the tales of brutality, seeing in the anticlericalism of the Communards an almost lubricious desire to desecrate what was holy: 'At the seminary of St-Sulpice, three days ago everything was pillaged, the church ransacked, by the nocturnal orgies of women. They drank from sacred vessels, made sacrilegious processions, broke everything.'[18] Bailly saw such behaviour as epitomizing the moral collapse of society, and was particularly shocked by the 'frightful heroines of murder and arson'.[19]

This picture of feminine danger was contrasted with an equally idealized portrait of 'good', 'Christian' women who opposed the Commune and the Thiers government. In essence, Bailly believed that there was a constituency of women from 'le populaire' who were both deeply Christian and instinctively patriotic, and whose ideals matched their own.[20] In fact, the Assumptionists believed as much in 'the people' as their leftist counterparts, and were convinced that they would lead them to a new and better society in the aftermath of the destruction. Consequently, a major part of their programme particularly targeted women and envisaged their recruitment in a white army to counter the 'scarlet' women with 'red' politics.

Their view of Commune was hardly unique, nor was their abhorrence of the heinous acts of the *pétroleuses*.[21] Their rhetoric differed only in its explicit reference to religious themes and metaphors of witchcraft and Satanism. The high level of contamination, they argued, required a correspondingly extreme purification. Constant reference to the blood of massacred priests resonated with allusions to the martyrs of the past. In fact, red became part of the symbolism, with the fiery destructiveness of the communist reds contrasted repeatedly with the red blood of redemption. In this eschatology, different kinds of women were seen as struggling for two different visions of society. Picard made the juxtaposition explicitly to the ladies of high society whom he hoped to enrol in his Catholic army:

Under the Commune, secret societies launched the *petroleuses* onto Paris . . . [he then went on] Women in a high places due to their social position, their fortune and their rank and sometimes by their name or birth . . . wish to form a league of devotedly Catholic women, who will affirm their faith through prayer and works, and who will wave valiantly the flag of the supernatural.[22]

Stalwart, pious and feminine, the leading organization for this counter-revolutionary movement became Notre-Dame de Salut, and its most public and prominent expression was pilgrimage. The mention of the flag once again demonstrates the Assumptionists' vision of the movement as a standard which rallied the faithful against the red hordes.

Picard and Bailly launched their women's organization with the whole-hearted support of some of the greatest aristocratic ladies in France.[23] The period immediately after the Commune brought in waves of female sup-porters, and the Assumptionists saw Notre-Dame de Salut as a national umbrella organization dedicated to fund-raising, charity and prayer. As the spiritual directors of the group, the priests sought to remind the women constantly of the difference between their activities and those of, for example, the *Comité Catholique des hommes*, a group which united legitimists – especially deputies – against the Republicans. Notre-Dame de Salut was meant to be apolitical as befitted a woman's organization.[24] But such a limiting prescription went against the tenor of d'Alzon's thought, which attempted to break down the division between the spiritual and temporal arenas. For the women inspired by his message no such division could be maintained, and despite their warnings, the priests were ambivalent about women's role. Along with charity came the desire to moralize the workers, to emulate Mary in forming a new generation of Catholic apprentices.[25] Such ambitions self-consciously sought a Catholic alternative to the exploitation of capitalism on the one hand and the seductions of revolutionary doctrines on the other. Even prayer became highly politicized in 1872 when the National Assembly, urged along by its legitimist deputies, voted for obligatory public prayers the Sunday before the return of the Chamber. Notre-Dame de Salut transformed this token proposal into a massive public vigil, with a fast and nation-wide novena anticipating the symbolic show in the capital.[26] The movement was a success, and was an early demonstration of the ability of these women to organize effectively on a national scale.

While the president of Notre-Dame de Salut was the venerable Madame de la Rochefoucauld, Duchesse D'Estissac, *née* Ségur, a woman of illustrious family and tremendous fortune,[27] the activists of the organization were either lesser aristocrats or pious women of good name and smaller resources. The biographical details are sketchy, although their personalities emerge vividly from their missives to the priests. These letters are fascinating, not least because they reveal clearly the complex web of spirituality, emotion and simple hard work that induced these women to devote themselves to what they clearly saw as a cause of overwhelming importance. Although not all the women involved enjoyed such intimacy, there were important examples in which the relationship between priests and the women of Notre-Dame de Salut generated erotic flirtations of the most intense kind, relationships which charged the imagination with fantasies of intimacy which could never be attained. Surrounded by an aura of voluntary labour and godly inspiration, emotion soared, and what would have been unseemly if not scandalous in any other context became appropriate and was even encouraged.

For example, Mme Laforest – the budding secretary of the organization – found her faith and her vocation simultaneously through Père Picard's influence. She was hopelessly in love: 'Why is it that I avoid the theatre and visits as much as possible (even too much, perhaps)? It is because you have changed everything. . .'.[28] She laboured like a slave and dedicated the work to him: 'Each time you leave, Father, it seems that I lose everything . . .

Father, can you tell me you are pleased with me? And also what displeases you? My intention is to write to you as a secretary, not as a child, but with you it is so difficult for me to be reasonable.'[29] Her passion for Picard was intimately tied up with the trying exactions of a new piety. Moments of observance were mixed with relapses, but by 1874 she could write to him with pride: 'But it must be admitted that to conquer me you had to use the most terrible means; you almost killed me.'[30] She was jealous and did not seek to hide it, showing her envy of a Mme de Damas in Dijon who was going to take care of him during one of his frequent illnesses. She went so far as to suggest that people might be more devoted to him than to the service of God: 'It is our Lord that we must serve, yes, but can't you admit, for some pious souls, that their dedication to the service of God can be doubled by the confidence they have in his minister?'[31]

An equally avid correspondent was Mme Dumont, who directed her letters to Vincent de Paul Bailly. If Mme Laforest's relationship to Picard was, above all, characterized by adoration, in which she was the patronized 'enfant' of a older and wiser man, Mme Dumont had a greater sense of her rights and expectations. She frequently hectored Bailly, and the tone here was much more of a disgruntled wife looking for acknowledgement and approbation from a neglectful husband. Repeatedly she asked him to ask her counsel: 'When you have some worry about the *œuvre,* speak about it with me; I don't think there is anyone whose judgement and clarity is as good as mine.'[32] But the relationship was highly ambivalent, and she revealed rather more when she contrasted her own lay direction of 'men who are very religious but too luke-warm', with Bailly's negligent approach regarding her. With her men she was pleased 'to chain their feet and ankles to the chariot of [her] imaginary saintliness'.[33] She seemed here to desire Bailly's similarly strong focus on herself. In any case the imagery of bondage which she used showed again a sexualized fantasy of desire only half-hidden by religious language.

These relationships thus do seem to confirm the most phantasmagoric of Michelet's fears: women confide in priests not husbands, and reveal their emotional and spiritual turmoil to men who, in turn, use their influence to channel their considerable energies towards serving the needs of the church and against the republican vision of society. The tone of the letters – in which Mme Dumont went so far as to fantasize about dosing Mme Laforest with deadly nightshade – reveals the ultimate fantasy, the murder of a competitor. In psychological terms, the struggle suggested an imaginary triangle of intense sibling rivalry or a legitimate wife fending off the advances or an unworthy opponent in the battle for the favours of an elusive father or husband. Moreover, it suggests a pettiness and subordination so corrupt and demeaning that it seems to justify the Republicans' preoccupation with excluding Catholic women from the body politic. A second glance, however, indicates a more complicated picture. The feelings of the men who were the objects of this intensity are harder to know, for their letters in reply were not always safeguarded by the archives. Letters to brother priests, however, show a clear ambivalence: pleasure in the presence of active, passionate women and the shared sense of mutual idealism,[34] as well as intense exasperation when the competition between them undermined the smooth functioning of the organization.[35]

There was also a titillating side to their spiritual direction. Women were not merely manipulated by the priests; the priests themselves were as bound up in the erotic fantasy world. D'Alzon, for example, was something of a legend for the volume of his correspondence with such women, and in his letters he seems entirely unaware of the ambiguity of his messages. To one of his virginal charges, he wrote:

Your little note, short though it is, my dear Valentine, gave me great joy. I have many things to tell you, and to write you about them on your return from Lourdes seemed perfect. Our Lord wants you closer to him every day. There is great delicacy in your soul, which he wishes to penetrate entirely. You have to open up to him, and, when you are open, you have to open still further, because our Lord is insatiable in his desire for your love and most intimate sacrifices . . .[36]

Of course, d'Alzon had no monopoly over the expression of divine love in eroticized terms, as this was famously an area of mystical writing in which medieval and early-modern women specialized.[37] What is jarring here is his use of such language to a young woman whose 'penetration' must necessarily come through his spiritual direction. The letter reveals more than the flowery language of epistolary romanticism; it conjures up his own unacknowledged sexual fantasies.

I think that such missives reveal the treacherous unconscious territory both women and priests entered. To characterize their interaction only in negative terms, however, misses other important dimensions which Michelet did not appreciate. Spiritual direction gave women a chance to talk about their inner quest and religious preoccupations and enabled them to confront issues which the dry diet of secular thought proscribed. In these encounters they also acted out and played with many different imaginary roles, becoming needy children, querulous mistresses and – in other letters that I cannot explore here – high-society patronesses reduced to the lowest state of spiritual abnegation.[38] Nor were their relations static. The early letters of Mme Laforest show an almost infantile regression and naked adoration, but also present her basking in the security and love which Picard offered. A later letter of 1884 telling him of her imminent move to a new home with her husband, however, reveals her as calm and mature with her spiritual director.[39] In sum, the relationship had withstood the intense transference and had now settled into an adult exchange. Mme Laforest 'grew up' within the context of her association with Picard, and its positive role in her life should not be dismissed.

Finally, such women were released momentarily from their 'real' roles as daughters, wives and mothers, finding another in an awkward, but none the less rewarding discipleship. While they were clearly the subordinate partner in the relationship, these women pressed for their vision of a regenerated France through Christian solidarity and to a considerable extent made an impact. It may perhaps be labouring the point, but it is difficult to think of any sphere in the parallel universe of the republic where women had such constant, institutionalized, influence. In sum, they were subordinate but still powerful, their authority in fact largely deriving from the moral stature which came from the secondary, servicing role they played. For example, Mme Laforest was an assiduous secretary who went on the earliest pilgrimages to Lourdes, and was ever after an enthusiastic advocate of the shrine. She was also an assiduous fund raiser – indeed, her colleagues were distressed by the way she dropped the names of the aristocracy to urge greater generosity, a habit which they condemned as both vulgar and out of keeping with Notre-Dame de Salut's image. Nor was she without courage; she made her way into the schools in the working-class *faubourgs*, trying to establish a regime of prayer among the poor.[40]

Mme Dumont had a larger sense than her colleague of the charitable scope and political agenda of Notre-Dame de Salut. She was, for example, actively engaged in the administrative systems designed to bring all of Catholic France into its orbit and was a constructive critic who questioned the sensationalist and populist tone employed in *Le Pèlerin*, the weekly journal associated with the *œuvre*.[41] Finally, like d'Alzon yet again, she was a tireless advocate of the need to evangelise the poor. When she felt that Notre-Dame de Salut was *too* engaged in contemporary struggles and propaganda, she said so, and repeatedly returned to the long-term charitable project of the *œuvre*. Moreover, she understood the special role of women in the struggle, and felt no compunction in reminding Bailly of their importance.[42]

This frenetic pace of activity and emotional involvement were integral to the two-fold project of the early 1870s which, as suggested, sought to unite the rechristianization of France with the restoration of the Bourbon monarchy. The history of the National Pilgrimage, however, is particularly interesting because it only took on its special character after the *failure* of the legitimist agenda, first when the Comte de Chambord turned down the tricoleur in 1873 and later when most legitimist deputies lost their seats in 1876/7. The pilgrimage was launched by the disasters of 1870/1 but it only became institutionalized when hopes of more orthodox political advance dissolved. No longer in the mainstream of national politics, these men and women did not give up their convictions but rather elaborated a form of 'spiritual politics', which channelled their energies and rallied the faithful. In sum, it was the 'feminine' side of the movement, with its emphasis on the tending of the sick, which culminated in the week of national pilgrimage once a year. This goal could not have been realized without the passionate interactions I have just described, which served as the micro-foundations for the larger spiritual politics which infused pilgrimage.

Until the turn of the century, going on national pilgrimage was always a religious enterprise charged with political overtones. Pilgrims protested about the Ferry Laws, secularism, freemasonry, Dreyfus and the crises surrounding the Separation of Church and State in 1901 and 1904.[43] Indeed, 1905 – the year of the separation – continued a campaign initiated in 1902 and 1904 to validate the cures at the grotto with episcopal commissions.[44] Pilgrims refused to celebrate Bastille Day and instead proposed the Assumption of the Virgin on August 15 as a more appropriate festival.[45] In sum, Republicans and Catholics continually fought on the symbolic terrain of the irrational, competing for political adherents in the age of the masses.

Above, all pilgrims celebrated the intimacy of the supernatural and the ubiquity of miracles in the age of positivism, the bodies of both sick and healthy pilgrims literally enacting resistance to the secularizing creed. The *malades* on their stretchers prayed with arms in crucifix position, imitating the passion (see figure 1);[46] helpers forgot to eat or sleep in their frenzy; and the leader of the National Pilgrimage, Père Picard, dramatically drank from the pools where the sick and dying were bathed, proclaiming the infected water to be most refreshing.[47] In the full flush of Pasteurianism, such a gesture attested to the power of faith over science. Such people were defiantly emotive and sentimental, modelling their devotions on highly-stylized conceptions of medieval, saintly mortification. In other words, both men and women practised an extravagant public piety which we now see as particularly characteristic of 'feminized religion'.

As suggested, the most 'feminine' aspect of all was the elevation of the care of the sick to be almost the defining characteristic of the pilgrimage movement. The Assumptionists had first tried the idea of national pilgrimage to Notre-Dame de la Salette in the Alps. But La Salette disappointed for several reasons: the visionaries changed their story and grew up to be drunks and hysterics; the mountain site made access difficult; and the radicalism of the Grenoblois made for an inauspicious political climate for the discharging of train passengers.[48] None of these difficulties arose at Lourdes, where Bernadette's behaviour was exemplary, the piety of locals estimable, and the site of the shrine – with the train link established at the end of the Second Empire – all contributing to its growth. But it was only after 1875 when around fifty *malades* joined the ranks that Picard realized that something novel and important was afoot. Prompted

Figure 1: 'Aspect de la grotte de Lourdes pendant les grands prières du 20 au 23 août.' Dessin de V. Urrabieta, *Le Pèlerin*, 4 September 1880

by the women of Notre-Dame de Salut, he increasingly came to see the spiritual and propagandistic possibilities of such a development.

While the elite women of Notre-Dame de Salut provided the funds, the Petites-Soeurs de l'Assomption, a sister order founded by Père Pernet, were the pioneers who tended the sick.[49] Devoted in their daily activities to helping the poor and sick in their homes, the Petites-Soeurs were able to penetrate working-class quarters, establishing missions in Leavallois-Peret and even in Belleville, and earning respect for their self-sacrifice. In calling on their help with the sick of Lourdes, Pernet was employing their virtues of humility, devotion and heroism, the last quality one of the leitmotifs of his direction, to the task of tending the sick during the difficult passage from station to train, and from the train to the hospitals and the grotto.[50] Their founder, Mère Marie de Jésus, came to Lourdes from the early 1870s to her death in 1883, and her *religieuses* continued this tradition long after her demise. They were devoted to the most impoverished and benighted, aiming to serve selflessly and to take nothing in return: 'in the person of the poor man who suffers on a miserable pallet, you see Jesus Christ, the divine leper'.[51] They were a familiar sight of humility and inspiration at Lourdes, dressed in a 'large black robe, a white cap and wimple, and for the novices, a black veil, the form of which recalls the *capulet* of Bernadette'.[52]

But the special role of neither group of women lasted long. While the devotion of the Petites Sœurs to the poor was legendary – even Zola acknowledged them unstintingly – both the direction of the pilgrimage and many of the charitable tasks were increasingly taken over by the new, but related, *Hospitalité de Notre Dame de Salut*. This organization, again dominated by men but serviced by women, transformed the character of the pilgrimage after its foundation in 1880. The idea for the Hospitalité came from aristocratic activists and its origins quickly became part of pilgrimage mythology: once, while observing the sick crying out in pain on the station platform at Lourdes, a group of men proposed to take them to the grotto. From then on they became, in Picard's words, the 'servants of the poor', and soon fashioned themselves after the crusading knights.[53] They were the latter-day Hospitaliers of St John, who helped the sick on their way to the holy places, and they presented themselves as chivalric, militant and manly in both their faith and politics.

The Assumptionists were thrilled by this army of new, male recruits. They were, it seemed, men of the right, many of legitimist and ultramontanist principles, and their annual pilgrimage to Lourdes increasingly became a means of re-consolidating the creed of opposition to the republic. Indeed, it seems that they became a haven for members and sympathizers of the Action Française, the ultra right-wing monarchist and integral-nationalist organization.[54] They became the brawn and the brains of the pilgrimage, in some areas displacing the Petites Sœurs. These relationships were represented in *Le Pèlerin* (See figure two).[55] On the left was a courtly, mature aristocratic man in top hat and elegant coat, holding a chair in which sat an inert *malade* clutching her rosary. On the other side she was accompanied by a Petite Sœur recognizable by her distinctive clothing. The three figures are presented in partnership, with the leadership of the man evidenced by his forthright gaze. Instead, the sick woman has her eyes towards heaven in a searching look of supplication and/or pain, while the Petite Sœur has eyes only for her charge, her face virtually invisible to us. Above the three figures are the three theological virtues – faith, hope and charity – each associated with the person they embody. Masculine faith is joined to the hope of cure and redemption, and in turn held by the charitable embrace of the nursing sister.

As the pilgrimage movement matured, the gendered division of labour became more evident. The ethos underpinning Notre-Dame de Salut – in which militant men directed and the women supported – was increasingly transposed onto the working life of the Hospitalité in a way which idealized gender relationships through a certain vision of the Christian family. While men were to excel at moving, carrying and organizing, the women were meant

Figure 2: 'Foi, Espérance, Charité.' Anon., *Le Pèlerin*, 13 août, 1881.

to feed, nurture and tend. Children were used as pages to bring messages to and from the grotto and hospitals, while the *jeunes filles* were only allowed to enter the wards if accompanied by their mothers, so horrible were the sights that they might behold. To protect their modesty, they were responsible for the refectories, preparing the food to feed the sick and the helpers.

In essence, heavy labour was men's province, while the more polluting jobs dealing with the waste products of the sick were by and large left to the *religieuses* and the *grandes dames*. There was a fundamental divide over who had close physical contact with the diseased bodies, only bridged in the bathing pools at the fountain's waters. Much was made of the astonishing sacrifice of the *grandes dames* who dirtied their hands and polluted their femininity with the sick. Certainly, this was no mere token gesture: while Lourdes today specializes in non-infectious neurological ailments – especially multiple sclerosis – the pilgrimages of the nineteenth century had a large proportion of infectious diseases, tubercular conditions and especially deforming lupus. Purulent abscesses were common in an age before antibiotics, and all who came to Lourdes were distressed by the often pustulent, decaying bodies which they saw there.

Much has been made by social anthropologists of the strangely liminal quality of such journeys.[56] Betwixt and between, the pilgrims make their way from home to the destination, losing all affiliations of class and status *en route*. Not only did individuals undergo initiatory religious experiences, they also experienced intense feelings of solidarity reinforced by the need to focus on the sick and leave other petty considerations aside. The ideal was indeed marred by the persistence of first-class carriages in the pilgrimage trains, and the occasional group of *révoltés* who escaped the pious ambience and human misery to picnic in the mountain countryside. On the whole, however, the pain of the *malades* of Lourdes did have the effect of turning the world upside down, albeit very temporarily. The sick and dying, usually relegated to the unseen margins of society, became the focus of attention. The attentive hands of the *grandes dames* astonished precisely because they were normally protected from such contamination. Women competed to show their heroism in the harrowing atmosphere of the trains, hospitals and pools. In sum, Lourdes made the disgusting elevating and brought the hidden into the open. The rich acted like servants, and servants were tended by the rich. In this way, women in particular heightened their moral and spiritual authority by revelling in an exaggerated version of their subordination, which in turn became the source of even greater admiration.

The paeans of praise to the society ladies could therefore be seen as part of the strangely carnivalesque world that the pilgrimage created. I would argue, however, that such an analysis would miscategorize the Lourdes experience. Carnival is about bodily excess and the celebration of disinhibition,[57] whereas the rituals at Lourdes were highly formalized, and the body's miseries wrapped in layers of spiritual cushioning. This is not to deny the centrality of the physical in the Lourdes pilgrimage, as participants – both the sick and the *hospitaliers* – bonded through the intense bodily experience of touch, consolation and care. Moreover the strong feeling of community generated by the religious and spiritual rites should not blind us to the exclusionist ethos on which the Lourdes pilgrimage was based. Under the Assumptionists, Christian collectivity was as much defined by its struggle against its enemies as by its positive attributes. *Le Pèlerin* not only illustrated miraculous cures, but regularly and often brutally caricatured Jews, Freemasons and Republicans, all of whom were outside the perceived spiritual circle of grace inhabited by *malades,* ladies and gentlemen alike.

Finally, the gendered division of labour in Notre-Dame de Salut, the Hospitalité and in the management of pilgrimage itself, was in some sense present in the theological underpinnings and devotional practices at the sanctuary. Lourdes was the site of the Virgin's appearance, and all who came sought to celebrate this miracle. The church, and especially the Assumptionists, were dedicated to increasing the cult of the Virgin, and were themselves key architects of this extravagant piety. However, in their development of ritual they needed to steer a course between the potential mariolatry of the faithful and the animistic tendencies of local belief and practice. Let us concentrate on the second pitfall for the moment. The grotto and the fountain, their location on the border between civilization and the forest beyond, the many deeper chthonic associations of the site which conjured up an almost womb-like place of both of entry and protection – these were all aspects of the Lourdes cult which explains its great success but also its subversive potential.[58] The grotto was tamed by the massive construction works which paved over the area leading to it, and was marked off by iron grills, while the building of the basilica above the grotto sought to superimpose, almost literally, a symbol of orthodoxy.

But this physical transformation was not enough. The sacramentalization of such sites was a key means of absorbing this popular, one might even say 'folkloric', piety into the mainstream of Church practice. At Lourdes, one of the most important devotional aspects of this process was the introduction by Picard of the eucharistic procession in 1888, an innovation which brings us back to questions of gender, the body and the relationships between subordination and authority. Bishops or archbishops carried the elevated Host from the basilica to the grotto, a procession which powerfully associated the fundamental tenets of Catholic belief with the pilgrimage's mission.[59] Under Picard's direction, the processions became moments of intense religious feeling, as the *malades* got up, discarded their crutches and walked, following the elevated host with gratitude and praise (See figure three).[60] In these moments, they celebrated Christ's power as a miracle worker, but also identified deeply with his human suffering and broken body. Picard made an implicit link between the Host and both the 'passions' and the 'resurrections' among the sick and dying. The unique circumstances of Lourdes thus made the bridge between the physical and spiritual, which was at the heart of Catholic belief, an ever more palpable reality.

The great success of the eucharistic procession suggests that a Christocentric orthodoxy was successfully re-asserted over the excesses of Marian piety in much the same way that the gendered division of labour within the pilgrimage movement rigidified with time. But such a parallel – in which

Figure 3: 'La procession du Saint-Sacrement récolte des miracles et les traîne à sa suite.' Anon., *Le Pèlerin*, 12 September, 1894.

the masculine directed the feminine – is far too neat and reductive in both cases. As I have suggested, women in pilgrimage seemed to accept and live out their subordinate role with enthusiasm, but it was precisely this position which strengthened their moral authority. Similarly, the devotion to the body of Christ which the eucharistic procession represented was perfectly compatible with an intensification of the Virgin's cult at Lourdes. While people acknowledged Christ's divinity and his accessibility during the eucharistic procession, at other times He remained the remote judge, at the centre of an ascetic and juristic system of salvation. The appearance of Mary on earth to direct and console made her a more immediate presence, and in the yearning for her help, the faithful could reach sometimes mariolatrous heights.

However, as with Christ, who was both divine judge and suffering humanity, the system of identification with the Virgin was complex. She was Mother of God, Queen of Heaven, Immaculate Virgin, titles which suggested her many different attributes and the dogmatic accretions which surrounded her.[61] At different moments and in different places the faithful would emphasize her different aspects. At Lourdes the Church adored her as the Immaculate Conception, a designation of stainless and pure perfection which contrasted markedly with the damaged and diseased bodies of those who came to seek her aid. Her perfection gave her power but also distanced her. The comforting humanity of the Mary of earlier centuries who suckled Jesus at her breast gave way to an image more like alabaster. In more human terms she was like the woman on a pedestal, powerful as an ideal but cold to the touch. Alongside this image of perfection, however, there was another strand which perpetuated Mary as the compassionate mother or gentle *jeune fille,* more like the ministering angel of domestic ideology, active in her concern for suffering humanity. These aspects predominated in the *piscines* when naked and vulnerable pilgrims sought her aid without any priestly intervention. While the eucharistic procession produced its share of miracles, the bathing pools – filled with the water that she had Bernadette discover – generated as many.[62]

The Virgin's ubiquity in the religious psyche of the period meant that often Mary, not Christ, was seen as *the* intermediary between God and his suffering people. The clergy were not always able to control the impulses of the pilgrims who seemed to worship Mary as a deity in her own right, and some priests even seemed to countenance such mariolatrous deviations in an effort to galvanize popular piety and, perhaps, to give expression to their own intense Marian adoration. This tendency was demonstrated most extraordinarily in an image in 1895 in *Le Pèlerin* (Figure four).[63] The image showed an impoverished woman of moribund aspect releasing her crutches into the stylized picture of death, a skeleton waiting with a shroud. But rather than falling into Jesus's arms, she is shown coming to greet the youthful embrace of *Marie Immaculée.* In this instance, the Virgin is not shown as a gentle intercessor, but rather as the worker of miracles herself, a vision of divine intervention rather at odds with Catholic teaching.

I hope I have shown that in the three instances discussed – the intimate, the institutional and the spiritual – women were subordinate, but that the considerable power and influence they exercised was strangely facilitated by that subordination. Priests directed women, but the defining characteristic of the pilgrimage was the vocation to care for the sick, which the women generated. While on pilgrimage, men directed yet again and others served humbly as *brancardiers,* but the heroines of the operation were the Petites Sœurs and the society ladies, the latter especially confirming their moral authority by jettisoning their social position, albeit only for a week. Christ was worshipped but Mary was adored and, except for the emotional moment of the eucharistic procession, she, not her son, was foremost in the prayers of pilgrims.

Finally, I would like to suggest that the development of Lourdes offers pointers which can used to re-consider the politics of the early Third Republic which at the moment are above all defined by great men, ideologies and the mechanics of party struggle. I would like to make two simple points. Firstly, we may begin to re-assess the very category of 'political catholicism' if we can take into account the passionate microfoundations on which it was built; and secondly, that these spiritual foundations were not

Figure 4: 'La mort préparait déjà un linceul, mais Notre-Dame de Lourdes rend la vie.' Dessin de Montégut, *Le Pèlerin*, 4 September, 1895.

only in large part generated and sustained by women, but were also the most developed expression of their political aspirations. They shared with the men a resistance to the Republican spirit of the age, proposing instead one based on Christian solidarity. The care of the sick on pilgrimage did not merely enable the National pilgrimage to continue after the politics that created it had been defeated. Rather, these political aspirations lived on in the spirituality of the movement, and the spirituality became a form of politics.

NOTES

1 For a broad social analysis of legitimism see Steven D. Kale, *Legitimism and the Reconstruction of French Society (1852–1883)* (Baton Rouge and London, 1992), especially pp. 263–328.

2 For a classic scholarly account see R. Aubert, *Le Pontificat de Pie IX (1846–1878)* (Paris, 2nd ed., 1963) pp. 72–106, pp. 311–67 and pp. 369–73; a newer interpretation is Yves Chiron, *Pie IX: Pape moderne* (Paris, 1995) pp. 445–67.

3 The *Annales de Notre-Dame de Lourdes*, established in 1868 by the Garaison Fathers under diocesan jurisdiction, give some sense of the still unformed nature of the pilgrimages. Processions were still generally of local regional origin, with groups coming from Bayonne, Toulouse and Bagnères, rather than from Paris or other regional capitals; narratives of healing filled the pages of these early volumes, but there is no sense of a national diffusion of such miraculous tales which the later Catholic, and especially Assumptionist, press would so successfully promote.

4 *Le Catholicisme au féminin: les congrégations françaises à supérieure générale au XIXe siècle* (Paris, 1984).

5 For this institutional efflorescence and the special role of feminine spirituality in its development see Olwen Hufton, *The Prospect Before Her: A History of Women in Western Europe 1500–1800* vol. 1 (London, 1995) pp. 366–96; for a brilliant examination of the spiritual well-springs of this movement and its intellectual bases see Linda Timmermans, *L'accès des femmes à la culture (1598–1715)* (Paris, 1993), pp. 393–811.

6 For this view see Ralph Gibson, *A Social History of French Catholicism, 1789–1914,* (London, Routledge, 1989) especially his remarks pp. 134–57 and pp. 180–90; for sympathetic portrayals of women's devotion to religion in the face of revolutionary persecution see Olwen Hufton, *Women and the Limits of Citizenship during the French Revolution* (Toronto, Press, 1992) and Suzanne Desan, *Reclaiming the Sacred: Lay Religion and Popular Politics during the French Revolution* (Ithaca, 1990).

7 Bonnie Smith in her pathbreaking *Ladies of the Leisure Class: the Bourgeoises of Northern France* (Princeton, 1981) demonstrates the ideological divide between the sexes which Catholicism created within elite families in the Nord. Scathing remarks about the piety of poor women fill the treatises of ethnologists, positivists and republicans.

8 For the enduring impact of such modes of thought on French political culture see Paul Smith's *Feminism and the Third Republic: Women's Political and Civil Rights in France, 1918–1945* (Oxford, 1996), pp. 63–162, especially. This work demonstrates the left's continued refusal to countenance the vote for women on anti-clerical grounds right through the interwar period. For a more intepretive account see Pierre Ronsanvallon, *Le Sacre du citoyen: histoire du suffrage universelle en France* (Paris, 1992), pp. 393–412.

9 See Gérard Cholvy, 'Emmanuel d'Alzon: les racines', in René Rémond and Emile Poulat eds., *Emmanuel d'Alzon dans la société et l'Eglise du XIXe siècle* (Paris, 1982), pp. l5–41.

10 See Louis Secondy, 'Aux origines de la maison de l'Assomption à Nîmes (1844–1853), *ibid.*, pp. 233–56; on the importance of the papal military forces in ultramontanist circles see 'Cinquantième anniversaire de la création du régiment des zouaves pontificaux: Allocution de Monseigneur de Cabrières', Montmartre, 5 June 1910 (Montpellier, 1910).

11 For d'Alzon's almost personal relationship to the Virgin, and his conviction that the miracles at Lourdes in 1877 were a sign of the Virgin's favour for his order and the forthcoming dogma of the Assumption, see Archives des Assomptionistes de Rome (from now on AAR), Père D'Alzon to Père François Picard, 3 Sep. 1877; for his fondness for eucharistic devotion, a stance often in contrast to the rigourism of his clerical forbears, see G. Cholvy 'Emmanuel d'Alzon: Les racines', quoted on p. 33; for more on the growing enthusiasm for eucharistic devotion see below; for the classic account of papal infallibility see Dom. Cuthbert Butler, *The Vatican Council, 1869–1870* (London, 2nd edn, 1962).

12 For this reason he ardently championed the Pope's temporal power over the papal states; see Père Touveneraud, 'La participation du Père d'Alzon à la défense des états pontificaux, 1859–1863', *Pages d'archives,* Oct. (1960), 385–410.

13 See Père Désiré Deraedt, 'Le Père d'Alzon et les droits de Dieu sur la société', typescript, 17pp. + notes AAR.

14 For the promotion of many symbols and the orchestration of commemorations see Pierre Nora, ed. *Les lieux de mémoire: la république,* (Paris, 1984) vol. 1.

15 Nonetheless, as time went on, the success of this initiative would surprise even him, and he worried lest the national pilgrimage take too much of his priests' limited energies. See his letter in AAR to Père Picard on 8 Sep. 1875; 'J'estime le moment est venu de laisser aux evêques la direction des pèlerinages. C'est ma plus profonde conviction. . . . Nous sommes trop peu pour nous tant éparpiller. On peut prier sans pèleriner ou sans diriger soi-même les pèlerins'. D'Alzon continued to waver in his enthusiasm, although this would not stem the movement's tide, especially after his death.

16 For background see E. Lacoste, *Le P. François Picard* (Paris, 1932) and P. Rémi Kokel, *Le Père Vincent de Paul Bailly: journaliste et pèlerin (1832–1912)* (Paris, 1943).

17 AAR Picard to d'Alzon no. 797, 10 Apr.1871.

18 AAR Bailly to d'Alzon, no.1155 12 May,1871.

19 AAR Bailly to d'Alzon, no. 1159, 31 May, 1871.

20 AAR Bailly to d'Alzon, no. 1151, 12 Apr. 1871, He was particularly impressed by those who were 'furieuses contre la Commune, ayant appelé Versailles à grands cris de femmes, bonnes chrétiennes indignées des églises fermés etc., etc; viennent et encore ce matin nous apporter des malédictions contre Versailles, ils n'ont pas eu, disent-elles, tant de courage pour nous délivrer des Prussiens et le reste'.

21 See, for example, Susanna Barrows, *Distorting Mirrors: Visions of the Crowd in Late Nineteenth-Century France* (New Haven, 1981), pp. 7–92.

22 Picard, 'Notre-Dame de Salut', no. 490, *Sermons et allocutions,* vol. 5, pp. 190–200, AAR.

23 The contacts were made with the help of the Mother Superior of Les Dames de l'Assomption, the sister order with its *maison-mère* in Auteuil. D'Alzon held a twenty-year correspondence with this woman, who is often credited with many of the Assumption's inspirations. See Sr Thérèse Maylis, 'Marie-Eugénie et le Père d'Alzon: Intuitions communes, influence réciproque?' typescript, AAR, p. 31.

24 Vincent de Paul Bailly, *Association de Notre-Dame de Salut, rapport général,* (Paris: Au sécretariat rue François 1er, 1874), p. 11.

25 For a copy of the manifesto see A Pépin, 'Le P. François Picard, directeur de l'Association de Notre-Dame de Salut et des pèlerinages nationaux', *Pages d'archives* Nov. (1963) pp. 183–4; for more on the prescribed division of labour based on gender see V.-P. Bailly, *Association de Notre-Dame de Salut, rapport général* (Paris, 1874), pp. 11–12.

26 A. Pépin, 'Le Père François Picard' . . . pp. 189–92; in this campaign of 1872 Notre-Dame de Salut called for a nation-wide novena and fast to anticipate the public prayers in the Chamber. Parishes across the nation were enjoined in various *Semaines religieuses* to make this sacrifice, and the Pope, on the urging of Père d'Alzon, accorded a plenary indulgence to all who followed suit. The movement was a success, and fifty bishops urged their faithful to pray for the Church and the conversion of sinners (although a few, like the archbishop of Paris, remained sceptical of the movement and shocked that their own authority seemed temporarily usurped by this small group of activist priests and lay women). This campaign articulated the major preoccupation of the Catholic right, concentrating above all on the theme of the nation's guilt.

27 See 'Madame de la Rochefoucauld, duchesse d'Estissac, née de Ségur, présidente du conseil de Notre-dame de Salut', *Hospitalité de Notre-Dame de Salut: membres décédés* (Toulouse: Imprimerie St Cyrien, 1906), pp 24–6; and 'Mme La Duchesse d'Estissac', *Bulletin de Notre-Dame de Salut,* 36(1905) pp. 115–20; A wealthy and accomplished Catholic, whose

condescension was highly prized by the less elevated women who did the work, Madame de la Rochefoucauld lent an air of unquestionable aristocratic grandeur and Catholic virtue to the enterprise. She tended the sick herself at the Hôpital Saint-Joseph and was known affectionately as 'la bonne Duchesse' by the small army of 'clients' – workers, orphans, the sick and the poor – whom she aided with her purse and sometimes with her attention. Above all, her influence was felt in the diocese of Orléans where her chateau, Combreux, was situated. So great was her love for the grotto at Lourdes, that she had a rather large facsimile re-created in the park, and once a year opened her *demeure* so the locals could come on pilgrimage.

28 AAR UB 203, Mme LaForest to P. Picard, 14 Feb. 1874.

29 AAR FF 62/1, Mme LaForest to P. Picard. 10 Sep. 1873.

30 AAR UB 211, Mme LaForest to P. Picard, 2 Dec. 1874

31 AAR FF 63/1, Mme Laforest to P. Picard, 23 Oct. 1874.

32 AAR UB 192, Mme Dumont to P. Vincent de Paul Bailly, 1874, no specific date; 'quand vous aurez une affaire qui vous donnera quleques soucis pour l'œuvre, causez en avec moi, pour le jugement la lucidité d'une situation quelconque, je ne pense pas que personne puisse vous aider plus que moi'.

33 AAR UB 190, Mme Dumont to P. Vincent de Paul Bailly, 1874.

34 For an example, see Picard's to Alexis P. Dumazer in AAR no. 967, 30 mai 1872.

35 See for one example among many, AAR Picard to d'Alzon no. 979, 26 Jan. 1873; in this letter he expressed his extreme irritation with one of the women and the need of the Duchesse d'Estissac's help in sorting out the situation.

36 AAR d'Alzon, to Mlle Valentine Chaudordy, 15 Jul. 1873.

37 See the classic discussion in Caroline Walker Bynum's *Holy Feast and Holy Fast: The Religious Significance of Food to Medieval Women* (Berkeley, 1987), see especially pp. 189–218 and pp. 245–59, as well as the more recent, Elizabeth Alvilda Petroff, *Body and Soul: Essays on Medieval Women and Mysticism* (New York, 1994).

38 See, for example, the following letters between Picard and Mme la Baronne de Bastard; ARR no. 865 12 Apr. 1871;1059 6 Aug.1873; no. 1060 21 Oct. 1873. Their relationship lasted for years, and was interspersed with mutual consolation over the political turn of events and Mme la Baronne de Bastard's frequent contributions to the Assumption. As she sank increasingly into solitary invalidism, he praised her willingness to embody the passion of France in her own person. Although a woman of fortune from a distinguished house, she sought only anonymity when she offered funds, an embodiment of Christian humility and physical suffering that gained Picard's true loyalty. Both priest and penitent gained much from their emotional interaction, the former the edifying spectacle of a 'good death', the latter a firm belief in her ultimate heavenly reward

39 AAR FF66, Mme LaForest to Picard, 10 Mar. 1885.

40 AAR UB 210, Mme Laforest to P. Picard, 31 Nov. 1874.

41 AAR UB 193 Mme Dumont to P. Vincent de Paul Bailly, 1874, no specific date.

42 AAR UB 195 Mme Dumont to P. Vincent de Paul Bailly, 1874, no specific date.

43 For a graph and figures which show approximate high-water marks see Thomas A. Kselman, *Miracles and Prophecies in Nineteenth-Century France* (New Brunswick, NJ, 1983), p. 165.

44 Paul Miest, *Les 54 miracles de Lourdes au jugement du droit canon* (Paris, 1958), pp. 8, 10–12.

45 See *Le Pèlerin*, 17 Aug. 1885.

46 See *Le Pèlerin*, 4 Sep. 1880.

47 A. Pépin, *Le Père François Picard*, pp. 224–5.

48 For the vicissitudes of the shrine, see P. Pierre Touveneraud, 'Le premier pèlerinage national à La Salette de passage à Grenoble, en août 1872', see pp. 9–11 (text counted from p. 3), unpublished manuscript, AAR UD 185. From the outset, Picard had expressed his personal disappointment that the grotto had not been chosen, perhaps

echoing d'Alzon's uneasiness with the Alpine shrine and the controversy it had generated: AAR Picard to d'Alzon, no. 882, 13 May 1872. As early as 1868, d'Alzon had contrasted the two sites: 'La Salette m'a laissé, ne ne sais pourquoi, incrédule ou au moins dur et sec, Lourdes m'a apporté je ne sais quel parfum de paix, de confiance et d'espoir que je convertirai un jour': AAR d'Alzon to Mère Marie-Eugénie de Jésus 16 Aug. 1868.

49 For the history of the movement, see Anon, *La Mère Marie de Jésus: fondatrice des Petites Soeurs de l'Assomption, garde-malades des pauvres à domicile* (Paris,1908), pp. 235–40, 264–66, 288–97.

50 Anon, *Hospitalité de Notre-Dame de Salut: Documents, Statuts, Coutumiers, Historique* (Paris, n.d.), p. 121.

51 Gaëtan Bernoville, *Le Père Pernet: Fondateur des Petites Soeurs de l'Assomption* (Paris, 1944), p. 117–18.

52 *Ibid.*, p. 127.

53 Rapport du 6 mars 1887 Anon, *Hospitalité de Notre-Dame de Salut,* (Paris, 1887), pp. 121–2.

54 Teasing out the relations of this elusive organization is often difficult, as it split in the early 1880s with another Hospitalité de Notre-Dame de Lourdes organized to greet pilgrims outside the period of the great national events. The series 5H in the Archives de la Grotte, Lourdes, contains some of the founders' correspondence. For the general story, albeit written in hagiographical terms, see André Rebsomen, *Cinquante ans d'Hospitalité (1880–1930)* (Paris, 1930), which describes the mission of the Hospitalité and the network of relations between the Hospitalité de Notre-Dame de Salut and that of Notre-Dame de Lourdes; in this volume, Rebsomen acknowledges the link between the Hospitalité and the Action Française and claims that the former was purged of this political 'deviation' when the pope put the Action Française on the index in Dec. 1926; see pp. 158–9. One might wonder how many maintained their political views despite these proscriptions. The proximity of the relations between the Hospitalité de Notre-Dame de Salut and the Action Française is once again confirmed by the holdings of AAR SW, UC 74–5, K61, especially.

55 *Le Pèlerin,* 13 Aug. 1881.

56 See for example Victor Turner and Edith L.B. Turner, *Image and Pilgrimage in Christian Culture: Anthropological Perspectives* (New York, 1978), pp. 1–39. In this introductory chapter, the authors discuss the concept of liminality and, perhaps, exaggerate the distinction between Christian individual pilgrimage and rites of passage associated with tribal groups. As I suggest, the feelings of social solidarity were an integral part of nineteenth-century pilgrimage.

57 For the way carnival mixed these themes see Peter Stallybrass and Allon White, *The Politics and Poetics of Transgression* (London, 1986); see also M. Bakhtin, *Rabelais and his World* (Cambridge, Ma., 1968).

58 For an exploration of these themes, see my forthcoming *Lourdes: Body and Spirit in the Secular Age* (London, 1998), chs. one and two especially.

59 A. Pépin, *Le Père François Picard,* p. 220.

60 *Le Pèlerin,* 2 Sep. 1894.

61 For the contemporary debate and systems of identification surrounding Mary, Barbara Corrado Pope, 'Immaculate and Powerful: The Marian Revival in the Nineteenth Century', in Clarissa W. Atkinson, *et al., Immaculate and Powerful: The Female in Sacred Image and Social Reality,* (Boston, 1985) pp. 173–200; for the changing perceptions of Mary and the dogmatic accretions see Marina Warner, *Alone of all her Sex: The Cult of the Virgin Mary* (London, 1976); Giovanni Miegge, *The Virgin Mary,* trans. W. Smith, *The Virgin Mary: The Roman Catholic Marian Doctrine* (London, 2nd ed.1961); and Hilda Graef, *Mary: A History of Doctrine and Devotion,* 2 vols (London, 1963–5).

62 For more on the different types of cures see my forthcoming *Lourdes: Body and Spirit in the Secular Age,* ch. 8.

63 *Le Pèlerin,* 4 Sep. 1895.

10 The Sacred Memory: Religion, Revisionists and the Easter Rising

Michael Laffan

'In the name of God and of the dead generations'. The opening words of the 1916 proclamation illustrate two distinctive features of Irish nationalism: its use of religious imagery and the sanction which it sought from a vision of the past. These characteristics had flourished long before the Easter Rising, and the rebels themselves would soon become venerated saints in the nationalist litany, mythical figures who would be assured of an honoured place among the dead generations.

Myths tend either to advocate a certain course of action, or else to justify the acceptance of an existing state of affairs. In Henry Tudor's words, they are believed to be true,

> not because the historical evidence for them is compelling, but because they make sense of men's present experience. . . . And events are selected for inclusion in a myth, partly because they coincide with what men think *ought* to have happened, and partly because they are consistent with the drama as a whole.[1]

In this sense much writing and speechmaking about the Irish past was mythical rather than historical. The myth had a hard core in generally accepted facts: centuries of English or British conquest, repression and exploitation, which provoked in turn widespread Irish dislike of the details (or even the very existence) of continuing links with Britain. This undisputed core was elaborated, oversimplified and distorted as circumstances might require. The Easter rebels, for example, referred to six insurrections against British rule in the previous three hundred years. This was effective propaganda, which was all that mattered at the time, and the objection that it was bad history would not have concerned them – although it might be of interest to later historians.

Alvin Jackson has pointed out that the Irish past is continually and ritually sacrificed to a caricature of the present,[2] but it has also been sacrificed to an image of an idealized future. It was useful because it was both present-centred and forward-looking. Pearse might claim that the Gaelic polity of nearly 2,000 years ago had the best and noblest educational system that has ever been known among men, but as Joseph Lee remarked, 'it is only when one turns to the content of Pearse's imagined Gaelic world that one realizes he has recreated in it the image of his ideal Ireland of the future'.[3] He gift-wrapped the gospel of the future in the packaging of the past.[4]

As visions of an idealized future were projected back many centuries, and thereby acquired a patina of venerable age, they appeared less fanciful and unrealistic; it seemed reasonable to imagine that if certain qualities or attitudes had already flourished in earlier times, they might do so again. For example, Michael Collins claimed that in the ancient days of Gaelic civilization the people were prosperous without being materialistic, while Arthur Griffith, the great apostle of national self-reliance, was able to link his cause with what he assumed to have been a similar movement led by Brian Boru in 1014.[5] From a different standpoint James Connolly viewed the Irish clan system, which had been destroyed in the seventeenth century, as 'founded upon common property and democratic social organization'.[6] In a similar fashion Sean O'Casey believed that in Gaelic Ireland the king 'affixed no gaudy seal on the grinding of the poor, but where the nation shared his greatness and his splendour; where great men were the concentrated Name of the Nation's soul. . . . Life was good for all their people as it was good for themselves'.[7] The virtues of earlier generations were both a distraction from current discontents and a stimulus to escape from them, while the bonds between past and future tended to isolate and even marginalize the unworthy present.

Irish nationalists tended either to avoid the weaknesses and failures which were revealed by a study of the historical records, or else defended them with obvious signs of embarrassment. One instance is an apologetic article in D. P. Moran's *Leader* rejecting the slur that 'of the twelve kings who ruled in the sixth century all but two were murdered or fell in battle'. It examined their reigns, life by life, to prove that a few rulers helped salvage national honour by their peaceful deaths. (One of these must be regarded as a dubious case; the king who 'drowned in a vat of wine while endeavouring to escape being burned'.)[8]

A study of history could provide absolution for present failings; if Irish Catholics were less industrious than Protestants, this was because of their landlords' policies and the effects of the Penal Laws.[9] It could be used to exhort or shame the faint-hearted – as in a stanza written by a republican Dáil deputy during the debate on the Anglo-Irish treaty:

> Hear ye not dead heroes taunting,
> 'They were weak when brought to bay',
> Steel your hearts and Heaven will chorus,
> 'As the Dead were so are they'.[10]

He could use the prospect of incorporation into the ranks of the elect to root out compromise and to foster intransigence. And a few days later one of his colleagues declared in the same spirit that 'we were the heirs of a great tradition, and the tradition was that Ireland had never surrendered, that Ireland had never been beaten'.[11]

Such appeals to the memory of the dead not only inspired and reassured; if the past were interpreted *correctly*, it would also provide lessons for the present, and its study would help banish hesitation or error. A leader-writer in the IRB newspaper *Irish Freedom* was refreshing in his blunt honesty when he declared that 'to us it seems that this is the true line of development, and we turn to history to prove that it is so.'[12] Clio would be the judge in a court of appeal whose verdict was pre-ordained.

This appeal to the sanction of dead heroes was complemented by a tendency to intertwine nationalism and religion, and the terminology of Irish radical movements, their accounts of dead heroes' virtues and endurance, were saturated in Catholic imagery. This was hardly surprising in a country where the Catholic faith had endured centuries of suppression and discrimination, and where (most notably in the case of O'Connell's Emancipation campaign) national feeling and self-expression had been linked to a religious cause. An oppressed people and an oppressed church reinforced each other, and the close links between Catholicism and nationalism survived the ending of formal religious discrimination. The radical Fr Michael O'Flanagan was able to pronounce of O'Donovan Rossa that while he was a criminal in the eyes of the British government 'his crimes were the title deeds of sainthood in Ireland's patriotic litany'.[13] Even the socialist *Irish Worker* could address Robert Emmet, executed more than a century earlier, in terms not unworthy of a Christian martyr or a Biblical prophet:

oh, wise beloved one, you, the far-seeing one, knew that no bondsman could write your epitaph. The meaning of your life must remain still unspoken until the fulfilment of the word. . . . Let the life of the beautiful one be an inspiration to us; let his death be our consolation. In life and death we are one with you. In the body we suffer with you; in the soul, to us, is the same sacred fire of discontent that burned so fiercely in yours. You are of us and we of you. Let us then rejoice that it was vouchsafed to this nation that such a man was given unto us as an example for us to imitate, and as an inspiration, to uplift us. . . . Emmet, great as you were in life, greater are you still in death.[14]

Arthur Griffith entitled his manifesto *The Resurrection of Hungary*, while James Connolly wrote shortly before the Rising that 'in all due humility and awe we recognise that of us, as of mankind at Calvary, it may truly be said "without the shedding of blood there is no redemption"'.[15] The seepage of religious terms into political language was widespread and instinctive.

This pattern reached its climax in the Easter Rising. Virtually all its leading figures were Catholics, and the two most prominent Protestants connected with it – Casement and Markiewicz – were soon converted to the majority faith. Accounts of the rebels' piety were soon disseminated throughout the country. Perhaps the most blatant annexation of Christianity by nationalism occurred in the opening lines of Pearse's *A Mother Speaks*, a poem which he sent to his own mother shortly before his execution:

> Dear Mary, that didst see thy first-born Son
> Go forth to die amid the scorn of men
> For whom He died,
> Receive my first-born son into thy arms,
> Who also hath gone out to die for men. . . .[16]

The Church went halfway to meet the republican revolutionaries. Bishops were surprisingly tepid in their response to the insurrection; while seven members of the hierarchy were outrightly critical, and one issued a qualified condemnation, another effectively condoned it and an astonishing twenty-two remained silent.[17] The Jesuit journal *Studies* and the *Catholic Bulletin* were among the first to publicize the rebel leaders. Only weeks after the Rising had been suppressed General Maxwell wrote to Archbishop Walsh protesting about the political demonstrations which followed requiem masses for the executed leaders.[18] A year later Fr O'Flanagan was elected a vice-president of the new Sinn Féin party, and soon afterwards Bishop Fogarty of Killaloe became a trustee of the Dáil loan.

The survivors of the Rising continued to use religious rhetoric, and during his imprisonment Thomas Ashe wrote a poem entitled 'Let me carry your Cross for Ireland, Lord!' According to the *Catholic Bulletin* a few years later, 'allegiance to the Irish Republic has come as a reawakened faith blessed and purified by our struggle of seven centuries'.[19] In the course of the debates which followed the Treaty of 1921, nationalism and sanctity were linked ever more closely together, and patriots of the past were summoned to reinforce the beliefs of their living colleagues. For one Dáil deputy the uniform in which Terence MacSwiney had been buried was 'a sacred thing; nothing less than the habit of a martyr, with a truer title to be so regarded than the purple or scarlet of Bishop or Cardinal: the habit of Francis or of Dominic'.[20] In another extreme case, a Maynooth professor remembered how 'we have rightly been accustomed to appeal to the men who laboured or suffered or died for Ireland in the past whenever we renewed the struggle for freedom, just as theologians and preachers recall the examples of Christ and the martyrs'.[21] The military and political campaign against the British was hallowed as a godly struggle.

Such imagery and such habits of thought were virtually unaffected by the achievement of independence for most of Ireland in 1922. As has been the case in many successful revolutions, the past was amended or doctored so that it might conform to new needs and realities. An Irish form of the Whig interpretation of history was sanctified with state approval. Former rebels who now enjoyed the pleasures of power calculated the inheritance which they wished to extract from their dead predecessors, and they exploited an appropriate image of Irish history to sustain their rhetoric and their values. In many cases this process also served conveniently to enhance their own honoured rôle in society as the survivors or successors of the new state's 'founding fathers'.

The realities of freedom might be drab and disappointing, but, following the pattern of earlier days, glorious and noble predecessors could provide both comfort and distraction. In particular the 'revolutionary years' – the Easter Rising and its aftermath – became enveloped in a cloying hagiography and remained untouched by serious examination for decades. Pearse and others were welcomed into a new Valhalla, and the respect with which they were viewed was untinged by any doubt or criticism. They were attached to the litany of past insurrections and were distanced from mundane realities as they became part of 'history' or 'myth'. The state felt that it was safe to honour their aims and methods since there seemed to be little risk that later generations would follow their example; the long struggle was now over, and the history of Irish insurrection had come to a triumphant conclusion. The cult of the Easter rebels was fostered by both church and state. Although bishops and priests remained vigilant against present unrest they were prepared to bless rebels when they were safely dead; 'as nationalistic violence receded in time so might it be the more safely sanctioned'.[22] In 1916 Cardinal Logue had condemned the Rising, but as part of the anniversary ceremonies fifty years later Cardinal Conway presided at a solemn High Mass in Armagh Cathedral.

The 'Catholic' beliefs and practices of the revolutionaries were emphasized in books, speeches and illustrations; thereby nationalist propagandists maintained the time-honoured links between religion and nationalism, and they also satisfied a pious generation's need for pious heroes. For example, when de Valera addressed Republicans at Bodenstown cemetery in 1925 he declared:

you have come here today to the tomb of Wolfe Tone on a pilgrimage of loyalty! By your presence you proclaim . . . your unaltered devotion to the cause for which he gave his life . . . you who were privileged to repeat your vows at this shrine . . . are here to bear witness to that which is living and true.[23]

The extent to which Patrick Pearse was singled out as the model of a devout Catholic hero is illustrated by an obituary of his mother which was printed in de Valera's *Irish Press*. It proclaimed that:

the home of the Pearses was one typical of Catholic Ireland. That good mother moulded the souls of her children in the historic pattern of patriotism, simplicity, humanity and simple piety. . . . Pearse's letter to his mother is one of the great documents of Irish nationality. He has just received Holy Communion. . . .[24]

The Pearse cult reached such proportions that the Easter Rising could almost be seen as the culmination of his career, rather than as an event with a complex history of its own. The most influential school textbook history of Ireland for many decades, James Carty's *Class Book of Irish History*, not only described Pearse as the greatest of the rebel leaders and as one of the noblest characters in Irish history, but it also devoted more space to his life than to the Rising itself or to the combined lives of all the other six signatories of the proclamation.[25]

For many decades the Irish people could find it difficult to escape from the praise of noble and holy rebels. The writings of survivors and partisans were often regarded as sacred texts, and until the 1960s generations of young people were influenced by zealous nationalist apologists such as Brian O'Higgins.[26] In the first edition of his *Wolfe Tone Annual*, he was able to write of Irish separatists that:

they perished for an imperishable cause, they died for an undying truth, they were degraded to be exalted for ever, and we can only truly honour them by accepting what they taught as the gospel of Irish Nationality. No class war was theirs, no party strife, no mean intrigue, no degrading compromise, but a God-like struggle for the spiritual and material welfare of their people.[27]

Some years later Pearse was singled out for special praise:

never in all the history of Ireland have we heard or read of a better man than Pádraic MacPiarais, the golden-tongued spokesman of the 1916 soldiers. . . . Clarke and Connolly, MacDermott and Ceannt and MacDonagh and Plunkett were great and true men, but with unerring instinct they recognised in Pádraic Pearse one who was of Heaven as well as of earth, one whom God had sent to do a deed that needed sorely to be done, to raise a people from slavery to freedom, from degradation to manhood.[28]

As late as 1966 a study of the executed leaders was entitled *Sixteen Roads to Golgotha*.[29] The fiftieth anniversary of the Rising was characterized by hyperbole, and for most people it brought the pattern of uncritical veneration to an extravagant climax. Within a few years, however, the martyrology of 1916 ceased to be fashionable, and attempts by priests and patriots to equate the Resurrection and the Rising came to be seen as at best superstitious and possibly blasphemous.[30]

It was natural that Catholics should form the great majority of those who linked their faith with a glorified image of nationalist rebellion. Nonetheless, on a much smaller scale, Marxists could also look back to 1916 and to the Irish revolution to confirm their beliefs; the socialism of the few could be linked to the nationalism of the masses. For Desmond Greaves, Connolly's determination to fight in 1916 'showed how completely he had identified himself with historical necessity'.[31] Greaves seemed determined to avoid complexity and ambivalence, and he argued that the looting in Dublin which accompanied the Rising was carried out by the *same* lumpen-proletariat which booed the defeated rebels. The number of working-class villains must necessarily be small.[32] His narrow approach contrasted with the warmth of the first writer to comment on the same subject, James Stephens, who had remarked that:

until the end of the rising sweet shops were the favourite mark of the looters. . . . Possibly most of the looters are children who are having the sole gorge of their lives. They have tasted sweetstuffs they had never toothed before, and will never taste again in this life, and until they die the insurrection of 1916 will have a sweet savour for them.[33]

Although a rich and humane interpretation of the Rising had been available from the very beginning, it could easily be ignored or dismissed as capitalist history. But for Greaves, just as working class heroes were to be exalted, villains existed to be hissed and booed; 'the storm-troopers of Unionist reaction were recruited from the brazen hoodlums of the Belfast slums. The leaders who directed them were mostly the brainless pups of aristocratic families.'[34] Like the present, the past was populated by good guys and bad guys.

Many Marxists must have been embarrassed by such depths of crudity. And even within the faith, internal divisions reflected those of Ireland in general; Protestant, Ulster unionist Marxists feuded with their Catholic, nationalist counterparts. The British and Irish Communist Organization, for example, attacked those who 'refer for support against historical reality to the mistaken statements made by Connolly and Lenin in 1912 when the partition situation was just developing', and a few years later it could declare, with full dogmatic confidence, 'it is already certain that all future writing on Irish history, which has the slightest pretension towards objectivity, will be along the lines laid down by the B&ICO'.[35]

But things had begun to change by the time that these sectarian battles were being fought, and in the course of the 1960s traditional images of 1916 were undermined and shattered. A loss of faith in the nationalist myths coincided with the emergence of a better informed, more sceptical, and less reverent generation of historians. They disentangled and reassembled the complexities of the revolutionary years, tried to relate the receding past to their own rapidly changing environment, and swept away many of the state-sanctified legends. One idiom seemed particularly appropriate for all these activities: irony.[36]

Some simplistic accounts have ascribed these historiographical develop-ments solely to the revival of conflict in Northern Ireland and to a fear by the Republic's 'establishment' of radicalism and conflict spreading south. In turn this was seen as leading to an attitude in which the violence of 1916 was linked to, and even blamed for, the Northern 'Troubles' after 1968–9. Unfortunately for those who held such theories, the new and less dutiful interpretations of the Rising and its aftermath *preceded* the re-emergence of violence; events in the South provided a more satisfactory background or explanation for the reassessment of the sacrosanct 'revolutionary years'.

During the 1960s old values were supplemented or supplanted as citizens of the Irish Republic became more aware of the outside world and, for better and worse, became more influenced by other cultures and customs. The transformation of the Catholic Church encouraged a new flexibility and self-criticism. Ireland played an active role in the United Nations, applied to join the European Community and established free trade with Britain. In the words of a harsh critic, 'the rebel image didn't suit a new class, absorbed with status-seeking'.[37] By now it was clear that in many respects independence had been vindicated, and that it no longer needed the apologists who had served it well in the past. As Gearóid Ó Tuathaigh remarked, the apparent diminishing significance of national sovereignty (economic and cultural, no less than political) seemed to portend the coming obsolescence of a large part of the rhetoric of Irish nationalism.[38] John A. Murphy, defining nationalism as a frustrated expression of a thwarted aspiration to independence, wrote of the Republic that 'already by the 1960s this State had outgrown the emotional manifestations of nationalism. These had given place to a quiet and assured acceptance of nationality.'[39] Patriotic reverence and flagwaving lost much of their appeal, and the recent past became something to be absorbed, studied, or even transcended, rather than merely (and endlessly) commemorated.

Even critics of the new historical approaches accepted the importance of the changes which took place in the 1960s; Desmond Fennell argued that the boom years 'led to a general ideological reaction against the nationalist programme inherited from the revolution', and Luke Gibbons conceded that 'Lemass's appointment as Taoiseach in 1959 is generally credited – or blamed, depending on one's standpoint – with ushering in the "revisionist turn" in Irish history and culture'.[40]

Partly encouraged by these trends, but to an extent quite independently of them, Irish historians began reassessing the origins of the state. The British government led the way in releasing records which enabled historians to research the revolutionary years, and gradually those who controlled Irish archives and documents followed their example. Ronan Fanning has pointed out the coincidence (and it *was* such) that new material became available, permitting the first serious examination by historians of the years between 1912 and 1923, just before the question of violence became once more topical after an interval of nearly half a century.[41]

One of the historians' early achievements was to enrich our understanding of the 1916 Rising. The first to challenge accepted orthodoxies was F. X. Martin, who presented Easter Week from the vantage point of an unfamiliar and unfashionable source: Eoin MacNeill. In his examination of the rôle played by Chief Secretary Augustine Birrell and of Dublin Castle Leon Ó Broin revealed unsurprisingly that British rule in Ireland before Easter 1916 was not (as claimed by Greaves) despotism softened by slovenliness,[42] but was in fact well-meaning and incompetent. William Irwin Thompson (like Ó Broin not a professional historian, and like him a scholar who has done much to enrich our understanding of the revolutionary period) examined the interaction of literature and revolution in a work which is widely regarded as a classic. Maureen Wall probed the divisions within the IRB and demonstrated the relative importance of Clarke and MacDermott rather than of Pearse and Connolly. These works were all published in the 1960s – and yet, so little of scholarly value had been written before this decade that they are now among the earliest books consulted by scholars and students of the period.[43]

The result of these developments has been to make possible a vastly more sophisticated study of the recent Irish past, and complexity was restored after decades of unnatural, implausible simplicity. Some people were dismayed by the undermining of their nationalist ideals by those whom they called 'revisionists', just as many were shattered by the desecration of their conservative Catholicism in the name of the Vatican's new *aggiornamento*. And, as suggested above, the two patterns were interconnected. Both churchmen and scholars may on occasion have displayed insensitive zeal, and they may have caused some unnecessary offence to the conservative faithful.

Post-nationalist history is normally viewed most clearly in the context of '1916 and All That'; the Rising and its aftermath have remained the area in which most of the battles have been fought. This is only natural. It was an event of particular importance to those who valued a nationalist or a socialist revolution, and it is the period which has been most thoroughly reassessed since the 1960s in the light of new evidence and values. It has inspired not only veneration but also mockery and iconoclasm. For example, at the end of the 1980s the London *Independent*, in its 'Anniversaries' column for 29 April, recorded bleakly 'Sinn Fein terrorists burned the Dublin Post Office, 1916'; while later, in *The Irish Times*, Kevin Myers wrote as follows about the Rising: 'I maintain it was a deplorable thing, with deplorable consequences since. It was a triumph of anti-democratism and militarism over democracy and civicism, of evil methods over peaceful ones.' He argued that virtually everything to do with it was horrible, from the homicidal manipulation of its preparatory stages, through the carnage and agony of Easter Week, to its hideous aftermath.[44] Such remarks were designed to irritate, but historians have tended to be more balanced and circumspect in their judgments. Nonetheless some of their writings have provoked attacks on them from those whose faith and values they were deemed to have traduced. In particular they have been accused of being unpatriotic and anti-national.

Common to all those who pine for a traditional, predictable, unchanging past is a dislike of those whom they criticize as 'revisionists'. But the word 'revisionism' itself is misleading and should be avoided – a point which is accepted even by some of those who use it with enthusiasm. A better term might be 'post-nationalist', even though it makes a gesture towards the trendily fashionable *fin-de-millénaire* terminology of literary criticism in which all is 'post this, post that. Everything is post these days, as if we're all just a footnote to something earlier that was real enough to have a name of its own'.[45] Naturally such a term would not imply a failure or an unwillingness to accept the importance of nationalism; no-one could think so who had watched the eruption of flag-waving xenophobia at the end of the twentieth century. Nor does such a term necessarily involve acceptance of Conor Cruise O'Brien's conclusion that nationalism has many negative aspects and should therefore be rejected.[46] There is no need to be *anti-nationalist*. What is meant by it is that most Irish historians have outgrown the need to *justify* Irish nationalism and the achievement of independence, to act as its mouthpiece, to treat Irish nationalists as being in need of positive discrimination. They have moved on from such pieties, keeping pace with the majority of historians throughout the world, and they cherish the right to cause offence to those who want the practice of history-writing to model itself on religious observance or the accumulation of folklore.

A critic of recent history-writing used revealing language when he complained that 'revisionism is like a despoiled church full of smashed images. That which formerly enthused and guided lies in fragments with nothing put in its place. The effect is thus bleak and dispiriting.'[47] In similar mood Owen Dudley Edwards remarked that the new attitude of historians 'seems to chip so much away that it sometimes seems almost impossible to retain a sense of the original reality. We strip away the myth; we may be left with a vacuum at the kernel. For the myth itself supplies a reality'.[48]

Denis Donoghue lamented the passing of the mythical version of Irish history, which he saw as a way of making sense of both the past and the present. It was a story, he wrote, which was told over and over again for the comfort of the community which received it, and it was therefore hard to dislodge. The new emphasis on social history he viewed as:

an attempt to remove from Irish history the glamour of its sacrifices and martyrdoms. Revisionism is a project of slow history, or confounding the drama, thwarting the narrative. Unfortunately, Ireland without its story is merely a member of the EC, the begging bowl our symbol.[49]

Another literary critic, Seamus Deane, also mourned the loss of a clear story line. According to him revisionists rejected any totalizing concept or system of metanarrative, and they replaced it with a series of monographic, empiricist studies which result in a plurality of narratives and disintegrate the established history of Ireland.[50] Donoghue and Deane might revel in the complexity of their own discipline, but they sought lower and less demanding standards when examining aspects of the Irish past; they seemed to want a story which would be stark and simple, in which there would be no subtlety, no ambivalence, and – above all – no censure of the heroic dead. Political Correctness became a fad (or even an obsession) in the United States and elsewhere during the 1990s, and, in a similar fashion, Irish historians were expected in some quarters to be Patriotically Correct.

One Fianna Fáil Dáil deputy, Dermot Ahern, described 'revisionism' neatly as 'a type of history which seeks to undermine the significance of the 1916 Rising and the struggle for independence'.[51] Anthony Coughlan believed that the historians provide an apologia for British government policy in Ireland, while Brendan Bradshaw claimed that they reject the substance of the Irish historical experience, and deprive the Irish people of 'heroes and heroic moments and movements'; they apply fudge and misrepresentation 'with a view to ridding nationalists of their supposed "victim complex"'.[52] Seamus Deane attacked what he saw as some historians' efforts to legitimize partition, and argued that 'by refusing to be Irish nationalists, they simply become defenders of Ulster or British nationalism'.[53] The reaction to Easter 1916 was seen as being part of the reaction to the Provisional IRA.[54]

Post-nationalist historians are also seen as capitalists, a taunt particularly popular among literary critics. Deane believed that they 'sing in chorus, if not in unison, against anything that threatens to upset the established structures'.[55] Terry Eagleton dismissed 'the knee-jerk superciliousness with which revisionism tends to travesty the slightest outcrop of popular militancy', while according to David Lloyd imperialist and revisionist histories were 'perhaps much the same thing'.[56] For Declan Kiberd the revisionists, like their conservative nationalist counterparts, were both 'sponsored by rival sections of the bureaucratic middle-class', and he complained that they can write whole narratives of Irish history which contain no reference whatever to colonialism or imperialism.[57] He believed that historians who downplay the significance of the colonial past, or even better, deny it utterly, are fêted and rewarded.[58] Those who study the events of the past may have dethroned most of the old gods, but students and scholars of English have moved in to reinforce the dwindling ranks of the devout; as Fintan O'Toole has remarked, 'in recent years, the epic version of Irish history has taken refuge in theories of post-colonial literature'.[59]

The post-nationalists have also been seen an organized faction engaged in developing an agenda. Whiffs of conspiracy have been detected, as in Desmond Fennell's belief that 'once Lemass had given the go-ahead, the media swung into action'.[60] Luke Gibbons has referred to 'the revisionist enterprise' (one aim of which was to insulate Irish society against 'the theoretical voltage of Marxism, psychoanalysis and post-structuralism'), and has suggested that historians sought to establish myth, violence and Catholicism as coordinates of militant nationalism because 'the task of forging a new set of cultural values for a liberal, modernizing society is easier if the ideology it is trying to replace is shown to be insular, illogical and narrow-minded'.[61] Blinded by their sensitivity to slurs on their dead heroes they seem not to consider the possibility that what historians are most intent on revising is one another's work.[62] They share a methodology, not an ideology.

Post-nationalist historians have caused offence by their assumptions, as well as by their iconoclasm. By and large they have tended to be not unhappy with the Republic of Ireland's place in the world: a state more prosperous and more secularized than in the past; as sovereign as are most other European countries; 'Western'; closer to Continental European states than to former British colonies in Asia or Africa; not conventionally 'post-colonial' because, in recent centuries its experience was not conventionally colonial; and inclined towards political rather than military measures to solve the Northern Irish question. They have chronicled, assessed and (in most cases) lamented its various failures, such as emigration, but while they sometimes wrote in sorrow and in anger in general they tended to see its path as relatively *normal* – however twisted that path might have been and however belatedly it might have been followed.

Many of their critics have been uneasy about some (perhaps in a few cases, even about all) of these characteristics of the state. Unhappy with Ireland's present (Deane, for example, described the country as steadfastly imprisoned within its colonial past[63]) they were critical of efforts to reassess the old comforting and inspiring vision of earlier centuries. The mythical heroic age was in danger of losing its value as a weapon against present opponents. Desmond Fennell has criticized historians (quite fairly) for not sharing his own 'allegiance to the essential tenets of Irish nationalism', and for abandoning the conflict between *good* and *bad*.[64] By and large the historians *have* committed these faults, and make no apology for them. But some responses to new history writing have been disproportionate. They reveal anger at what they see as a betrayal, as an attempt to undermine a belief – whether that be faith in a Catholic Ireland, or the struggle against

Britain, or the victory of the progressive working class, or the virtues of neutrality; or hostility to the lures of liberal humanism, or opposition to the European Community in particular and to the West in general. To varying extents those who hold such views have tended to look to the past for reinforcement, and any assault on past examples or models weakened the cause in the present and future.

One example is provided by the headline of a newspaper article on the 1916 Rising by Sean MacBride which read 'the Proclamation is now the bedrock of our neutrality'.[65] MacBride (or, possibly, a sub-editor who provided his article with its title) should have known that the proclamation explicitly repudiated neutrality in 1916 by referring to their 'gallant allies in Europe'. It would seem that the doctrine of neutrality needed to be legitimized by the manufacture of a rebellious lineage. Another commonplace example is the sustained effort by Sinn Féin and the Provisional IRA to present themselves as the sole legitimate heirs of the Easter Rising, the inheritors of the apostolic succession.

Because of their nationalist (or, much more rarely, Marxist) sympathies, such critics have concentrated their efforts on trying to salvage their vision of the Irish revolution which props up and gives depth to their present and future ideals. And for some the achievement of a nation state has not (following the normal pattern elsewhere) removed the need for nationalism; as long as the island is partitioned 'unfinished business' will remain. Another grievance has been the fact that the Irish choose to speak English, which remains the language of the people even though Irish is decreed to be the language of the state.

The content and tone of much recent history writing has caused offence to several different (and sometimes mutually hostile) elements in Irish society. Of course some attacks on the work of 'post-nationalists' are accurate and reasonable. For example, Joseph Lee pointed out that Francis Shaw, in his controversial article 'the Canon of Irish History', surmised that 'Pearse, one feels, would not have been satisfied to attain independence by peaceful means', and he then quoted Pearse, chapter and verse, to prove the contrary.[66] In a similar fashion to Lee, Luke Gibbons has suggested that Pearse represented only one strand of the Irish cultural revolution in 1916, and that the writings of Thomas MacDonagh reveal a warmer, more humane, more generous and inclusive vision of Irish traditions and Irish literature.[67] His arguments comprise an admirable exercise in historical revision. Other attacks, however, are both extreme and unfair.

One book which has provoked exceptional controversy and attack is Roy Foster's *Modern Ireland, 1600–1972*. In particular he has incurred the rage of Brian P. Murphy, who seems to imagine that only Foster's criticisms of Irish nationalists are worthy of comment, and that no attempt should be made to set such remarks in their context. Yet in his treatment of the Irish revolution Foster refers, *inter alia,* to the inhabitants of North King Street who were 'indiscriminately murdered' by British troops; the 'ludicrous' efforts of Dublin Castle officials to smear Home Rule leaders; the 'grisly executions' which followed the Rising; unionist 'intransigence' in 1917; the 'brutal regime' of the Black and Tans who behaved 'like independent mercenaries'; the 'horrific reprisals' of the crown forces; the 'berserk sackings of towns and villages'; the 'hard-line colonial attitudes on the part of the military'; and the fact that Northern Ireland 'was effectively a one-party state'.[68] To see him as an apologist for the British or the unionists would be absurd.

Despite his harsh comments on the British and the unionists it might reasonably be argued that Foster tends to be more severe on Irish nationalists than their opponents; this is a matter of opinion, which can be debated in a civil and productive manner. Yet Murphy denounces Foster as someone who justifies partition and makes it more respectable by branding the native Irish as racialist, revolutionary and sectarian. Foster's assessment of nationalists' attitudes towards unionists is dismissed 'not only as partial history, but also as a highly political statement'. He is attacked for having taken the side of the censor who did not wish the true history of Ireland's struggle to be recorded. He is attacked of projecting a revolutionary dimension on Irish nationalism, with the result that 'it becomes reasonable for Unionists to distance themselves from the nationalist movement. An argument for separation and partition is again advanced'.[69] In his book Foster suggests that the sectarian and even racialist emotions focused by the Irish cultural revival were in a sense a 'logical response to generations of English and Anglo-Irish condescension towards "priest-ridden", "backward" Ireland';[70] the initial fault is ascribed clearly to the British. Murphy pays no attention to this, and his outrage lures him into the imbalance which he is so anxious to see in his opponent.

Another such case is that of Brendan Bradshaw's critique of Ruth Dudley Edwards's life of Patrick Pearse. She is accused of writing a 'condescending and mean-spirited biography of that heroic figure', of attacking her subject for being vain to the point of megalomania, and of making no allowance for his considerable achievements.[71] This is simply untrue. His vanity and messianic qualities *are* stressed, and are illustrated, but Bradshaw ignores the other elements of Edwards's portrait which balance those aspects which he dislikes. He overlooks her emphasis on Pearse's dedication, enthusiasm, optimism, honour, idealism, kindness, courage and numerous other noble qualities. No-one would imagine from Bradshaw's attack that Pearse emerges from the biography as a flawed but rounded and *interesting* man, likeable except for his solemnity and limited sense of humour. The book's references are inadequate, but Edwards's remarks which Bradshaw dismisses as unsourced, *are* in fact documented. Even Declan Kiberd, no friend to post-nationalist history, concludes that she restored to Pearse an essential humanity.[72] Neither Bradshaw nor Murphy can bring himself to see the slightest merit in his opponent; they write as if an act of sacrilege has been committed, and as if the culprit is to be damned and excommunicated.

Objections to the interpretation of 1916, and other aspects of Irish history, are not based on mere scholarly disputes; they seem to reflect outrage at a loss of or an assault on *faith*. The links between the Church and rebellion may have been broken, and the use of religious terminology in political contexts has declined, but it seems as if nationalism has become (or has remained) a sort of religion in its own right. Critics are seen as heretics. Murphy attacks in their turn historians such as F. S. L. Lyons and Patrick O'Farrell, who influenced Foster's theories; error, like a cancer, must be traced back to its source before being extirpated. It seems as if some of the attitudes and characteristics which flourished in the years before the Rising have not quite disappeared. Anthony Coughlan has complained how, 'with the zeal of converts to a new religion the country's young liberal intelligentsia threw off the values of their fathers'.[73]

But there is nothing peculiar to Ireland, or to Irish history, in such concern or dismay at what is seen the historians' rejection of familiar and inspiring tales. In France, for example, as long ago as 1912, young nationalists attacked professors of the Sorbonne for 'Germanizing' French culture and replacing classical learning with Teutonic sociology and meaningless erudition; scholars such as Lavisse and Durkheim were accused of having failed to fulfil their mission of educating and shaping the nation's youth; of providing students with ideals or faith in the nation's future.[74] Many decades later, in 1986, David Cannadine was equally gloomy about the writing of history in Britain:

> the best that can be said is that we live in unheroic times, and it is small wonder that most of us succumb to the temptation to write unheroic history. The worst that can be said is that, with no real sense of national identity in the present, and little hope for a national revival in the future, it is an awesome task to ask historians today to construct a version of the national past which will be as usable and relevant in these times as the Welfare State version was in the 1950s, 60s and early 70s.[75]

In France, in Britain, in Ireland and elsewhere, confusion and distress have often resulted from the new approaches, the new irreverence, the new appreciation of ambivalence and uncertainty, and (crucially) the mere accumulation of details which bloat and blur the lean shape and the sharp lines of a narrative. Volume and complexity tend to impose an unheroic or even an ironic style or methodology; centrifugal tendencies stretch and tear apart the core of a simple heroic and moral tale; the more we know about the past the more varied and shapeless it can appear; it becomes less *mythical*; it is less *useful* for those who wish to exploit it, either to preserve or to undermine existing structures and beliefs.

It might be argued that all this does not really matter. Those Irish nationalists, literary critics and others who dislike the way in which many historians get on with their jobs (and get on with them in pretty much in the same way as their counterparts do in other countries) can be left to mutter in the wings, while those who research and write on Irish history and Irish nationalism can muffle their ears and continue to examine and inter-pret the sources. Historians should not worry about being called names – even though this is a besetting fear of academics, who tend, by and large, to be a craven lot. And after all, 'revisionist' is a mild term in the repertoire of abusive epithets.

Up to a point this is a reasonable argument. But occasionally (although not too often, lest they be distracted from other more important activities) historians should stand up and fight back and declare that the past must be rescued from myths and their manipulators. Not only must they continue producing varied, complex, ironic, post-nationalist history, but they must also be ready defy those critics who demand the restoration of inspiring or reassuring legends, who believe that history is too useful to be left to historians. Irony and complexity must not only be cherished; they must be advocated.

NOTES

1 Henry Tudor, *Political Myth* (London, 1972) p. 124.
2 Alvin Jackson, 'Unionist History', in Ciaran Brady ed., *Interpreting Irish History: the Debate on Historical Revisionism* (Dublin, 1994) p. 253.
3 Patrick Pearse, *Political Writings and Speeches* (Dublin, n.d.), p. 24; Joseph Lee, 'In search of Patrick Pearse', in Theo Dorgan and Máirín Ní Dhonnchadha eds, *Revising the Rising* (Dublin, 1991) p. 135.
4 Declan Kiberd, *Inventing Ireland* (London, 1995) p. 207.
5 Michael Collins, *The Path to Freedom* (Dublin, 1922) p. 127; *Sinn Féin*, 7 Jan. 1911, leader.
6 James Connolly, *Labour in Irish History* (Dublin, 1910) p. 76.
7 *Irish Freedom*, Mar. 1913, p. 8.
8 'Seaghan Eireannach', *Leader*, 30 Mar. 1912, pp. 162–3.
9 P. J. McDonnell, *Leader*, 5 Mar. 1910, p. 61.
10 Sean Etchingham, *Republic of Ireland*, 3 Jan. 1922, p. 3.
11 Harry Boland, *Dáil Eireann, Debate on the Treaty* (Dublin, n.d.) p. 304 (7 Jan. 1922).
12 *Irish Freedom*, Nov. 1912, leader.
13 *Freeman's Journal*, 29 July 1915, p. 8.
14 *Irish Worker*, 8 Mar. 1913, leader.
15 John Newsinger, '"I bring Not Peace But A Sword": The Religious Motif in the Irish War of Independence', in *Journal of Contemporary History*, XIII, 3 (1978), 616.

16 Ruth Dudley Edwards, *Patrick Pearse: the Triumph of Failure* (London, 1977), pp. 315–16.
17 John Whyte, '1916 – Revolution and Religion' in F. X. Martin ed., *Leaders and Men of the Easter Rising: Dublin 1916* (London, 1967), pp. 221–3.
18 General Maxwell to Archbishop Walsh, 19 June 1916, Dublin Diocesan Archives, Walsh MSS, 1916, 385/5.
19 *Catholic Bulletin*, May 1919, p. 222.
20 J. J. O'Kelly, *Debate on the Treaty*, p. 135 (22 Dec. 1921).
21 Patrick Browne (later Monsignor Padraig de Brún) to Erskine Childers, 27 Dec. 1921, Childers MSS, National Library of Ireland, MS 15,444(1).
22 Oliver MacDonagh, *States of Mind: A Study of Anglo-Irish Conflict, 1780–1980* (London, 1983) p. 98.
23 Maurice Moynihan ed., *Speeches and Statements by Eamon de Valera, 1917–1973* (Dublin, 1980) pp. 118–19.
24 *Irish Press*, 23 Apr. 1932, p. 6, cited in Shauna Gilligan, 'Image of a Patriot: the Popular and Scholarly Portrayal of Patrick Pearse, 1916–1991' (MA dissertation, University College, Dublin, 1991) pp. 35–6.
25 James Carty, *A Class Book of Irish History*, IV (London, 1943) pp. 111–19.
26 F. X. Martin, '1916 – Myth, Fact and Mystery', *Studia Hibernica* 7 (1967) p. 21.
27 *Wolfe Tone Annual*, 1932, p. 6.
28 Brian O'Higgins, *Easter 1916* (Dublin, 1941) p. 19.
29 Martin Shannon, *Sixteen Roads to Golgotha* (Dublin, 1966).
30 Tom Garvin, 'The Rising and Irish Democracy', in *Revising the Rising*, p. 27.
31 C. Desmond Greaves, *The Life and Times of James Connolly* (London, 1961) p. 328.
32 Greaves, *1916 as History: the Myth of the Blood Sacrifice* (Dublin, 1991) p. 29.
33 James Stephens, *The Insurrection in Dublin* (Dublin, 1916) pp. 25–6.
34 Greaves, *James Connolly*, p. 230.
35 British and Irish Communist Organization, *Connolly and Partition* (Belfast, 1970), p. 6; *The Two Irish Nations* (Belfast, 1975), p. 4.
36 See Ciaran Brady, ' "Constructive and Instrumental": the Dilemma of Ireland's First "New Historians" ', in *Interpreting Irish History*, pp. 25–6.
37 Ulick O'Connor, in Dermot Bolger ed., *Letters from the New Island* (Dublin, 1991), p. 201.
38 Gearóid Ó Tuathaigh, 'Irish Historical "Revisionism"', in *Interpreting Irish History*, p. 306.
39 John A. Murphy, 'Further reflections on Irish Nationalism' in Mark Patrick Hederman and Richard Kearney eds, *The Crane Bag Book of Irish Studies*, (Dublin, 1982), p. 308.
40 Desmond Fennell, *The State of the Nation: Ireland since the Sixties* (Dublin, 1983), p. 14; Luke Gibbons, 'Introduction', in Seamus Deane ed., *The Field Day Anthology of Irish Writing* (Derry, 1991), III, 561.
41 Ronan Fanning, 'The Great Enchantment: uses and abuses of modern Irish history', in James Dooge ed., *Ireland in the Contemporary World: Essays in Honour of Garret FitzGerald* (Dublin, 1986) p. 136.
42 Greaves, *James Connolly*, p. 337.
43 F. X. Martin ed., 'Eoin MacNeill on the Easter Rising', *Irish Historical Studies*, XII, 47 (1961); Leon Ó Broin, *Dublin Castle and the 1916 Rising* (London, 1966) and *The Chief Secretary: Augustine Birrell in Ireland* (London, 1969); William Irwin Thompson, *The Imagination of an Insurrection: Dublin 1916* (New York, 1967); K. B. Nowlan, ed., *The Making of 1916* (Dublin, 1969).
44 'Anniversaries', *Independent*, 29 Apr. 1989; 'Irishman's Diary', *The Irish Times*, 16 May 1995 and 14 Mar. 1996.
45 Margaret Atwood, *Cat's Eye* (London, 1989), p. 86.

46 Conor Cruise O'Brien, 'Nationalism and the reconquest of Ireland', in *Crane Bag Book*, p. 95.
47 Daltún Ó Ceallaigh, 'Reconsiderations', in Daltún Ó Ceallaigh ed., *Reconsiderations of Irish History and Culture* (Dublin, 1994), p. 22.
48 Owen Dudley Edwards, *Éamon de Valera* (Cardiff, 1987) p. 145.
49 Denis Donoghue, *Warrenpoint* (London, 1991) pp. 169–70, 172.
50 Seamus Deane, 'Wherever Green is Read', in *Revising the Rising*, pp. 96, 100.
51 *The Irish Times,* 9 Mar. 1991, p. 5.
52 Anthony Coughlan, 'Ireland's Marxist Historians', in *Interpreting Irish History*, p. 304; Brendan Bradshaw, 'Revising Irish History', in *Reconsiderations,* pp. 28, 37; Bradshaw, *Times Literary Supplement,* 16 Dec. 1994, p. 17.
53 Deane, 'Wherever Green is Read', p. 102.
54 *Ibid.*, p. 95.
55 Deane, 'Introduction', *Field Day Anthology*, III, 685.
56 Terry Eagleton, 'A Postmodern Punch', in *Irish Studies Review,* 6 (Spring 1994), p. 2; David Lloyd, *Anomalous States: Irish Writing and the Post-Colonial Moment* (Dublin, 1993) p. 125.
57 Kiberd, 'The Elephant of Revolutionary Forgetfulness', in *Revising the Rising*, pp. 15, 10.
58 Kiberd, 'Post-Colonial Ireland: "Being Different"' in *Reconsiderations*, p. 96.
59 *Observer,* 7 Jan. 1996, Review, p. 15.
60 Fennell, *The State of the Nation*, p. 91.
61 Gibbons, 'Introduction', *Field Day Anthology*, III, 568, 566.
62 Tom Dunne, 'New Histories: beyond "Revisionism"', *Irish Review*, 12 (1992), 6.
63 Deane, 'Introduction', *Field Day Anthology*, III, 681.
64 Fennell, 'Against Revisionism', in *Interpreting Irish History*, p. 184.
65 *Irish Press*, 24 Apr. 1986, p. 13.
66 Lee, 'In Search of Patrick Pearse', in *Revising the Rising*, p. 129.
67 Gibbons, 'Introduction', *Field Day Anthology*, III, 562–6.
68 R. F. Foster, *Modern Ireland, 1600–1972* (London, 1988) pp. 484–6, 498, 504.
69 Brian P. Murphy, 'The Canon of Irish Cultural History' in *Interpreting Irish History*, pp. 228, 229, 232.
70 Foster, *Modern Ireland*, p. 453.
71 Bradshaw, 'Revising Irish History', p. 37.
72 Kiberd, 'The Elephant', pp. 5–6.
73 Anthony Coughlan, 'Ireland's Marxist Historians', in *Interpreting Irish History*, p. 290.
74 Robert Wohl, *The Generation of 1914* (London, 1980) p. 6.
75 *Times Literary Supplement*, 10 Oct. 1986, p. 1140.

11   Religious Conflict in Twentieth-Century India

C. A. Bayly

Religious conflict has taken innumerable forms in colonial and independent India. In addition to the most obvious and politically momentous conflict between Hindus and Muslims, there has been an underswell of antagonism between Sikhs and Hindus, Hindus and low caste neo-Buddhists, and, in the far south of India, between Hindus and Christians. Rivalries within religious communities have been equally violent at times. Sunni Muslims, for example, have battled with the Shia minority; zealous Akali Sikhs with more 'broadchurch' Nankpanthi Sikhs; different groups of Hindu renouncers and sects have also come into collision.

This chapter mainly concerns the conflicts between Hindus and Muslims across the subcontinent. Indians, Pakistanis and Bangladeshis tend to see these as the paradigm of all other 'communalisms', that is to say deep-rooted religious or caste conflicts.

I shall illustrate in the case of India that religious conflict has social roots. It has fed on the protest of declining elites, on the desire for status of aspiring elites, and on the passionate resistance of the poor and underprivileged. To examine the discourse of religious violence outside the context of its social meaning would therefore be false. I want additionally to stress, however, the importance of two other determining conditions of religious conflict in modern India: firstly the role of the state in initiating religious discord and in giving it institutional form; secondly, the role of associations in mobilizing religious traditions. The significance of associations and the values they propagate cannot, I believe, be reduced to matters of social protest: they have an autonomous role in maintaining symbols of faith and identity; these are markers of difference, though not necessarily harbingers of antagonism.

Certainly, there is the danger of perpetuating stereotypes. For some commentators, simply to focus on this topic betrays an orientalist cast of mind in its pejorative, modern sense. In recent years, Edward Said and Ronald Inden have both deplored the tendency of Europeans to construct Asian histories and societies in terms of religious categories which deny individual agency and rationality to their people.[1] They have a point. When two years ago Hindu extremists demolished a Mosque at Ajodhya in northern India, the western press seized on an issue which was assumed to be what India, or Pakistan, or for that matter 'the Middle East', was all about: namely, religious conflict. The correspondents and editors knew that Asians are prone to rehearse for ever ancient religious conflicts. They knew that India's weak civil society is always on the verge of disintegration in the face of religious zealotry or the irrationalities of caste. The West has customarily lost sight of almost everything else about India: economic change, industrialization, the rise of Indian capitalism, the persistence of Indian democracy, let alone art and intellectual history.

The corrective offered by Said and Inden has been valuable. Writing on communalism, particularly in the west, has often failed to notice the malleability and fickleness of supposed primordial religious identities. Within eighteen months of the Ajodhya incident, when the western press was predicting the permanent division of Indian society into mutually hostile Hindu and Muslim blocs, self-proclaimed class movements swept to power in the most populous Indian state and displaced the Bharatiya Janata Party which had been associated with the demolition of the mosque. The 'Hindu wave' had apparently broken on the rocks of economic and political contingency. Studies of earlier communal riots have also shown how quickly antagonisms could subside, to be replaced by the solidarities of region or social class.[2] In such a shifting world, historians must avoid assuming the existence of fixed identities and rigid communities.

On the other hand, it would be a mistake to underrate the persistence in south Asia of ideas and traditions which can, and do, give rise to periodic conflict. The memories of past wrongs are as bitter as the recollections of past harmony idyllic. When I was first in India in the 1960s, not so long after the Partition of 1947, and in the midst of a series of Indo-Pakistan wars, I was astonished by the level of mutual distrust, even hatred I sometimes encountered between members of different religions. Perhaps these were feelings that Indians would reveal to a foreigner sooner than to each other. Non-Muslims spoke with venom to me about Muslims: 'I can smell a Muslim from a hundred yards', 'the Muslims always smile when they stab you', 'we learnt their language, Persian, and worked for them, but always hated them'. Muslims, then more self-confident, responded in kind. These were the sentiments of educated citizens of Allahabad, a High Court Centre and seat of a University during the palmy days of Congress 'secularism'. Perhaps what has happened in the last five years is that such views can now be openly stated, not that they did not exist before. While we must beware of the orientalist fallacy, it is equally important to avoid a sentimental image of a harmonious Indian society, wickedly divided by colonialists, priests or capitalists. To replace the image of a land riven by ancient religious conflicts with a facile 'Merrie India', would be of little value, least of all those who deprecate religious conflict.

The writings of contemporaries and of historians on the origins of communalism have been strung between polar opposites. On the one hand, there is what can be be called the false-consciousness argument. This sees all religious conflict as a manifestation of class or political interest. Opposed to it is the 'primordialist' position which stresses the all-encompassing nature of doctrine and argues that Muslims and Hindus, Hindus and Sikhs are bound by the precepts of their religions and the lessons of their history to keep their distance from each other.

The false consciousness argument has long been strongly held within the Indian National Congress. According to this view, where Hindu was pitted against Muslim, this was a consequence of manipulation by feudal interests, or lately, by capitalists.[3] Alternatively, it was the result of conspiracy by malign British power, or more recently by Pakistan, Iran or Saudi Arabia. Jawaharlal Nehru was a sophisticated proponent of this view.[4] It seems to explain why he did not do more to compromise with the separatist Muslim League in the later 1930s when its rise to influence might have been averted.

Amongst academics, it has inevitably been the traditional Marxists above all who have seen in all communal violence and division the spectre of class-conflict. The argument was first advanced, ironically, by an American historian, Wilfrid Cantwell Smith, who in his *Modern Islam in India* of 1943 argued that Muslim separatism in India was driven by what he called 'the Muslim bourgeoisie expanding during the Second World War'.[5] Later in his career Smith regretted this youthful materialism and emphasized the autonomy of faith with almost equal vigour. Today the main vehicle of the intellectual left in India, *The Economic and Political Weekly*, still carries many articles which seem to subscribe to the argument of false consciousness, that mobilized religions are masks for class interests.

The other extreme, the argument for primordial religious identities, was equally prominent among the ideologues of the Muslim League who asserted that Hindus and Muslims in India represented 'two nations'. These nations might temporarily ally in the anti-colonial struggle but could never merge. This view found favour amongst many Islamic modernists and was expounded initially by the nineteenth-century Muslim leader, Sir Syed Ahmed Khan, founder of the Anglo-Muhammadan College at Aligarh in north India.[6] To a lesser extent it was found among the purist Muslims who rejected the moral and educational influence of the West. Its political home today is Pakistan, a state which has become increasingly theocratic since independence and has replaced the study of history with what are called 'Pakistan Studies', thus projecting the history of the Islamic republic back to a period before Islam existed.

In academic circles outside Pakistan itself, the primordialist position – that religion was prior and social conflict a surface phenomenon – has been less acceptable. But sophisticated versions lurk in some recent studies. A number of American historians of Indian religion imply that a purist Islam is the inevitable long-term trend of social and doctrinal changes throughout the subcontinent. Though few of them actually argue that conflict beween Hindus and Muslims has been inevitable, the notion that scriptural doctrines and beliefs are likely increasingly to structure everday life seems to point in that direction. Farzana Shaikh, a Pakistani resident in Britain, has also argued a strong case against a contingent, or socially-located understanding of the Pakistan movement.[7] Islamic societies in her interpretation necessarily seek to be political societies, because there can be no doctrinal and practical difference between secular and religious law. In India, such views have not gained much academic respectability, but they are strongly held amongst the supporters and ideologues of the Hindu right-wing parties, notably the BJP and the Shiv Sena of western India. In this reading, the land of India – Bharat – was always essentially Hindu. Muslims and Christians may reside in it, but because nation, race and religion are congruent, minorities live in India only on sufferance.

There have been some challenges to the notion of religious conflict as false consciousness even among Indian academics of the left. Here I am referring to recent changes of direction among people writing history from below – the so-called Subaltern Studies Group, who have used Gramscian terminology but have often been trying to find an elusive common ground between E.P. Thompson and Jacques Derrida in their studies of Indian peasants, tribals and workers.[8] Understandably, the subtler historians of this group have found difficulties with the false-consciousness doctrine. If one is to argue for the agency of peasants and workers in their own histories, it has become increasingly embarrassing to insist that their religious differences were purely the result of manipulation by British officials or Indian elites. The work of Gyanendra Pandey epitomizes the strengths and weaknesses of this position most clearly. His *The Construction of Communalism in Colonial North India* argues that Hindu-Muslim antagonism was 'created' from above by colonial policy-makers and, to a lesser extent, by elite politicians. At the same time, however, agency must be reserved for the peasantry, even in matters of belief. Pandey argues, therefore, that rural Hindus rallied around the sacred cow as a symbol of community and harmony. The problem was that protecting the cow from hurt came to involve attacks on Muslim neighbours who had begun to slaughter her on days of religious festivals, affirming their own respectability within a revived Muslim community.[9] Both of Pandey's positions are plausible. The problem is how to reconcile them. Another former historian of the Subaltern Studies group – the historians from below – has displayed a sinister consistency in this respect. As columnist for a Delhi news-magazine, he argued during the Mosque incident of 1992, that the wave of Hindu activism was a genuinely popular movement, rather than just a 'constructed' plot by big business or Indian expatriates.

I want now to go on to try and strike a balance between a view of twentieth-century religious conflict in India which stresses the autonomy of religious values and one which sees antagonisms as socially and politically constructed. I want to consider the matter at three levels. First, I will discuss the *institutional* politics of parties and constitutions. Secondly, I will discuss the level of traditional and voluntary organizations and the *traditions* they embody. Thirdly, I will consider *popular actions* and reactions, concentrating especially on religious riots and mass demonstrations.

It seems to me that the links between these three levels of political action have been, and remain extremely weak. When actors at these three levels find common cause – as they did during the Partition riots of 1946–7 or during the Ajodhya Mosque incident of 1992 – the notion that India is irremediably divided on the ground of community achieves a degree of plausibility. However, this contingency is quite rare. Equally, over the long periods when these several levels of politics do not mesh with each other one may get the impression that the 'communal problem' has disappeared. This is not true either, since at the level of organization and tradition, groups with a commitment to emphasizing religion continue to promote a sense of exclusive identity.

First, then, let us consider the level of institutional politics. Here there has been a consistent pattern since the later nineteenth century. It has been declining or embattled elites both among Hindus and Muslims who have been the prime movers in the politics of religious community. The most striking example of this was the Muslim League, founded in 1906, which argued for special electoral representation for Muslims within the British colonial system and, after 1940, raised the demand for an ill-defined Pakistan. The politicians and patrons of the League may well have struck a chord with poorer Muslims from time to time. They may have held sincere religious opinions. But their prime and often stated aim was to protect Muslims, by which they meant elite Muslims, from the new competitive world which the Crown's government had inaugurated in 1858. Fearing the rise of Hindu commercial and professional classes, they wanted to preserve their position in government service.[10]

In the twentieth century the Indian National Congress came into alliance with a predominantly Hindu peasantry over much of north India. After 1937 a revamped Muslim League drew on the support of landed interests in many parts of northern India who feared the populism and agrarian radicalism of the Congress leadership. The institutional politics of the Muslim League was driven, above all, by Muslim gentry and professional people, fearful of competition, industrialization and the end of rural privilege.[11]

The same type of analysis applies to many of the constituencies which self-consciously Hindu leaders sought to make their own. Hindu apologists wrote, and still write, as if Hindus were always the down-trodden masses seeking emancipation. In the later nineteenth century, however, many of those Hindu leaders who were conspicuously hostile to constitutional compromise with the Muslim League were concentrated in Bengal, the urban Punjab and western Indian outside Bombay. The high-caste Hindu professional and commercial groups, the people who became associated with the Hindu Central Association or provincial Hindu associations, were also staring decline in the face. For instance, they included Hindu traders and professional people of the towns of the Punjab who faced being politically swamped by a largely Muslim hinterland. In western India, formerly dominant priestly and writer groups similarly channelled their fears of decline into an intransigent religious politics.

This theme has been expertly developed by Joya Chatterji in *Bengal Divided*.[12] Until recently most historians sought the origin of the push for Pakistan between 1944 and 1947 in the Muslim League, especially in the provinces of Muslim majority (Punjab and Bengal) which feared the emergence of a central authority in independent India dominated by Congress Hindus. Chatterji, however, has identified a powerful impetus to Partition within the ranks of the predominantly Hindu Bengal Congress. Bengali Hindus of high status had become increasingly disillusioned with the policy of the all-India leadership. Since 1900 they had seen influence slipping from their grasp. It was the assertive Muslim sub-tenure holders of eastern Bengal who called the shots in local politics. Anticipating the crumbling of their influence as landlords and the decline of their Hindu gentry culture, a division of the province seemed attractive. In this way, a poverty-stricken Muslim east could be cut away from a predominantly Hindu west, which would retain the city of Calcutta, its industries and international trade.

Not all the institutional politicians and magnates who favoured communal politics and religious reservations could, of course, be classed as declining or embattled elites. Wealthy nouveaux riches, commercial communities or middling people provided both money and organization for avowedly 'communal' organizations among the Hindus. Tobacco sellers, west coast merchant communities and even proud and impoverished weavers gave the Muslim League a network of connections below the level of the landholders and literati. Such groups were important in sustaining Muslim candidates in local politics and providing recruits for defensive organisations. If we are considering party and institutional politics, however, religious difference and religious antagonism could better be seen as an aspect of the social protest of the embattled masters than the revolt of the helots, at least up to the 1960s.

It is here that the role of the colonial state must be introduced. The British were, after all, the ultimate declining elite in twentieth-century India. For the British 'rallying the moderates' meant rallying the conservatives. The aim was to disable the nationalist movement by splitting it down to a regional level and fragmenting it into interest groups. The British had always regarded India as an amalgam of castes and religious communities. The Muslims were a distinct 'race' to them as much as they were to Muslim leaders such as Sir Syed Ahmed Khan. Their aim, however, was not directly to stimulate religious discord. This might impede trade and revenue collection and would certainly bring down on the government of India the hostile scrutiny of parliament and the British government. Instead, the creation of religious categories in electoral politics and in institutions would help to advance the cause of those conservative forces in India which might support them.

We can see this clearly in the case of the decentralized electorates created in 1909 under the terms of the reforms of Lord Morley and Lord Minto. This piece of legislation created elected majorities in provincial assemblies, based on a tiny electorate. Notoriously, it entrenched the principle of separate electorates for Muslims and hence consolidated an emerging separatist Muslim politics. Once the British had conceded this principle and the Muslim League had accepted it, Congress could never banish it from India until independence. When we look at the small, direct Muslim electorates created at this time, though, we see that the state's strategy was only religious division in the formal sense. What it was really looking for was a conservative constituency. Most of the people enfranchised in the so-called Muslim electorates were retired policemen or non-commissioned Indian officers, small landlords and members of subordinate administrative families.[13] These were natural loyalists.

Elsewhere where the British gave, or sought to give, special privileges to religious or ethnic groups this usually reflected a search for conservative allies. It was as true in electoral arrangements as it was in the Indian army regiments, which had become after 1857 the preserve of particular religions or castes. Richard Fox pushed the argument to the limits in his book on the Sikhs, *Lions of the Punjab*, where he argued that the modern identity of this religious community owed almost everything to the patronage of British Indian Army officers who codified the rituals and marriage practices of their Sikh soldiery whose allegiances before this intervention had been much more malleable.[14] Needless to say, the implication that the British created modern Sikhism was not too popular in the Punjab.

The institutional politics of religious difference in the colonial period can reasonably be seen, then, as a defensive tactic by the British and certain declining elites. Does this analysis hold for independent India with a mass electorate, ferocious political conflict and uneven economic growth? In ideological terms the Republic of India has been deeply opposed to any hint of religious communalism. The British separate electorates were abandoned and single community parties were discountenanced. But beneath the surface, the commitment of the state to 'secularism' has been less solid, and its policies have sometimes seemed to perpetuate those very divisions which its early leaders so deprecated. For one thing, positive discrimination in government employment and education has been targetted on the basis of caste, another colonial legacy; and this has raised questions about the status of religious minorities. Next, post-colonial politicians have tended to play a more subtle game of religious politics than their colonial predecessors, but one which nevertheless privileges religion as a political category. Mrs Gandhi seems to have conceded much to Islamic intransigents in Kashmir and Sikh radicals in the Punjab because she feared the moderate, but better organized regionalist parties in those states. As Congress has forfeited the Muslim vote which it has held since independence, its tendency to accentuate religious politics has increased.[15] Muslims supported Congress because they believed its secular credentials. When support drifted away, Rajiv Gandhi acquiesced in Muslim demands that their personal law, in matters of divorce, should supersede that of the Indian Union. This in turn infuriated the Hindu right. Recently political competition forced the Congress to play safe on the matter of Hindu temples supposedly demolished to make way for mosques under Muslim rule. Muslims have responded by turning away from the Congress in droves since 1992. All this shows that democratic and avowedly secular governments can be prisoners of competitive religious politics if they once bow their heads to it.

Having discussed the importance of declining elites and the role of the state, I now pass on to the second category which I want to discuss in regard to religious conflict. This is the role of institutions, both traditional and modern in sustaining religious identities. I would agree with the premise of much of our discussion, that religious conflict expresses, often quite directly, fears and aspirations which derive directly from social and economic inequalities or changes. I do not, however, believe that religious conflict can be reduced to these conditions. The sense of different identity which underlies it in India and elsewhere has been constantly nurtured by organizations which train, educate and indoctrinate special bodies of devotees and the public. These cannot be understood without taking account of the meanings of the doctrines and traditions which these groups claim to represent. So, for example, Richard Fox's argument that the colonial state created Sikh identity is too absolute, because it cannot explain why it was a Sikh identity that people valued. We need to supplement it with a discussion of the tradition of Sikh disciplehood, represented particularly by the Akali cult, which survived as an autonomous force even at periods when the boundaries between Sikh and Hindu were palpably weakening. This has been superbly accomplished by Harjot Singh Oberoi who writes about the strong sense of purity and pollution which underlay the beliefs of the devoted Sikh and served to energize them in their resistance both to Muslim competitors and to the colonial state. Oberoi's testimony is all the more powerful because the drift of his argument is to show how looser, pre-colonial identities were hardened up in the later nineteenth century.[16]

When we consider *organization*, I have in mind two separable but interconnected types. What I have to call traditional organization, with all the difficulties of that adjective, here, for Muslims, I would class the organizations associated with the mosque and the sufi mystical orders, or old international contacts of learning linking India to central and West Asia. For Hindus and Sikhs, these are represented by the classes of Brahmin teachers and ascetics associated with temples and by the ancient ties linking families and castes to the holy places of Hinduism and Sikhism. These organizations have remained vital, and often flourished during the colonial and post-colonial years. Hindu temples and monasteries receive veneration and huge sums of money from wealthy businessmen and ordinary people. Financial support for Muslim institutions has come directly from Indians who have worked in the Middle East, or indirectly from Arab and Iranian trusts and government sources. Over the past century pilgrimage within and outside India has become easier with a resulting increase of donations from wider and wider circles of pilgrims.

Representatives of these revived traditional institutions have played a low key role in most of the modern movements of Hindu and Muslim regeneration. The Shankaracharyas or abbots of the major Hindu monasteries were involved in the first Hindu associations which emerged after 1880.[17] Their political activity has recently become more public. The Shankaracharya of the southern temple town of Kanchipuram held a number of prominent all-India political pilgrimages in recent years, and these have notably raised the temperature of religious politics.[18] On the Muslim side, the role of the *ulama*, the learned ones, was always more circumspect. Some important teachers opposed the foundation of Pakistan on the grounds that it would strand too many Muslims in India. After Independence many of the Muslim leadership continued to support Congress. Recently, however, with the festering Kashmir issue and the resurgence of political Hinduism, some clerics have become more politically assertive. The leadership of the Great Friday Mosque in Delhi pushed hard for the reintroduction of Muslim family law.

Alongside these traditional organizations are the modern voluntary associations of religious politics. These also emerged after 1880 and existed in a symbiotic relationship with the major political parties, the Congress and the Muslim League. Although priests and learned men were associated with them, they were largely recruited from professional and commercial people and emphasized education and community help over and above worship. They ranged from relatively moderate Hindu or Muslim associations and conferences to cell-like organizations with rigid ideologies and authoritarian mien. I am here thinking of the RSS, a Hindu supremacist organization founded in the 1920s whose aim is to convert India into a Hindu state.[19] Muslims and Christians can have a part in the country, the RSS argues, but only if they 'recognize Lord Ram as hero'. Rama is the virtuous warrior divinity who has represented the personal morality and social regeneration of Hindus for many centuries, but in modern conflicts has been assigned a more aggressive and intransigent role, supported by almost racist ideologies. It was particularly important that the demolished mosque of Ajodhya was said to have been built over the birth place of Lord Rama. The RSS had links to the assassin of Mahatma Gandhi, who was blamed for partition. More recently, its cells have underlain the political organization of the BJP, though many of that party's supporters find it too extreme and the appeal of its homogenizing creed to its present allies among the militant traditionalist sects is in question.

Now here some caveats need to be entered. I am not claiming that these organizations are always or necessarily involved in an aggressive promotion of communalism. Some like the RSS or the youth cadres of the Shiv Sena of Bombay are. Others, however, simply see themselves as propagating correct or purified forms of their own faith and ensuring the education, health or welfare of the young. I would argue, however, that the cumulative impact of these organizations has increased religious difference, though not necessarily overt conflict. It has privileged religious over other identities, especially those of local community. These movements have often targeted syncretic religious cults in towns and country which previously sustained a commonalty of feeling between ordinary people, beneath differences of confessional affiliation. These organizations might well disavow any intention to divide people along religious grounds. They do so nevertheless.

Secondly, I am not arguing that these organizations exist outside the field of economic and social conflict. Traditional religious institutions and the modern cadres of religious politics have both recruited from identifiable social groups. Many of the leaders come, once again, from old established families under pressure, oppressed perhaps by stringent quotas for the lower castes in government employment. Conversely, many of the followers have been recruited from frustrated and impoverished youth in town and country. The western Indian Hindu chauvinist party, the Shiv Sena, which recently won the elections in the state of Maharashtra, made a definite effort to recruit

unemployed youths of lower caste to its support. Many of the Sikh militants
who took the Golden Temple, and sustained a guerilla war against the Indian
army, appear to have hailed from rural families in areas which did not benefit
from the fabled Green Revolution of new seed varieties in the 1960s. They
were sons of families without electric pump-sets and tractors.

All the same, autonomous weight must be given to the strength of taught
and learned religious affiliation. It is difficult to put a price on pride of
family or lineage. It is also difficult to underestimate the power of new media
of consciousness-raising: the religious soap opera and oleograph print for
Hindus; the tape-recorded sermon for Muslims. The institutional persuaders
appear to have a better story and a fresher appeal than the tired proponents
of secularism and tolerance.

The final dimension of religious conflict in India to be discussed is the
popular movement, and particularly the so-called communal, or Hindu
Muslim riot. We now have an almost continuous record of such riots from
the late seventeenth century through to 1995. Large amounts of scholarly
time have been spent on analysing them following the models of Rudé,
Hobsbawm, Thompson and le Roy Ladurie.[20] At one time historians saw
these riots as unique windows into society through which to gauge social
relations in general and relations between religious communities in particular. Proponents of the 'social history' school of the 1960s took the view that
riots were often a mask for other, deeper changes in material patterns of life.
In the towns of north India riots between Hindus and Muslims were
portrayed as 'really' riots between weavers, butchers and other artisans, who
were mainly Muslim, and money-lenders, shopkeepers and professional
people, who were mainly Hindu. In the countryside, rising middle peasant
groups rioted against old established or declining landholding families.
These were thought to have masqueraded as conflicts between Hindus and
Muslims. For example, there were many riots in Bengal in the 1930s depression, when Muslim tenants were pitted against usurious Hindu landholders,
whose credit networks had been damaged by the collapse of land prices.[21] In
other parts of India, the situation was reversed, with Hindus as tenants and
Muslims as small landowners. In any event, according to this view, communalism was often determined by underlying class conflict.

Another version of this socially reductionist view was that Hindu-
Muslim conflict was 'really' all about the clashes of local faction-leaders
vying for supremacy in local political arenas which had been created by the
colonial power. Studies of riots in independent India have focussed more
often on the role of immigrant communities, or on struggles between urban
landholders over high-rent slums. This was one explanation given for the
savage upsurge of rioting between Hindus and Muslims in the slum areas of
Bombay in 1993.[22]

In the later 1980s and 1990s, historians have come to question some of these views from a number of different perspectives. First, they have argued that policing and the apparatus of the state must be given much more weight.[23] It was heavy police or administrative intervention which gave the appearance of inter-community conflict. Secondly, recent writers have emphasized the ritualistic dimension of these conflicts. According to Sandria Freitag, an American historian, the public demonstration and riot of the twentieth century represented a novel projection of the idea of community into a public arena.[24] Face-to-face relations of belief were transformed into demonstrations of community.

More radically still, some commentators have abandoned the social science agenda of finding a social or social structural 'cause' for riots and instead have looked at them in terms of the discourse of community which they reveal.[25] We can never know what really happened goes the argument; all we can do is to show how people represented communities in conflict. This approach is interesting, though self-limited. Certainly, the representation of the Muslim in India has appeared to change in recent years. Once they were regarded as a fanatical and conservative Other. Now, Hindu zealots often describe Muslims in terms which we recognize from our own parochial racisms: they are said to account for ninety per cent of the crime in India; they are terrorists with Middle Eastern connections; they bring AIDS into the country, and so on. The question which all these positions need to answer is: how significant are communal riots anyway?

I must confess to some scepticism about any attempts to find a set of 'causes' for riots, or even to define very adequately what was and what was not a religous riot. Certainly, a huge variety of different phenomena are involved. In some cases policing or administrative interventions were critical; in other cases social tensions and the insurgency of suppressed groups against the privileged coloured them. In some cases, again, clashing religious calendars, or chance happenings set off entirely unexpected events. In some cases politicians deliberately manipulated volatile constituencies for electoral or pecuniary gain. In my opinion religious tensions have a long history in India stretching back even to the pre-colonial era when religious boundaries were fluid and much religious practice was syncretic.[26]

While one can point to certain periods of greater tension, notably the 1930s, the period of the Partition and the last ten years, it is doubtful if the incidence of communal riots in themselves will tell us much about the growth of decline of communal mentalities, or the direction of South Asian politics as a whole. In general the links between popular explosions of this sort and the politics of institutions or of organizations which I was talking about earlier have been quite tenuous. Quite often compacts between local leaders or bosses have been able to prevent the export of conflict from high politics to the localities. The Bengal Communist governments have been quite successful, for instance, in preventing rioting in the aftermath of conflict at the all-India level. The opposite has also been true: all-India leadership has sometimes been able to take the sting out of local rioting when the political will has been there. Historians, politicians and the press have, in short, often over-interpreted the events which we call communal riots in India. Of course, they leave memories of hatred and bereavement; they are inscribed in histories; they tell us about some popular attitudes. It would, however, be wrong to try to deduce the direction of politics in India from them now or in the past. It would even be hazardous to posit any stable mentalities by examining them.

The three levels of religious conflict discussed – the institutional political level, the level of organization, and the level of popular conflict – are interconnected. But those connections are often distant, they are contingent and they are malleable. This offers some degree of comfort. Strong leadership at the political and organizational level has been able, and may yet be able to prevent the permanent polarization of religious communities that many in South Asia fear. Equally, there are some signs that the relationship between these domains is undergoing a shift. And that shift may presage deepening conflict.

One ominous feature is the relative decline of the state, especially the Union state, and the growing power of organizations. We have tended to see the Indian government in the colonial and post-colonial periods as a powerful one. But the apparent power of the centre masked growing weaknesses which have become more and more marked in recent years. The Indian state now commands a declining part of the Indian GDP in relative terms; its control over wealth, the means of production and employment are now more limited. Since economic deregulation, the impotence of Delhi has become more pronounced. The Indian central state has declined along with the Congress Party which once seemed almost indistinguishable from it. By contrast the wealthy middle class, expatriate Indians, and aspiring groups from below, have funded and fostered sectarian and communal organisations. This strength has flowed into the political parties such as the BJP or the Shiv Sena which play host to them. The campaign to demolish the mosque at Ajodhya was supported with huge funds from merchant groups, for example. This has an effect, too, on popular politics. If it is the local RSS cell, or Shiv Sena boss, or the abbot of the Hindu monastery who can provide jobs, food or a patch of land, the recruitment of the underprivileged, bored or enraged into these institutions will increase. The relative decline of the state may yet provide the conditions for the forging of stronger links between popular discontents and the politics of religious identity. Therein lies the danger. In Pakistan, the mullahs, the sectarian leaders and the radical religious cells have been able to snatch the government of the city of Karachi away from the state. In Bombay an alliance of local chauvinists and right politicians has consolidated its hold over state government. Of course, in its play for power at the Centre, the BJP may yet soften its line and become a broad-church party like the Indian National Congress before it. Again, sectarian and regional differences within the Hindu right may fracture its unity. Zealotry can only take you a little way in a country like India. The auguries are mixed, nevertheless.

NOTES

1 Edward Said, *Orientalism* (New York, 1978). Ronald Inden, *Imagining India* (Oxford, 1990).
2 See, for example, Vinita Damodaran, *Broken Promises, Popular Protest, Indian Nationalism and the Congress Party in Bihar 1935–46* (Delhi, 1992) pp. 284–369.
3 Bipan Chandra, *Nationalism and Colonialism in Modern India* (Delhi, 1979).
4 Jawaharlal Nehru, *An Autobiography* (Bombay, 1962 rpr. of 1936 ed.) pp. 605–6.
5 Wilfred Cantwell Smith, *Modern Islam in India* (Lahore, 1943) pp. 12–13.
6 Francis Robinson, *Separatism Among Indian Muslims. The Politics of the U.P. Muslims, 1860–1923* (Cambridge, 1974).
7 Farzana Shaikh, *Community and Consensus in Islam. Muslim Representation in Colonial India, 1860–1947* (Delhi, 1986).
8 Ranajit Guha, *Subaltern Studies* (Delhi, 1980–95), 8 vols.
9 Gyanendra Pandey, *The Construction of Communalism in Colonial North India* (Delhi, 1990).
10 Francis Robinson, *Separatism Among Indian Muslims. The Politics of the U.P. Muslims, 1860–1923* (Cambridge, 1974).
11 David Page, *Prelude to Partition. The Indian Muslims and the Imperial System of Control, 1920–32* (Delhi, 1982). Lance Brennan, 'The Illusion of Security; the Background to Muslim Separatism in the UP', *Modern Asian Studies*, 18, 2, 237–72.
12 Joya Chatterji, *Bengal Dividend. Hindu Communalism and Partition, 1932–47* (Cambridge, 1994).
13 C. A. Bayly, *The Local Roots of Indian Politics. Allahbad, 1880–1920* (Oxford, 1975), pp. 202–5.
14 R.G. Fox, *Lions of the Punjab. Culture in the Making* (Berkeley, 1985).
15 Manini Chatterjee, 'The BJP: Political mobilisation for Hindutva', *South Asia Bulletin*, 14, I, 1994, 14–23.
16 Harjot SIngh Oberoi, 'Brotherhood of the Pure. The Poetics and Politics of Cultural Transgression', *Modern Asian Studies*, 26, I, 157–97.
17 Bayly, *The Local Roots*, pp. 107–11.
18 S. Bayly, 'History and the Fundamentalists. India after the Ajodhya crisis', *Bulletin of the American Academy of Arts and Sciences*, 46, April 1993, 7, 7–26.
19 B.D. Graham, *Hindu Nationalism and Indian Politics* (Cambridge, 1990).
20 Katherine Prior, 'The British Administration of Hinduism, 1780–1900', unpub. PhD thesis, University of Cambridge, 1990. Gyanendra Pandey, *The Construction of Communalism in Colonial North India* (Delhi, 1990). Sandria Freitag, *Collective Action and Community. Public Arenas and the Emergence of Communalism in North India. 1870–1940* (Berkeley, 1989).

21 Sugata Bose, *Agrarian Bengal: Economy, Social Structure and Politics, 1919–47* (Cambridge, 1986).

22 J. Masselos, 'The Bombay riots of January 1993; the politics of urban conflagration', *South Asia*, 17, 1974, special issue, pp. 79–95.

23 P. McGinn, 'Governance and Resistance in North India Towns, c.1860–1900', unpub. PhD thesis, University of Cambridge, 1993.

24 Freitag, *Collective Action and Community.*

25 See, for example, Peter Van der Veer, 'The Foreign Hand: Oriental Discourse in Sociology and Communalism' in C. Breckenbridge and P. Van der Veer, *Orientalism and the Postcolonial Predicament* (Philadelphia, 1993).

26 C.A. Bayly, 'The Pre-history of "Communalism"? Religious Conflict in India, 1700–1860', *Modern Asian Studies*, 19, 2, 177–203.

12 Bible Prophecy Belief in Modern American Culture

Paul Boyer

For fifty-one days in the spring of 1993, media attention worldwide focused on Waco, Texas, as federal authorities besieged a tiny religious sect known as the Branch Davidians. On 19 April some eighty Davidians and their leader David Koresh died fiery deaths in an apocalyptic finale as the tanks rolled in.[1]

Precisely two years later, 19 April 1995, a bomb destroyed the US federal building in Oklahoma City, killing nearly 200 people. A month earlier, in March 1995, attention focused on Tokyo, where a subway nerve-gas attack killed ten persons and sickened more than 10,000. The attack was soon linked to a shadowy cult group, Aum Shinriko, with many followers in Japan and elsewhere.

Somewhat obscured in the media coverage of these events was the apocalyptic world-view of the groups involved. While Aum Shinriko's beliefs remain obscure, the apocalyptic strand emerges in the leader's stark warnings that the world will end in 1997.

As for the American groups, the Branch Davidians represented a heretical offshoot of the Seventh Day Adventist Church, a group saturated in Bible prophecy. As one former Davidian recalled: 'Their main concern was getting the message out to the world of Christ's second coming.' The two suspects who were quickly arrested and charged in the Oklahoma City bombing proved to have links to the 'Michigan militia', part of a complex network of right-wing, anti-government paramilitary groups that had recently sprung up in the United States. Along with white supremacist and anti-semitic ideologies, these groups often embrace interpretations of Bible prophecy that foresee the rise of a demonic world government at the end of history. The head of the Michigan Militia warns of the coming battle with an evil 'New World Order' – a sinister global system of which the US government is simply one component. The leader of another far right group warns of a 'one-world government, with a one-world religion, where some of us will be annihilated.'

These groups have been much influenced by *The Turner Diaries*, a futuristic novel published in 1978 by one William Pierce under the pseudonym

'Andrew MacDonald'. After earning a PhD in physics, Pierce joined the American Nazi Party and espoused anti-semitic and racist causes. *The Turner Diaries* pits a group of white patriots, the Organization, against a sinister Jewish- and black-dominated government, the System. In one scene, the Organization bombs the FBI headquarters as an act of anti-government terrorism. As the Organization gains power, first in Southern California then across America and finally the world, it launches a program of racial cleansing, systematically exterminating all the world's non-white peoples.

The Turner Diaries is, in fact, an apocalypse, with righteousness eventually triumphing over evil after a cosmic struggle involving massive violence and bloodshed. At his initiation into the Organization, the eponymous hero Turner muses:

I understand now why we *cannot* fail, no matter . . . how many of us must perish in doing it. We are truly the instruments of God in the fulfilment of His Grand Design.[2]

I am no expert on cults or antigovernment fringe groups in contemporary America. But I can offer some thoughts on the soil from which these movements arise: the larger world of Bible prophecy belief in US culture. From 1987 to 1991, researching what became the book *When Time Shall Be No More*, I immersed myself in this world, reading some 300 paperbacks; interviewing prophecy writers; listening to prophecy expositors on TV and radio; and attending services in prophecy-oriented churches. In the process, I learned a lot about a belief system that seems alien to many academics, even students of American culture. It is, nevertheless, a world of belief inhabited not just by cultists or fringe groups, but by millions of Americans.

This essay offers a brief overview of the origins and evolution of Bible prophecy belief, argues for its pervasiveness in American culture; explores its political and cultural implications, both in the Cold War era and beyond; and, finally, suggests a few reasons for its tenacious grip on the popular mind.

First, then, the historical context. From around 200 BC to AD 100, a literary genre known as *apocalyptic* flourished in Judaism and early Christianity. Jewish apocalyptic thought emerged from the earlier prophetic tradition, but is distinct from it. The historian Norman Cohn has recently traced the genre to what he believes to be its ultimate source: Persian Zoroastrianism of the fourteenth century, BC.[3] The Greek word *Apocalypse*, of course, means an *unveiling* of that which is hidden. (The word originally described the erotic performance in which a dancer seductively removes veil after veil.) The writers in this genre produced texts rich in imagery of future events, some of which found their way into the Christian Bible – notably the Book of Daniel; the 'Little Apocalypse' in Christ's Mount of Olives sermon recorded in Mark 13; and the Book of Revelation, the Apocalypse of John, written in Asia Minor around AD 100 to assure the tiny communities of fearful and persecuted Christians of Christ's imminent return in glory.

Although Origen, St Augustine, and other Church Fathers downplayed eschatology and historicized or allegorized the apocalyptic scriptures, popular prophecy belief spawned a rich interpretive and artistic tradition in medieval Christianity. Portrayals of the Apocalypse in sculpture, stained glass, and illuminated texts rank among the treasures of medieval art. The twelfth-century Calabrian monk Joachim of Fiore produced a vast corpus of prophetic interpretation. Hildegard of Bingen recorded her apocalyptic visions in works of startling originality.

Apocalyptic speculation soared during the Reformation, as Protestant polemicists portrayed the Pope as Antichrist – a charge the Rev. Ian Paisley and a few other Protestant fundamentalists perpetuate to this day. Catholic polemicists, of course, returned the favour and proclaimed Martin Luther as the Evil One. Prophetic imagery pervades seventeenth-century English Puritanism, including countless Puritan sermons and tracts and the poetry of John Milton. Sir Isaac Newton distilled years of prophecy study into his *Observations upon the Prophecies of Daniel, and the Apocalypse of St John,* published posthumously in 1733.

The most popular prophetic system in modern America is *premillennial-dispensationalism,* formulated by the nineteenth-century British dissenter John Darby, who left the Church of Ireland to found the Plymouth Brethren, and further elaborated by the American Cyrus Scofield, whose *Reference Bible* has sold as many as 12 million copies since it first appeared in 1909, vastly enriching the coffers of its publisher, Oxford University Press.

Premillennial means that Christ will return before the millennium, the thousand-year reign of peace alluded to in the Book of Revelation. *Dispensational* means that God has dealt with mankind in a series of distinct epochs, or dispensations. Popularizers buttress this belief system with proof texts drawn from Daniel, Ezekiel, Matthew, Mark, II Thessalonians, II Peter, and Revelation – works written over a span of hundreds of years but believed in prophecy circles to unveil a coherent sequence of end-time events that can be pieced together by a careful study and appropriate arrangement of the key texts.

According to this scenario, as history nears its climax, probably very soon, a series of 'signs' will alert the faithful that the end is near. Wickedness will grow worse, natural disasters will increase. The 1918 Balfour Declaration, the founding of the State of Israel in 1948, and Israel's recapture of Jerusalem in 1967 are cited as vitally important prophetic signs.

These signs will culminate in the *Rapture,* when all true believers will join Christ in the air. Though silent and secret, this event will quickly become known – especially to airline passengers flying with a raptured pilot. Those left behind will endure the seven-year *Great Tribulation,* a brief but nightmarish dispensation when the *Antichrist,* also referred to in Revelation as the *Beast,* will rule the world.

After the Tribulation, Antichrist's forces will gather in Israel to fight a 200-million-man army that will march from the East. The armies will converge on the lush plains of Jezreel near the hill of Megiddo (*har-mĕgiddô*), an ancient battlesite some miles southeast of present-day Haifa – hence the *Battle of Armageddon.* As the armies assemble, Jesus Christ will return with His saints as avenging warrior to destroy his foes and launch His thousand-year earthly reign – the *Millennium* – from His seat of government, the restored Temple in Jerusalem. After a final battle with Antichrist and a solemn *Last Judgement,* human history ends. A New Heaven and a New Earth arise, with Christ reigning forever.

How widespread in America is the belief system I've just sketched? Despite erosion in the twentieth century, it remains deeply rooted. Forty per cent of Americans profess to be biblical literalists, regarding the Bible as 'the actual Word of God, to be taken literally, word for word'. Another 45 per cent view the Bible as divinely inspired. Sixty-two per cent profess to have 'no doubt' that Jesus Christ will come again.

Several large evangelical and fundamentalist denominations embrace premillennial doctrine, as does the fast-growing pentecostal movement, spearheaded by the 2.2-million member Assemblies of God Church and by various charismatic offshoots. Though the fifteen-million-strong Southern Baptist Convention has historically eschewed binding creedal pronouncements, many individual Southern Baptists embrace premillennial-dispensationalism or some other variant of end-time Bible prophecy. Prophecy belief pervades the many independent Bible churches and fellowships that are spreading rapidly across America, such as the Rev. Charles Swindoll's sprawling First Evangelical Free Church of Fullerton, California, a bastion of prophecy teaching. The Mormons, Jehovah's Witnesses, and Seventh Day Adventists, with millions of members in all, espouse particular versions of end-time belief.

A torrent of prophecy paperbacks feeds an apparently insatiable market. Hal Lindsey's *The Late Great Planet Earth,* the non-fiction bestseller of the 1970s, with sales now in the millions, offered a slangy, jazzed-up version of premillennial-dispensationalism. Lindsay followed this work with a succession of prophecy books, including *Planet Earth, 2000 AD* (1994) and *The Final Battle* (1995), which became big sellers in their turn. Boasts such as 'over 100,000 sold' or '250,000 in print' adorn many prophecy paperbacks. These beliefs are also spread by America's ubiquitous religious broadcasters, including such luminaries as Oral Roberts and Jerry Falwell. Pat Robertson, head of a vast TV and media empire and of the powerful evangelical political lobby the Christian Coalition, dwells heavily on Bible prophecy in his broadcasts and books, most recently *The New World Order* (1991) and *The End of the Age: A Novel* (1995).

The prophetic word is also spread by touring evangelists; by Christian bookstores (a three-*billion*-dollar business in America); by evangelical seminaries and Bible schools; by tape, film, and videocassette; by tracts, Christian comic books, 'Rapture' wristwatches that proclaim 'One Hour Nearer the Lord's Return', and automobile bumper stickers with such slogans as: 'Warning: If the Rapture Occurs, This Car Will be Driverless.'

Prophecy belief has seeped into mass culture through such Hollywood movies as *The Omen* of 1976 and *The Rapture* (1991). Apocalyptic lyrics pervade rock music, as evidenced by Barry Maguire's 'Eve of Destruction,' David Bowie's '[We've Got] Five More Years,' and many more recent songs.

Nor is Bible prophecy belief in America confined to a mythic southern 'Bible Belt'. These beliefs certainly pervade the South and West, with their Protestant concentrations, but they are not *confined* to those regions. Madison, Wisconsin, a university town and state capital in the Upper Midwest, boasts over fifty churches where prophecy is regularly expounded and seven Christian bookstores offering the latest prophecy paperbacks. Similarly, while prophecy belief is strongest among the poorer, least-educated Americans, it is found at all educational and income levels. Indeed, many prophecy writers have backgrounds in the space program, nuclear physics, computer programming, and electrical engineering.

And prophecy belief has penetrated to the highest level of American politics. President Ronald Reagan and several members of his administration, including Secretary of Defense Caspar Weinberger and Secretary of the Interior James Watt, were avowed prophecy believers. President George Bush's vice president, Dan Quayle, had close links to the Rev. Robert Thieme, a prominent premillennial-dispensationalist based in Houston, Texas.

Despite all this, students of US culture have largely ignored apocalyptic and prophetic beliefs. Scholars who discourse learnedly about Disneyland, Elvis, Madonna, or rap music stare blankly when one mentions Hal Lindsey, the Rapture, or the Great Tribulation.

But are these beliefs anything more than bizarre cultural vestiges? Do they merit all this attention? Decidedly yes! Millions of Americans' view of current events is influenced by their understanding of Bible prophecy. Of course, Bible prophecy is not the *only* factor shaping the world-view of believers. World-views arise from many sources, and are rarely wholly consistent. For example, President Reagan's prophetic beliefs helped convince him that the eventual destruction of Russia is foretold in the Book of Ezekiel. Yet Reagan ended his presidency by strolling in Red Square with Mikhail Gorbachev, ruler of the Evil Empire. But while Bible prophecy is obviously not the only way by which believers interpret world events, for millions of Americans it represents one *very important* source.

The point becomes clear as we look at some specific prophetic themes that directly influenced believers' view of the post-1945 world. In the decades after World War II, countless prophecy popularizers found nuclear war, the destruction of Russia, the fate of the Jews, the rise of a global economic order, and the takeover of the US government by the forces of evil all foretold in the Bible. Each of these themes offers rich material for consideration.

1. *The advent of the atomic bomb* in 1945 stimulated intense interest in prophecies of the earth's final destruction. As II Peter memorably puts it: '[T]he heavens shall pass away with a great noise, and the elements shall melt with fervent heat, the earth also and the works that are therein shall be burned up.' Zechariah 14:12 anticipates John Hersey's *Hiroshima*: '[The people's] flesh shall consume away while they stand upon their feet, and their eyes shall consume away in their holes, and their tongues shall consume away in their mouths.'

Scores of post-1945 prophecy writers interpreted such texts as forecasts of nuclear holocaust. Despite their claims to biblical literalism, these popularizers freely transformed the bows and arrows and spears of the apocalyptic scriptures into missiles, missile launchers, and ICBMs.

These writers insisted that they were not *advocating* nuclear war. They were simply pointing out a plausible way by which the prophecies of global destruction might be fulfilled. But in treating nuclear war as most probably foretold in the Bible, they encouraged passivity toward the nuclear threat. Why resist the inevitable, especially when it will probably come *after* the Rapture, when believers will be safe in the skies? Nuclear disarmament talks were a cruel deception, most prophecy writers agreed, offering a promise of peace when the prophecies foretold otherwise. 'Our hope does not lie in peace treaties', wrote one in 1962, amid negotiations for a nuclear test-ban treaty. Only the Second Coming, he said, would end the nuclear threat.[4]

The more scrupulous writers noted that Armageddon is not a human war, but a divine punishment of wicked humanity. But images of nuclear war and of Armageddon easily blurred in the popular mind. Indeed, a 1984 survey found that 39 percent of Americans believed that the Bible's end-time prophecies do, in fact, refer to thermonuclear war.

2. *Russia*, too, loomed large in Cold-War-era prophecy popularizations. This was, of course, not a new theme. The surge of Prussian patriotism that followed the 1807 Treaty of Tilset, by which Napoleon and Alexander I sharply reduced Prussia's territory and autonomy, created a favourable climate among German biblical scholars for finding Russia's destruction foretold in scripture, and sure enough, the Prussian Hebraicist Wilhelm

Gesenius soon identified Russia as 'Gog', the northern kingdom that according to Ezekiel 38 will one day invade Judea and be obliterated as a result.

Gesenius's fateful identification, reinforced by the fact that Moscow lies due north of Jerusalem, proved highly popular. The 'Meshech' and 'Tubal' mentioned by Ezekiel were linked to Moscow and Tobolsk. Some expositors argued that the phrase translated as 'chief prince' in the King James version of Ezekiel 38:3 actually meant 'Prince of Rosh' – another arrow pointing to Russia.

John Darby found Russia in Ezekiel, as did John Cummings, whose 1855 prophecy study *The End*, a big seller in England and America during the Crimean War, patriotically predicted on the basis of Ezekiel that Russian forces would soon invade Palestine where they would 'perish . . . amid tremendous scenes'. In America, Cyrus Scofield's 1909 *Reference Bible* further promulgated what had by then become the conventional wisdom in dispensational circles: Ezekiel 38 foretells Russia's doom.

This reading, strengthened by the 1917 Bolshevik Revolution, reached almost hysterical proportions during the Cold War. Paperback popularizers, TV preachers, and touring expositors endlessly proclaimed 'The Coming Destruction of Russia'. As Jerry Falwell wrote in 1983, when God destroys Russia as foretold in Scripture, 'the communist threat will cease forever'.

The prophecy writers I interviewed in the late 1980s denied any intention of fomenting war with the Soviets. Russia's foreordained end will be by *divine*, not human, means, they insisted. But their endless preaching of Russia's coming doom unquestionably added an eschatological dimension to many Americans' suspicions of Moscow, undercutting efforts to reduce Cold War tensions. If Russia's destruction was inevitable, why bestir oneself to interfere with the unfolding divine plan?

3. A third point of intersection between prophetic belief and the 'real world' relates to *the Jews, Israel, and the Middle East*. In Genesis 15:18, Jehovah promises Abraham and his people all the land from the Euphrates to the 'river of Egypt', often identified as the Nile. In this and other texts, fundamentalist prophecy popularizers find not only a divine warrant for Israel's existence as a nation but a foretelling of a vast expansion of its future boundaries to include all or parts of Lebanon, Syria, Iraq, Jordan, Saudi Arabia, and Egypt. Again the more scrupulous interpreters place this expansion in the Millennium, but the popularizers often blur or downplay this distinction.

Prophecy writers also cite scriptures that in their view foretell the rebuilding of the Temple in Jerusalem on the exact site of the Temple destroyed by the Romans in AD 70 – a site now occupied by the Islamic

Dome of the Rock, built over the spot where the Prophet Mohammed ascended to heaven. Writes one interpreter: 'How the Jews will surmount the problem of rebuilding a temple on the place now occupied by an Arab holy place is anyone's guess. But rebuild it they shall, for as Jesus said. [. . .] "The scriptures cannot be broken[. . .]".' (During the Persian Gulf War, some prophecy believers expected that Saddam Hussein's scud missiles would obliterate the Dome of the Rock, clearing the way for a rebuilt Temple.)

Again, these writers insist that they are simply interpreting prophecy, not making political judgements. Yet the anti-Arab implication is clear. As one author put it in 1975: 'When all the Jews return. [. . .], God [. . .] will lay the land of the Arabs waste, and it will be desolate. [. . .] This may seen like a severe punishment; but [. . .] [God's covenant with Israel] must be carried out to the letter.'

But the prophetic view of the Jews is complex. The same writers who predict Israel's territorial expansion and a rebuilt Temple also portray the grim history of Jewish persecution as God's 'chastisement' of His people for their failure to accept Jesus as the prophesied Messiah.

Pat Robertson's expositions of Bible prophecy, particularly *The New World Order*, contain coded allusions to the role of 'international bankers' and discuss 'the liberal, wealthy Jews [who] voted for [. . .] Carter, Mondale, and Dukakis'.[5] In fact, Robertson's discussion of the Jews' prophetic destiny draws heavily from *Pawns in the Game*, a 1955 antisemitic work by the Canadian William Guy Carr.

And things will get worse, the prophecy gurus preach. In a kind of cosmic Catch-22, the Jews will continue to be 'chastised' by God in the present dispensation for rejecting Christ, and then persecuted by Antichrist during the Great Tribulation for being God's Chosen People! Citing a cryptic passage from the Book of Zechariah, prophecy writers teach that during the Great Tribulation two-thirds of all Jews will be slaughtered. (A tiny remnant who at last accepts Christ as Messiah will die as well, though presumably they will fare better at the Last Judgement.)

This, too, of course, is all part of God's plan, beyond human power to avert. To be sure, the Tribulation will be no picnic for anyone, but Jews will be singled out for special vengeance. As one writer puts it: 'Antichrist's persecution will be much more terrible than Hitler's. [Hitler] got rid of six million Jews. But Antichrist's purpose will be to do away with *all* Jews. [. . .] God cannot act to save the Jews until the Jews keep their end of the covenant'.

Just as the prophecy popularizers portrayed nuclear war and Russia's destruction as divinely ordained, so they pictured Jewish holocausts past and future as part of God's plan – tragic and lamentable, but inexorably inscribed in the prophecies. The way this strand of prophetic interpretation can encourage a resigned attitude toward anti-semitism and even toward overt anti-Jewish persecution is only too clear. In 1990, when I visited Yad Vashem, the Holocaust memorial in Jerusalem with its horrifying record of the Nazis' slaughter of European Jewry, a fundamentalist prophecy believer with whom I had become acquainted whispered to me: 'Surely when Jews see this, they must realize what a terrible mistake they made in rejecting Christ.'

4. As we have seen, Bible prophecy popularizers also foresee a *standardized, regimented world order* in which all individuality will be ruthlessly stamped out. The technological sophistication of the modern global economy is anticipated, they believe, in the account of Antichrist's world rule and the dread 'Mark of the Beast' foretold in Revelation 13:

And [the Beast] causeth all [. . .] to receive a mark in their right hand, or in their foreheads. And [. . .] no man might buy or sell, save he that had the mark, or the name of the beast, or the number of his name. [. . .] Let him that hath understanding count the number of the beast; for [. . .] his number is Six Hundred three score and six.

The prophecy popularizers see computers, communications satellites, multinational corporations, laser scanners, electronic banking, and credit cards as the instruments of Antichrist's dictatorship. Citing passages from Daniel, they teach that Antichrist will initially rule a ten-nation European federation representing a revived Roman Empire. But he will soon extend his rule worldwide.

The mysterious number '666' rouses special fascination. The ancients often gave numerical values to names, and most biblical scholars view '666' as a cryptic allusion to the Emperor Nero, whose resurrection as an avenging tyrant and persecutor of Christians was widely anticipated in late first-century Asia Minor. Over the centuries, prophecy interpreters applied the fateful number to the Pope, Saladin, Napoleon, Hitler, Mussolini, Anwar Sadat, Don Carlos of Spain, Henry Kissinger, and many others. In the 1980s, some noted ominously that each of *Ronald Wilson Reagan*'s three names has six letters!

But the more typical strategy of recent prophecy writers is to link '666' not to an individual, but to the emerging global economic *system*. They document the use of the number on product labels, corporate logos, government documents, and so forth. One insists that the consumer product bar codes now found everywhere in US supermarkets and department stores are based on the numerals 666. Another points out that if you give the letter A the value 6, B the value 12, C 18, and so on through the alphabet, adding six each time, then the numerical value of the word 'COMPUTER' is . . . 666. (It works out; try it!)

The prophecy writers also cite television, the glitzy celebrity of rock stars, and the manipulative techniques of modern politics as ways we are being softened up for the Antichrist. The Evil One will not initially seem monstrous or evil, they suggest, but eloquent, caring, and charismatic – brilliantly using the electronic media to further his demonic purpose.

This strand of prophecy belief clearly taps into the sense of anonymity, alienation, and loss of individuality felt by vast numbers of people, whatever their religious beliefs, in an age of mass culture, multinational corporations, and media-driven politics. Radicals of the left seeking evidence of popular resistance to the modern corporate hegemony have missed an important source. Indeed, the conspiratorial, paranoid view of a demonic global system that one finds among prophecy believers (and in the militant right-wing groups burgeoning in contemporary America) uncannily resembles the New Left rhetoric of the 1960s, which also saw capitalism as an omnipotent world system with its tentacles in government and the mass media. The politics differs; the paranoid and apocalyptic sensibility is similar.

American society and the US government, the prophecy writers warn, are preparing the way for this demonic world order. Citing an array of evidence from secularism, materialism, and radical feminism to AIDS, abortion, pornography, and a sex-drenched media, they warn that the rising tide of wickedness in America offers compelling evidence that the end is near. The so-called New Age movement that arose in the 1970s, with its interest in eastern religions and its vaguely pantheistic emphasis on planetary consciousness, was demonized as part of a US-based plot to prepare the world for the Beast. Once in power, Antichrist will exploit electronic wizardry pioneered in America. As one writer put it in 1982: '[The United States] is leading the world down the primrose path to the "Mark of the Beast".' Even as they picture the world's downward spiral, these American prophecy writers display a perverse patriotism in insisting that the United States is leading the way.

The images of deepening chaos reach a crescendo in the accounts of the turbulence that will follow the Rapture. *The Beast*, Dan Betzer's 1985 prophecy novel, describes one character's horror as she drives through New York City after the Rapture:

She could see cars overturned and on fire. Trash littered the streets. Shop windows had been smashed and the merchandise inside stolen. It was like a scene from hell. [. . .] Some great restraining hand had been lifted from the earth. The delicate veneer that kept mankind from the laws of the jungle had been jostled. [. . .] [T]he ooze of primitive man was escaping.

These two motifs, social regimentation and social chaos, while superficially contradictory, represent two loci of anxiety in contemporary America:

the fear of crime, social disorganization, and incipient violence among the inner-city poor and the technologically displaced, on the one hand, and the fear of an emerging global economic and technocratic order, on the other. Structurally, the two themes converge in descriptions of the Great Tribulation, when an initial wave of post-Rapture social chaos and anarchy will quickly give way to the reign of Antichrist, whose new world order will be equally terrifying in its regimentation of every detail of life.

The view of the United States as a cesspool of evil represents a radical shift in prophetic interpretation. The New England Puritans, Jonathan Edwards in the eighteenth century, and many nineteenth-century church-men saw America as divinely favoured, perhaps even the site of the millennial kingdom. As Edward Johnson assured his fellow New Englanders in 1653: 'For your full assurance, know this is the place where the Lord will create a new Heaven and a new earth [. . .], new Churches and a new Commonwealth together.' In an 1857 sermon preached by invitation in the US Capitol in Washington, DC, a Tennessee prophecy expounder with the wonderful name Fountain Pitts found the Declaration of Independence foretold in the Book of Daniel and discerned a glorious destiny for the United States.

Except for the Mormons and certain other groups that still foresee a prophetic role for America as the New Zion, such blending of patriotism and prophecy is rare today. Most writers conclude sadly that America is irretrievably in the grip of the forces of evil. The federal government, once viewed as an instrument for promoting God's cause globally, is now in demonic hands, intent on oppressing the righteous, whether by permitting abortion, promoting 'secular humanism', banning school prayers, or pushing homosexual rights. In God's due time, Washington, DC will be unmasked as a centre of the conspiracy preparing the way for Antichrist's global tyranny.

Historically, apocalyptic/millennial rhetoric, adding a religious patina to a pervasive civic ideology of manifest destiny and divine mission, comprised a benign, fairly uncontroversial theme in American popular ideology and poli-tical speechmaking. In recent years, growing numbers of prophecy believers, alienated groups, and TV and paperback popularizers have espoused an apocalyptic end-time scenario that views America and its government not as divinely favoured, but as sinking in wickedness and rife with menacing eschatological significance. With this shift, the apocalyptic mindset, once easily assimilable to American civic ideology, stirs worried concern in the secular media and the political establishment.

But what of the present? The Cold War is over, the Soviet Union defunct; the nuclear threat has faded and Israel and its Arab neighbours are moving haltingly toward peace. Under such vastly altered world conditions, what is happening to the end-time scenario described in this essay?

In a word, it is thriving. Some prophecy popularizers and television expositors, clinging to the familiar scenario, still warn ominously of Russia. The apparent Soviet collapse and the enfeeblement of communism is just a passing phase, if not a trick, they caution. After all, does not the Bible say: 'For when they shall say peace and safety, then sudden destruction cometh upon them.'

Other expositors, while retaining elements of the familiar scenario, subtly shift its emphasis by reviving a very ancient prophetic theme: the Muslim world as the demonic end-time power. From the fifteenth through the nineteenth centuries, European prophecy expositors routinely identified the Islamic Ottoman Empire as the evil power whose destruction is foretold in Ezekiel 38. When the Ottoman Empire collapsed and the Soviet Union emerged, the prophecy popularizers quickly adapted to the altered realities. But the Islamic threat never wholly vanished from this literature, and it is now being dusted off and put to work again. During the 1991 Persian Gulf War, some opportunistic prophecy writers hastily fit Saddam Hussein into their end-time scenario, noting that Revelation 18 prophesies the fiery destruction of Babylon, the ancient city that Saddam is elaborately restoring. The most recent writings of the ever-resourceful Hal Lindsey point ominously to the upsurge of Shiite fundamentalism as a fulfilment of Bible prophecy. In *Planet Earth – 2000 AD*, Lindsey launches a chapter on 'The New Islamic Threat' by quoting God's curse against Ishmael recorded in Genesis 16:12: '[H]is hand will be against everyone, and everyone's hand will be against him'. Implicitly identifying Ishmael with the Arab world and with Islam, Lindsey goes on darkly:

The greatest threat to freedom and world peace today – is Islamic fundamentalism. [. . .] [T]he threat it poses to the whole world, and especially Israel, reinforces the idea that we are seeing the scene set for the fulfilment of Ezekiel prophecies about a future invasion of the Middle East by a coalition of Russian and Arab forces.[6]

The post-Cold War end-time scenario is being reconfigured to reflect not only fears of Islamic militancy, but environmental worries as well. As many recent prophecy writers note, the Book of Revelation describes the ultimate ecological catastrophe: earthquakes rock the globe, the sun and moon darken, the seas become 'as the blood of a dead man'. Searing heat, monstrous insects, and hideous sores make life a torment for suffering humanity.

Current concerns about oil spills, global warming, the greenhouse effect, radioactive wastes, ozone depletion, and toxic pollution of lakes and rivers all fit readily into the biblical scenario. As one commentator put it: '[The Bible] pictures ecological upheavals that challenge description. Generations of pollution [. . .] may contribute to the chaos of nature pictured [in

Revelation]'. And Hal Lindsey, that bell-wether of shifting themes in prophecy interpretation, begins a discussion of current environmental threats in *Planet Earth – 2000 AD* by asserting:

The physical tribulations of the Earth and its environment has been one of the most significant developments – prophetically speaking – since I authored *The Late Great Planet Earth* 25 years ago. You can scarcely read a newspaper or watch a television program without being bombarded with information about the crisis of the environment. [. . .] [And] many of these conditions [. . .] fit [. . .] exactly into the prophetic scenario for the endtimes.[7]

The new global economy, and especially the sinister role of the United States in furthering it, looms ever larger in post-Cold War prophecy popularizations as well. During the Cold War, the standard apocalyptic formula of dividing all reality between righteousness and evil was projected on a global stage, with Moscow the focus of evil. The prophecy interpreters of the 1990s shift this manichean formula to the domestic realm, with Washington, DC as the heart of darkness. Pat Robertson even suggests in his 1991 book *The New World Order* that the Cold War was a hoax perpetrated by US and European bankers (implicitly identified with the Jews) to increase their grip on world finance and prepare the way for the Antichrist.

The contemporary apocalyptic mindset thus reinforces more strongly than ever a deep vein of anti-government hostility in present-day America. The hatred of Washington has many sources, of course, but prophecy belief is surely one. For followers of the Darby-Scofield prophetic scheme, the coming rule of the Antichrist deepens the conviction that the federal government is not only inefficient, wasteful, and intrusive, but that it is, quite literally, demonic.

In short, prophecy belief has displayed a chameleon-like adaptability over the centuries. Whatever the precise balance of components in the post-Cold War end-time scenario, this belief system will almost certainly adapt itself to current realities as it has accommodated other vast historical changes in the past.

Finally, taking a broader view, how do we account for the remarkable hold of Bible prophecy belief in the contemporary United States, not only among paranoid fringe groups and obsessive individuals, but among millions of ordinary citizens? From one perspective, this phenomenon is simply a by-product of the high level of evangelical piety in America compared to the British Isles and Western Europe. This, in turn, relates to traditions of religious freedom and the absence of a state church. From the seventeenth century to the present, America has nurtured religious innovators: Anne Hutchinson and Roger Williams in Puritan New England; Joseph Smith, the founder of the Mormon Church; Mary Baker Eddy, the 'discoverer' of

Christian Science; Ellen White of the Seventh Day Adventists; Charles Taze Russell of the Jehovah's Witnesses; and the pentecostalist Charles Parham – all flourished in America's non-hierarchical, *laissez faire* religious environment. Hal Lindsay and his ilk are simply another manifestation of this larger phenomenon. Prophecy interpretation, after all, is the quintessential democratic theology: anyone may play. Even the great Cyrus Scofield had little formal education. Indeed, the lack of theological training and of institutional credentials is considered an asset, certifying one's freedom from the scepticism and relativism associated with secular universities and many seminaries.

Nor should one assume that the apocalyptic world-view will fade as America's technological infrastructure becomes more sophisticated. On one hand, the prophecy popularizers weave the latest electronic innovations into their scenario, as evidence that Antichrist's rule is drawing ever closer. On the other hand, the popularizers avidly adopt that same new technology to spread the word, from satellite TV to the Internet to sophisticated mass-marketing techniques.

Further, Bible prophecy belief flourishes in a *secular* discourse saturated in apocalypticism. Books with titles like *Future Shock, The Eco-Spasm Report*, and *The Population Bomb* warn of cataclysm ahead. A recent headline in my hometown newspaper warned: 'Earth's Time May Be Short'. The article did not, as I expected, tell of a sermon by a touring prophecy expounder, but summarized a scientific report documenting various global hazards. A 1994 TV report with the apocalyptic title 'The Fire Next Time' dealt with global warming.

The differences, of course, are profound. The secular apocalypticists promulgate their grim warnings as a stimulus to action; the religious apocalypticists see no hope short of God's divine intervention. As Hal Lindsay observes after his recital of environmental dangers in *Planet Earth – 2000 AD*: '[D]on't mistake anything I write here to suggest I am siding with those who use environmental scare tactic to incite strong-arm tactics by big government. [. . .] [T]here is not much any of us can do about the matter. It is in God's hands'.[8] Nevertheless, secular apocalyptic and religious apocalyptic genres *are* symbiotically linked, each reinforcing and strengthening the other.

If prophecy belief is rooted in America's religious history, thrives in our modern technocratic age, and gains strength from secular apocalyptic thinking, it also possesses certain intrinsic strengths. Perhaps the greatest strength is its flexibility – a flexibility enhanced by the allusive, symbolic language of the apocalyptic texts. While the core structure changes little, new events, as we have seen, are constantly incorporated, while events or individuals that fail to fulfil their designated prophetic roles are quietly dropped. From the 1920s through 1945, many prophecy writers built a persuasive biblical case for Mussolini as the Antichrist. With Il Duce's death, these books quietly vanished, and new interpretations quickly took their place. In 1930s' America, Social Security numbers, union labels, and the National Recovery Administration's Blue Eagle were seen as forerunners of Antichrist's rule. Today it is Mastercard, computers, electronic banking, and multinational corporations.

The historian, reading hundreds of prophecy books published over a 150-year span, can clearly see this technique of inserting current events and trends into a venerable system of eschatological interpretation. The ordinary believer, encountering the genre for the first time, is stunned by the amazing contemporaneity of the prophecies. The remarkable 'prophetic fufilments' that ingenious popularizers discern as they match the prophecies with current events help buttress evangelical faith. With the erosion of eighteenth-century natural theology, which found proof of God's existence in the harmony and symmetry of nature, prophecy belief finds evidence for the divine in the harmony and symmetry of history.

Prophecy belief also finesses the ancient dilemma of free will versus determinism by embracing *both* positions. In the prophetic scheme, history's *overall course* is wholly determined. But within this predestined order lies a crucial realm of freedom: by understanding the prophecies and accepting Christ, *individuals* can control their personal destiny and escape the horrors ahead.

Above all, prophecy belief gives meaning and even drama to history and to one's individual life. In place of the aimless, 'one-damn-thing-after-another' quality of secular historiography, prophetic history is ordered and purposeful. As one writer puts it: 'The twentieth century is a stream moving exactly in the pattern of the prophetic word.' In earlier times, 'secular' historians often smuggled divine providence into their work. With the banishment of supernatural causation from academic history, the prophecy interpreters stepped in to the meet the popular longing from meaning, drama, and purpose in history. Significantly, these writers often employ metaphors drawn from the theatre – 'the stage is set', 'the scenery is in place', etc. – evoking images of an exciting drama that the raptured saints will view from a safe distance.

And beyond the terror and bloodshed ahead lies a golden age. At heart this is a utopian system. The Tribulation and Armageddon are but way stations to the Millennium: a new age of peace, harmony, and justice – the antithesis of our present, all-too-flawed social order.

Yes, 'The End is at Hand' – for this essay, at any rate. Let me conclude, then, with a modest prophecy of my own as the portentous year 2000 approaches: so long as prophecy belief continues to meet important emotional and psychological needs, and so long as its purveyors display their accustomed ingenuity in weaving contemporary social trends into their end-time scenarios with a flourish of biblical citations, this ancient belief system will continue to thrive, powerfully influencing America's politics and culture. And as the 'globalization' of US mass culture proceeds apace, prophecy belief, too – along with McDonalds, Wendy's, and Burger King – may display surprising appeal in regions far beyond America's shores.

NOTES

1 Paul Boyer, 'Apocalypse in Waco: David Koresh and the Branch Davidians', in William Graebner, ed., *True Stories from the American Past*, Vol. 2 (New York, 1997) pp. 251–71.
2 Michael Barkun, *Religion and the Racist Right: The Origins of the Christian Identity Movement* (Chapel Hill, 1994) pp. 225–8. Quoted passage, p. 226.
3 Norman R. Cohn, *Cosmos, Chaos, and the World to Come: The Ancient Roots of Apocalyptic Faith* (New Haven, 1993).
4 Paul Boyer, *When Time Shall Be No More: Prophecy Belief in Modern American Culture* (Cambridge MA, 1992), p. 125. Except as otherwise cited, the sources and documentation for the quoted passages in this chapter, as well as the narrative history of prophetic belief and interpretation (apart from the most recent works and trends), will be found in *When Time Shall Be No More*, which is fully indexed.
5 Pat Robertson, *The New World Order* (Dallas, 1991) pp. 117, 123, 181.
6 Hal Lindsey, *Planet Earth, 2000 AD* (Palos Verdes, CA, 1994), pp. 171, 176.
7 *Ibid.*, pp. 90–1, 93.
8 *Ibid.*, pp. 93, 98.

Index

Contributors to this Volume

C.A. Bayly is Vere Harmsworth Professor of Imperial and Naval History and Fellow of St Catharine's College, Cambridge. He is the author of, among other works, *Indian Society and the Making of the British Empire* (Cambridge, 1988).

Paul Bew is Professor of Irish Politics at Queen's University Belfast. He is the author of, *inter alia, Land and the National Question in Ireland, 1858–82* (Dublin and NJ, 1978).

David Blackbourn, Professor of History and Senior Associate of the Centre for European Studies at Harvard University, is the author of, among other works, *Marpingen Apparitions of the Virgin Mary in Bismarkian Germany* (Oxford, 1993).

Paul Boyer, Merle Curti Professor of History at the University of Wisconsin-Madison and Director of the Institute for Research in the Humanities at the Universities of Wisconsin, is the author of, among other works, *When Time Shall be No More: Prophecy Belief in Modern American Culture* (Cambridge, Mass., 1992).

Nicholas Canny is Professor of History at University College, Galway. His first book was *The Elizabethan Conquest of Ireland: A Pattern Established, 1565–76* (Brighton, 1976), and the subject of his paper for this collection will be further developed in *Ireland and the English Colonial System, 1580–1650*, which he is completing for Oxford University Press.

Fergus A. D'Arcy, Dean of the Faculty of Arts, University College Dublin and Lecturer in its Department of Modern History is the author, among other works, of *Horses, Lords and Racing Men: The Turf Club 1790–1990* (Kildare, 1991).

Eamon Duffy is a Fellow of Magdalene College, Cambridge, and the author of *Stripping the Altars: Traditional Religion in England 1400–1500* (London and New Haven, 1992).

Ruth Harris is a Fellow of New College, Oxford, and the author of *Murders and Madness: Medicine, Law and Society in the Fin-de Siècle* (Oxford, 1989); she is currently completing a book for Penguin entitled *Lourdes: Body and Spirit in the Secular Age*.

Jacqueline Hill is Senior Lecturer in the Department of Modern History at St
   Patrick's College, Maynooth, and the author of *From Patriots to Unionists:
   Dublin Civic Politics and Irish Protestant Patriotism, 1660–1840* (Oxford,
   1997).
Michael Laffan is a member of the Department of Modern History,
   University College Dublin and the author of, *inter alia, The Partition of
   Ireland* (Dundalk, 1983).
James Livesey is Lecturer in the Department of Modern History, Trinity
   College Dublin, and the author of *From Virtue to Happiness: Creating
   Modern Democracy in the French Revolution*, forthcoming, Harvard
   University Press.
F. Donald Logan, Professor Emeritus of History at Emmanuel College
   Boston is the author of *inter alia, The Vikings in History* (London, 2nd ed.
   1991) and *Runaway Religious in Medieval England* (Cambridge, 1996).